The Catholic University of America
Studies in Canon Law
No. 211

The Right of Papal Legation

BY

Gino Paro, J.C.L.

Priest of the Diocese of Treviso (Italy)

A DISSERTATION

Submitted to the Faculty of the School of Canon Law of the Catholic University of America, in Partial Fulfilment of the Requirements for the Degree of Doctor of Canon Law

THE CATHOLIC UNIVERSITY OF AMERICA PRESS
WASHINGTON, D. C.
1947

Nihil Obstat:

LOUIS MOTRY, S.T.D., J.C.D.,
Censor Deputatus.

Washingtonii, die 3 *Junii,* 1948.

Imprimatur:

✠ THOMAS JOSEPHUS WALSH, S.T.D., J.C.D.,
Archiepiscopus Novarcensis.

Novarci, die 3 *Junii,* 1948.

THE CATHOLIC PROTECTORY
ARLINGTON, NEW JERSEY

TO

HIS EXCELLENCY

THE MOST REVEREND

THOMAS JOSEPH WALSH

ARCHBISHOP OF NEWARK

WITH RESPECT AND GRATITUDE

TABLE OF CONTENTS

CHAPTER VI

CHAPTER VII

CHAPTER VIII

FOREWORD

The right of papal legation has a twofold aspect: one has reference to the relations which the Pope has with the Catholic hierarchy and the faithful throughout the world, the other extends to the relations which exist between the supreme religious authority on the one hand and civil government on the other. This twofold aspect of papal legations is derived not so much from the double power, spiritual and temporal, of the Pope, as from the nature of the sovereignty of the Holy See, the supreme organ of authority in the Church and a legal person in international law. The author has sought to base the present work on this fundamental principle. From this standpoint also has resulted the division of the dissertation into two parts: in the first an attempt has been made to determine the juridical position of the Holy See in international law; in the second, after some general notions have been given, the historical deevlopment of the right of papal legation in its diplomatic and religious aspects is traced, and the principles which regulate it, recalled.

A considerable part of the present dissertation is concerned with questions predominantly historical. These questions however are valuable not merely as a record but also as bound up with juridical theories of very great importance; for this reason particular stress has been laid upon the controversy which arose during the period 1870-1929, regarding the international juridical position of the Holy See and on the historical development of the right of papal legation.

It is to be noted that once the juridical capacity of a sovereign ot send his representatives has been established, his capacity to receive the representatives of other sovereigns necessarily follows. Regarding the right of "passive" legation there is no question; it is rather a corollary of the right of "active" legation, and in these pages it receives only casual consideration.

The author is pleased on this occasion to express his deep gratitude to the superiors who permitted him to pursue his juridical studies at the Catholic University of America and he likewise wishes to thank the members of the Faculty for their helpful and enlightened direction; and he recalls with affection the memory of the many friends who extended him their valuable advice and constant kindness.

PART ONE

THE INTERNATIONAL PERSONALITY OF THE HOLY SEE

CHAPTER I

POSITION OF THE HOLY SEE IN INTERNATIONAL LAW BEFORE AND AFTER THE LATERAN TREATY

The right of legation is universally recognized as an attribute of the entities that form part of the international community; it constitutes an act of reciprocal recognition among the members who make use of it, and it is a means of preserving the relations which promote the common good.

In general it may be said that persons in international law are all those juridical entities which are not otherwise constrained by their respective internal laws. The arguments vindicating such a personality should, however, be based on a legitimate juridical title. Hence the question arises: Is the Catholic Church and, through it, the Holy See in possession of such a legitimate juridical title? This question is considered by authors from two different points of view.

1) Those who more or less follow the theories of the Positivist school of law enquire whether a certain number of positive elements, generally admitted, are *de facto* present in the Catholic Church, and answer the question accordingly.

2) Those who follow the principles of the Naturalist school enquire, on the other hand, whether there exists in the intimate constitution of the Catholic Church a fundamental right which, by its very nature, places it among persons endowed with international juridical capacity. For these latter the historical proof is nothing more than a confirmation of the juridical argument, which alone affords legitimate title.

Article I. The origin of a controversy

The problem of the international position of the Holy See did not present itself to jurists before the occupation of Rome on September 20, 1870 and the consequent extinction of the temporal power of the Popes.[1] Until that time no difficulty had existed, of course, in the minds of Catholic writers who, reasoning from the very nature of the divine institution of the Church and the spiritual sovereignty of the Pope, did not doubt that the Holy See was a juridical entity belonging to the international community by reason of its very position. Their adversaries, on the other hand, although arguing from another point of view, were compelled to arrive at the same conclusion. As a matter of fact, the Holy See possessed the characteristics then generally required for the recognition of juridical personality in international law, namely, a territory of its own and a people with an independent political organization. The Pope, a sovereign in the full sense of the term, performed functions which were in every respect commensurate with those of other rulers of peoples. The extension of his spiritual power gave him an unique position in the world, and was often violently attacked. But the arguments used were more or less of a sectarian character and broke down before the fact of his incontesable territorial sovereignty, which guaranteed his independence and contributed towards the fulfilment of his apostolic mission.

After September 20, 1870, as a result of the loss of his temporal power the Pope retired into the Vatican as a voluntary prisoner, and, protesting loudly against the injustice inflicted on him, refused every legal guarantee offered by the victors and demanded that the protection necessary for a real and visible independence should be restored.[2] Thus the *"Roman Question"* (*"La Questione Romana"*)

[1] The historical background of the *"Roman Question"* however goes back to the movement of the Italian Risorgimento. Cfr. Piola, *La Questione Romana nella storia e nel diritto. Da Cavour* al Trattato del Laterano, pp. 3-33; Jemolo, *La Questione Romana,* pp. 7-45.

[2] Diplomatic Note of Card. Antonelli (September 20, 1870); Concistorial Allocution of Pius IX (November 7, 1870)—Bastgen, *Die Romische Frage—Dokumente und Stimmen,* II, 655-659; Pius IX, Enc. *"Ubi Nos"* (15 Maji 1871)—*Fontes,* n. 560; Leo XIII, Enc. *"Inscrutabili"* (21

was opened and the problem of the international position of the Holy See automatically arose. Fed often by passion but more frequently by minds which were honest and desirous of truth the controversy was discussed for nearly sixty years. There was hardly an expert in international law who did not try to solve the problem. The difficulties were often more of a theoretical than of a practical nature. Even after 1870 the relations of the Holy See with other states were regularly maintained and could not be regarded as anything other than diplomatic relations between persons in international law. While being confronted with facts it was not difficult to recognize the personality of the Holy See, yet it was almost impossible to find the juridical *formula* which would completely save the position when it came to writing treatises on the question. The reconciliation which occurred on February 11, 1929, has put an end to many controversies; nevertheless it is a matter of interest to determine the principles by which, during the troubled period, the juridical personality of the Holy See was recognized or denied in international relations. The question is not purely historical, since, even if the international value of the Lateran Treaty cannot be denied, yet the fundamental reason why the Holy See belongs to the community of nations is not exclusively based on it. A brief exposition of the various opinions will show that the personality of the Holy See was for one reason or another recognized by the majority of authors; and though it may be claimed that territorial sovereignty is a good title for the juridical recognition of persons in international law, it will also be seen that it is neither the only title nor the most important one. Perhaps it is precisely the "*Roman Question*" and, better still, the solution of this question, which has done a great deal towards clarifying ideas regarding a point which was considered as a dogma by the adherents

Apr. 1878)—*Fontes,* n. 573; Epist. ad Card. L. Nina (27 Aug. 1878)—*Fontes,* n. 575; Enc. "*Etsi Nos*" (15 Febr. 1882)—*Fontes,* n. 583; Epist. ad Episcopum Cremonensem (G. Bonomelli) (29 Apr. 1889)—*Acta Leonis XIII,* IX, 89-90; Epist. ad Card. Rampolla (5 Oct. 1895)—*Acta Leonis XIII,* XV, 372; Pius X, Enc. "*E supremi*" (4 Oct. 1903)—*Fontes,* n. 653; Benedictus XV, Enc. "*Ad Beatissimi*" (1 Nov. 1914)—*AAS,* VI (1914), 580; Pius XI, Enc. "*Ubi arcano*" (23 Dec. 1922)—*AAS,* XIV (1922) 699; cf. Jemolo, *La Questione Romana,* pp. 129-163.

of the positivist juridical school namely, that a defined territory is the only foundation of international juridical capacity. For, as we shall see later the fundamental reason why international recognition is given to the Holy See is something else besides a small portion of territory. The State of the Vatican City, morally necessary for the liberty of action of the Holy See, is but a visible evidence of the independence of the Pope.[3] Temporal sovereignty is neither the sole nor the principal juridical title to membership in the international community. The real and absolute reason consists in the fact that, being the ruler of a perfect and independent religious society, the Pope is entitled to a spiritual sovereignty.

Article II: The international position of the Holy See before the Lateran Treaty

I. *The Regalist Theory.* Among the adherents of the positivist school of law it was taught with almost dogmatic insistence that only States with definite territories can form part of the international community since territorial power alone constitutes *summa potestas*. Religious power does not in itself enjoy sovereignty, since being distributed in various States it is necessarily subject to territorial sovereignty and is reduced to the level of private associations dependent on the internal laws of each State which regulate matters connected with worship. Hence it is outside the sphere of international affairs.[4] With regard to the Catholic Church since its Head was also the sovereign of a state, it enjoyed a right to be numbered among the members of the international community; but once the Papal States

[3] "Moraliter necessaria optimo iure habetur potestas civilis Romani Pontificis."

"Id iam sesuitur *er natura rei.* Nam plena et perpetua *libertas* R. Pontificis est Ecclesiae omnino necessaria. At *spectatis hominum* moribus praesertim principum in praesenti ordine *generis humani lapsi* (i.e. non tantum hoc nostro saeculo!) principatus civilis est medium moraliter necessarium, ut illa libertas *plena* et *perfecta,* ad quam Rom. Pontif. ius habet, *perpetuo* et *constanter* servetur."—Wernz-Vidal, *Ius Canonicum,* II, 425-426.

[4] Fauchille, *Traite de droit international public,* I, 208-210. However Fauchille admits the international personality of the Holy See by attribution: cf. infra p. 24.

disappeared his independence ceased with the loss of territorial sovereignty. He was nothing more tha na subject of the kingdom of Italy, and, as such, bound by the internal law of that State, and consequently entirely separated from the international community. If in fact some governments continued their relations with the Holy See, this was done, not because it was held to be a sovereign state, but merely as an act of international courtesy. The apostolic nuncios could not be regarded as diplomatic representatives since the juridical basis of their existence was missing. Furthermore Italy guaranteed to representatives sent by the Holy See or credited to it only those privileges which are generally granted in accordance with the Law of Nations, but it did not accord them recognition as diplomatic agents. To those who maintained that the Pope was part of the international community on account of his spiritual power these authors replied that the spiritual power has here no meaning since the Law of Nations is concerned only with political questions. If it was observed that the Law of Guarantees (13 May 1871) recognized and guaranteed the spiritual sovereignty of the Pope to the world, it was also justly answered that this was merely a concession of the Italian government, granted by a national and unilateral law incapable of juridical effects in international affairs. In conclusion, if before 1870 the Holy See enjoyed a personality in the Law of Nations, this was due entirely to the fact that the Pope was sovereign of certain territory and could avail himself of this position to carry on relations of a religious order with States. An international character was attributed to these relations by confusing the two sovereignties, temporal and spiritual, which were found united in the one person; but since the destruction of the Papal States and the sundering of the two powers, the relations between the Pope and the different governments were no longer international but only religious. There remained, therefore, no juridical foundation for the recognition of the Holy See in the Law of Nations.[5]

This theory will be refuted when it has been shown that territory is not the only basis of international personality.

[5] Despagnet, *Cours de droit international public,* (4th ed.), pp. 196-208; De Louter, *Le droit international public positif,* I, 164-167; Cavaglieri, *Corso di diritto internazionale,* pp. 109-115; Brusa, 'La *jurisdiction* du Vatican,' *RDILC,* XV (1883), 114-145.

II. *The Theory of the Vatican Principality.* Completely opposed to the Regalist Theory is the Theory of the Vatican Principality. Some Catholic authors maintained and still maintain that the Papal States continued to exist without interruption. In spite of the ocurrences of September 20, 1870 the Pope remained the legal sovereign of all the territory of which he had been previously in peaceful possession, and that he was both legally and in reality the sovereign of the Vatican territory. The Papal States continued to exist in the Vatican Principality.[6]

The arguments brought forward by the adherents of this Theory may be stated briefly as follows. No peace treaty was concluded between Italy and the Holy See in order to put an end to hostilities and to regularize the situation in the Papal States. In the armistice concluded between the generals of the two armies it was laid down that the Italian troops should not occupy the 'Leonine City.' The plebiscite to annex Rome as capital of the kingdom of Italy was invalid because it took place before the cessation of hostilities; and at any rate it was not the business of the people to decide, where there was clear injustice, the future of the supreme authority of the State. In fact the Pope exercised sovereign powers within the territory of the Vatican and adjacent places: he had subjects and retained a regular political administration over territory which, however small, was entirely dependent on him.[7]

[6] Diplomatic Note of Card. Jacobini (September 11, 1882): "On occupying Rome on September 20, 1870 the invaders respected the enclosure of the Vatican where the Pope with his guards and ministers, surrounded by the faith and love of his subjects, continued to exercise that sovereignty of rights with which he was invested before September 20,—thus since *legally he has never ceased to be sovereign of Rome and of all the other Papal States, so also he continued both legally and in fact to be sovereign of the enclosure of the Vatican*"—quoted by Pinchetti-Sanmarchi, *Guida Diplomatica Ecclesiastica,* I, 43.

[7] Giobbio, *Lezioni di Diplomazia ecclesiastica,* I, 103-121; Imhart Latour, *La papauté en droit international,* pp. 122-136; Pinchetti-Sanmarchi, *Op. cit.,* I, 171-239; Pasquazi, *Ius Internationale Publicum,* pp. 9-94; Müller, *Die völkerrechtliche Stellung des Papstes und die Friedenskonferenzen,* p. 59. Stefenelli, *Die Wahrheit über die römische Frage,* p. 38. Balladore Pallieri, "La Sovranità Temporale della Santa Sede e i Trattati del Laterano"—*Chiesa e Stato, Studi Storici e Giuridici per il Decennale*

The several positive arguments which may be urged against this Theory have been summarized as follows by Wagnon.[8] The Papal States were destroyed by *debellatio*, that is, by armed force and the occupation of the territory by the conqueror. Though the Italian

della Conciliazione tra la Santa Sede e l'Italia, II, 3-11.

Pietro Agostino D'Avak also defends this Theory when dealing with the "Qualifica giuridica della Santa Sede nella stipulazione del Trattato Lateranense" *RDI*, XIV (1935), 83-124; 217-236. He writes:

"That which moreover seems to us to be of importance is to determine not so much what was the preexisting effective position of the Holy See according to the principles of international law as what was its position according to itself and according to the Italian State" (p. 99). The ideas of the two contrasting parties were absolutely opposed and antithetical: the Theory of the Vatican Principality proclaimed the existence of a double international personality (spiritual and temporal sovereignty); Italian law recognized no such personality. "On account of this absolute antithesis it was necessary that one of the parties should abandon the stand it had taken to apporach the point of view of the other; that is to say, it was necessary that either the Holy See should submit to the Italian State and accept the juridical condition attributed to it unilaterally and as from a sovereign, or that the State should approach to the canonical point of view and recognizing the autonomy and sovereignty of the Holy See should treat with it on the same footing as it would with other States, agreeing to determine its juridical position in Italy by means of a bilateral act of an international nature (pp. 102-103). Arguing from the first articles of the Treaty, D'Avack holds that Italy contracted as a *Catholic state*, that is, as one which agreed with the point of view of the Theory of the Vatican Principality, which theory acknowledged the dual personality in the Holy See and accepted the independent existence of the remainder of the old Papal State, or at least that which would be the juridical situation created within the Vatican territory in the fairly long period between 1870 and 1929 (pp. 112-119). It should, however, be recognized that, by means o fthe Treaty, the Holy See and Italy have constituted a new state (pp. 217-225).

It may be observed that it seems beyond doubt that Italy did in fact incorporate the Papal States. On the other hand, for the juridical effects of the bilateral act of the Lateran Treaty, it is not necessary to seek territorial personality in the Holy See. If the Holy See has a spiritual international personality, why can it not conclude a pact juridically perfect from the point of view of Jus Gentium? Italy, precisely because she is a Catholic state, has recognized the just demands of the Holy See and withdrawn its dominion from the territory she had conquered by *debellatio*.

[8] *Concordats et Droit International*, pp. 48-50.

troops did not set foot in the Vatican, nevertheless, the military occupation could be called complete from the moment that the Papal fortresses and places of defense fell into the hands of the enemy. Italy had repeatedly expressed her intention of suppressing the Papal States, annexing their territory and bringing her capital to Rome. She had done all this by effective military occupation, and her warlike intentions were unequivocally confirmed and maintained after the occupation of the Eternal City. The European powers accepted the fait accompli, contenting themselves with the request that Italy should insure the spiritual independence of the Pope. Italy did this by the Law of Guarantees. Though this guarantee did not safeguard what was most important, the independence necessary to the Pope, still the fact of annexation was accepted by the nations of Europe. It is not surprising that the Law of Guarantees was unilateral: in fact Italy could not treat with an incorporated state.

On the other hand, the theory of the continuation of a Vatican Principality was belied by the very claims of the Pope which tended not to the increase and extension of a hypothetical and petty Papal State to its former boundaries but to the creation of a new state.[9]

Undoubtedly the Pope as Supreme Head of the Church remained independent of every other human power and there is no doubt of the injustice of the spoliation. Moreover, in political circles the independence of the Pope and the necessity of giving him a place among the members of the international community were affirmed;[10] but all this is very different from the question of the independent existence of a Papal State. According to positive international law the Papal States no longer existed.

III. *The Theory of artificial personality.* After 1870 it was evident that, in spite of the extinction of the temporal power of the

[9] Fedozzi, *Trattato di Diritto Internazionale*: *vol. I*: *Introduzione e Parte Generale,* p. 143. The theory of the survival of the Papal States is in absolute contradiction with the protests of the Pope himself, who has always complained of being deprived of temporal power and territorial sovereignty. — Falco, *The legal position of the Holy See before and after the Lateran agreements,* pp. 9-10.

[10] Cf. Mostaza, "Sanctae Sedis personalitas internationalis in Decretalibus et iure gentium," *ACII,* III (1936), p. 89; Pasquazi, *Ius internationale publicum,* pp. 94-100; Moore, *Peter's City,* pp. 71-78.

Popes, the position occupied in the world by the Holy See remained almost unaltered. Moreover its prestige continually increased, especially in respect of the right of active and passive legation [11] and the conclusion of agreements (concordats) with States in matters of common interest. If the Holy See took part in international affairs without having temporal sovereignty, it did so, according to this theory, not on account of any proper juridical title, but only by a concession of the States which alone are the creators and possessors of the norms and principles which constitute international jurisprudence. Then the idea of having *normal* and *artificial* international persons was excogitated. It was said that to the first class belonged the different States since they formed a political entity and constituted an organic unity capable of entirely satisfying the requirements of international personality. It is, however, to be observed that since the political unity varied in the different states, equal juridical capacity in international affairs was not to accorded to them all. To the second class belonged all those entities which in some way conformed to the rules of international law. The extension of their juridical capacity would vary according to the will of the normal international persons. The criterion for recognizing artificial international persons is found in what has been done in the past. Every State can recognize when a certain government has elements which come under the rules of international law. In the case of normal international persons the act of recognition is only a declaratory formality, but in the case of artificial international persons this act constitutes a juridical personality.[12] Consequently artificial persons would not have the qualification of subjects of international law except in the measure agreed on by the States; the recognition would be a completely gratuitous act and could be revoked at will. With regard to the Catholic Church, since she cannot be compared to a State, her international

[11] In 1899 the number of states to which papal representatives were sent was 16 and the number of states which sent diplomatic representatives to the Holy See was 20; cf. *Gerarchia Cattolica* (1899), 750-758. At the beginning of 1929 before the Lateran Treaty both of these numbers had risen to 30; cf. *Annuario Pontificio* (1929), 529-544.

[12] Gidel, "Quelques idées sur la condition internationale de la Papauté" *RGDIP* XVIII (1911), 604-609.

juridical capacity (which in fact exists) cannot be said to be inborn, but necessarily due to the assent of normal international persons.[13]

This Theory is based on the supposition that only States are by their very nature endowed with international juridical personality: a supposition which has never been incontestably demonstrated.[14] To say that States create the international juridical personality of the Holy See is, to say the least, an unpardonable anachronism. Many modern states arose when the Holy See for centuries had been exercising her influence in the international community. In certain historical periods her supremacy was uncontested [15] and if in our day a policy of co-ordination be observable, her international position is not thus any inferior than that of the States which profess to follow the same lines.[16]

IV. *Theory of the "sui generis" personality.* Jurists try in vain to discover in the Catholic Church the ordinary elements of international personality: the adaptations and analogies do not constitute a proof. Here there is no question of an international personality in the ordinary sense of the word, but of what is entirely a special position, *"sui generis,"* and sufficient to express the juridical character of the relations between the spiritual and temporal orders. The Church possseses a personality derived from its very nature, in as much as it is a distinctly organized unity. But since it is a society founded on religious beliefs and so differs from the State, it cannot enjoy the exercise of those rights which international law accords only to States. The title which it possesses in the Law of Nations belongs to it because of its entirely special position, since it constitutes an order of its own; which order cannot properly be classified according to the rules of international law.[17]

[13] Fauchille, *Traité de droit international public, I,* 208-210; 726-754; Strupp, *Elements du droit international public, I,* 12; 44-48. Oppenheim, *International Law: A Treatise, I,* 209-211.

[14] Wagnon, *Concordats et Droit International,* p. 51; Iannacone, *La personalità giuridica internazionale della Chiesa,* p. 9.

[15] Cf. Chénon, *Histoire des rapports de l'Eglise et de l'Etat,* pp. 87-102.

[16] Cf. Pennisi, "La personalità internazionale della Chiesa Cattolica ed il rapporto giuridico tra la Chiesa Cattolica e lo Stato della Citta del Vaticano," *ACII,* V (1937) 4, note 1.

[17] Diena, *Principi di Diritto Internazionale,* pp. 150-160; Rivier, *Principes de droit des Gens,* I, 120-121.

According to Wagnon,[18] this Theory does not touch the crux of the question and throws little light on the solution of the problem. It accepts the juridical position of the Holy See, but establishes an international order which is fictitious and therefore is incapable of giving account of the real state of things. In our case the question of fact is preceded by a legitimate right, a foundation necessary to and inherent in the nature of the Church.

V. *The Theory of "ius inter potestates."* Somewhat similar to the preceding Theory is that which places the relations between the Holy See and the different States in the juridical order of *"ius inter potestates."* This Theory perhaps first arose out of an expression in an enactment[19] of the first Peace Conference at the Hague (May 18—July 29, 1899). At the instance of the Tsar and Queen Wilhelmina of Holland the Holy See was invited to send a representative to the Conference. This invitation implied a formal recognition of the Holy See as a person in international law. According to the theory predominently in vogue at that time, the only persons in international law were the States, that is, the territorial sovereignties. Hence the presence of a representative of the Holy See could lead one to believe that the Conference intended to proclaim in some way the sovereignty of the Holy See over a part of the territory of Rome. Perhaps for this reason the Italian government opposed the participation of the Holy See in the Conference.[20] Then, on the proposal of the French delegate, for the word "States" used heretofore, was substituted the expression "Powers" (Puissances) to designate those taking part in the Conference.[21]

The Theory of *"ius inter potestates"* was elaborated by the Rus-

[18] Wagnon, *Op. cit.* p. 52.

[19] *Acte finale de la première conference de la Paix,* art. 60—Publications de l'Institute international de la Paix, n. 12 (Munich, 1910), p. 42.

[20] Cf. Leo XIII, Epist. ad Gulielminam (29 Maji 1899)—*Acta Leonis* XIII, XIX, 83; Concistorial Allocution (December 14, 1899), *ibid.* p. 261.

[21] Mostaza, *Op. cit.,* p. 89; cf. Eppstein, *The Catholic Tradition of the Law of Nations,* pp. 172-175; Le Fur, *Le Saint-Siège et le Droit des Gens,* p. 40.

sian Baron M. de Taube.[22] According to this Theory the international order is chiefly concerned with political questions and territorial boundaries. The Holy See, a universal spiritual power, rejects every limit based on territory and is thus placed both outside and above international law. However, since the Holy See does not refuse to treat with states and since she is the organ of an autonomous religious society, she must be acknowledged as having a juridical capacity. This juridical capacity can be compared only in part with that of States. Hence the relations between the Holy See and the different States should be subject to a special law, namely the *"ius inter potestates,"* that is, a law which governs the non-territorial sovereign powers.

This manner of conceiving the relations between the Holy See and States remained an experiment without issue; perhaps because the system appeared more speculative than practical, or rather because what is properly called international law confines itself to the discussion of questions of a territorial character.[23] It may also be noted that almost contemporaneous with the exposition of the Theory of Baron de Taube, on the occasion of the rupture of diplomatic relations with France, Pius X insisted on the international obligation of the parties bound by the Concordat, and stated expressly: *"illa pactio eodem iure ac caeterae quae inter civitates regitur, hoc est iure gentium,"* and he went on to add that the violation of such pacts was not only an injury to the Holy See but also an offence against the international order in as much as it discarded the inviolability of pacts solemnly concluded according to the rules of the Law of Nations.[24]

VI *The Positivist Theory.* In order to affirm that the Holy See belongs to the international community it is necessary to show that there exists a positive international law which can be applied to it, and that it contains within itself elements on which an affirmative

[22] "La situation internationale actuelle du Pape et l'idée d'un droit entre pouvoirs (*ius inter potestates*)," *Archiv für Rechts und Wirtschafts philosophie,* I (1907-1908), 360-368; 518 quoted by Chklaver, *Le droit international dans ses rapports avec la philosophie du droit,* p. 167.

[23] Wagnon, *Op. cit.,* pp. 54-56.

[24] Pius X, Encyl. *"Vehementer Nos"* (11 feb. 1906)—Fontes, n. 671).

conclusion may be logically based. The Positivist school denied the personality of the Holy See by reason of the fact that authors, in dealing with the subject of the Law of Nations, started by presupposing the necessity of territory. A negative conclusion was easily reached on the simple verification of the fact that after 1870 the Holy See had no territory over which soverignty could be exercised.

When, however, public international law, confronted by the evidence of facts, was forced to admit that institutions other than States possessed an international personality, the way was opened for the international recognition of the Holy See.

Investigation concerned itself with the consideration of those elements which positive law recognizes as an expression of juridical capacity in international affairs. The first elements to be found were of an historical nature, that is, derived from ecclesiastical tradition, such as the right of active and passive legation, the concluding of concordats, (which in many respects can be compared with international treaties), and acts of recognition on the part of other international persons.[25] Here again there are many controversies according to the point of view from which the authors started and whether they considered all these elements together or only some of them.

Furthermore there are some who see in the relations between the Holy See and the different states in the period 1870-1929 nothing more than a logical continuation of the historical international personality formerly attaching to the Pope as Head of the republic of Christian nations. All the business transacted between the Holy See and those powers retained, from the international point of view, a juridical character.[26] Article II of the Law of Guarantees implicity acknowledges the right of active and passive legation on the part of the Holy See in as much as these guarantees concede that the envoys of foreign governments to His Holiness and the envoys of His Holiness to foreign governments may enjoy, on the part of the kingdom of Italy, all the immunities and prerogatives in use in

[25] Fedozzi, *Trattato di Diritto Internazionale;* vol. I: *Introduzione e Parte Generale,* pp. 146-147.

[26] Romano, *Corso di Diritto Internazionale,* p. 68; cf. Jannaccone, "La personalità giuridica della Chiesa," *DE,* XLI (1930), 381-443.

international law. According to the opinion of Anzilotti,[27] however, no argument in favor of the juridical personality of the Holy See may the deduced from the recognition thus given by the Law of Guarantees. The right of legation, he argues, is to be considered as an attribute belonging exclusively to international persons, whereas the Law of Guarantees is an internal law and cannot grant international rights. In our case, however, we do not base our argument on the supposition that the Law of Guarantees grants the right of legation, but only that it recognizes and accepts an element inherent in international law. Facts go to prove that during the abovementioned period the right of legation, so far as the Holy See was concerned, remained unchanged in its juridical aspects. Nuncios continued to be accredited and received by governments in the traditional way. For these reasons there are authors who maintain that the right of legation is a proof that the international personality of the Holy See survived during the period of the suppression of the Papal States. In fact there is nothing to prove that the title of such a right was changed from a juridical into a gratuitous one, or that the foundation of such a right has passed from international law into the domain of the internal law of the different States, in as much as no such declaration had been made by the various governments and could not be even implicitly deduced from their attitude.[28]

Concordats constitute another argument advanced in favor of the international personality of the Holy See. Abstracting from speculative discussions in these agreements as to the true juridical nature of these acts, it cannot be denied that the Holy See and a particular State come together with the express will of concluding a solemn

[27] *Corso di Diritto Internazionale,* p. 138.

[28] Cfr. Ponce v. Roman Catholic Ap. Church in Porto Rico, decided June 1, 1908—Moore's, *Digest of International Law,* I, 130-131; Brown Scott, "The Treaty between Italy and the Vatican," *Proceedings of the American Society of International Law,* 23rd Meeting (1929) p. 18; Piola, *La questione romana nella storia e nel diritto. Da Cavour al Trattato del Laterano,* pp. 174-178; Petroncelli, "La Santa Sede e lo Stato della Città del Vaticano" *RISS,* XL (1932), 172-173.

pact. We should not deny, as do Ottolenghi,[29] Roman [30] and Falco,[31] that concordats have the juridical character of international contracts. These authors base their opinion on the supposition that the Church is devoid of juridical personality in international affairs. On the contrary, we should affirm the international character of the Holy See considering that concordats are to be referred to the international juridical order. No difficulty arises from the fact that concordats have remained historically distinct from international treaties, nor is any difficulty caused by reason of the subject-matter of concordats. It is the nature of the obligation that is important, and this obligation is governed by the international rule, "*pacta sunt servanda.*" Since, therefore, there exists in the Church a juridical element by means of which she is bound by an obligation which is a rule of the Law of Nations, it must be concluded that she is to be reckoned among the members of the international community.[32]

Finally there is yet another element of international personality in the exercise of the right of recognition and the mediation of the Holy See in international questions. In 1885 Leo XIII was the intermediary in the question which arose between Spain and Germany regarding the possession of the Caroline islands.[33] On September 2, 1905 the Republics of Columbia and Perù came to an agreement *d'arbitrage* by which the matters which could not be solved directly should be left to the decision of the Pope.[34] To quote another example, immediately after the Great War (1914-1918) the Holy See recog-

29 "Sulla personalità internazionale delle unioni di Stati," *RDI,* V (1925), 492.

30 Romano, *Corso di Diritto Internazionale,* p. 58; cf. Balladors Pallieri, "Il Rapporto fra Chiesa Cattolica e Citta del Vaticano," *RISS,* XXXVIII (1920), 208, note 1.

31 Falco, *The Legal position of the Holy See before and after the Lateran agreements,* p. 16.

32 Anzilotti, *Corso di Diritto Internazionale,* pp. 129-131; Morelli, "Il Trattato fra l'Italia e la Santa Sede," *RDI,* VIII (1929), 200-201.

33 Leo XIII, *Epist. ad Oth. Bismarck* (31 dec. 1885)—*Acta Leonis* XIII, V, 179; cf. Wagnon, *Op. cit.,* p. 165; Fedozzi, *Op. cit.,* p. 147.

34 Eppstein, *The Catholic Tradition of the Law of Nations,* pp. 184-186.

nized the independence of the new Republics of Esthonia, Lithuania and Latvia and established diplomatic relations with them.[35]

All these expressions of juridical activity on the part of the Holy See could not escape even the jurists who were accustomed to discuss international law on the basis of positive criteria. Confronted with the evidence of facts they found it necessary to recognize that, notwithstanding petty theories of theirs, the Holy See was a living and active force in the international world. The positivist school of law came thus to the conclusion that since the Holy See was acting as a normal person in international affairs, she had to be considered as a normal subject of the international community.

As a matter of fact, the Positivist Theory honestly recognized that the juridical value of the very same arguments, which are usually admitted for membership in the international community, stands likewise for the case of the Holy See. It does not, however, sufficiently demonstrate how this right *"iure suo"* actually springs out of the very nature of things.

VII. *The Theory of Spiritual Sovereignty.* While some Catholic authors have attempted to uphold the thesis of an independent Vatican Principality during the period 1870-1929, all agree in teaching that the real foundation of the international personality of the Holy See is its spiritual sovereignty. This theory had a certain number of adherents even among the "Internationalists." [36]

The Law of Guarantees recognized the spiritual sovereignty and certain prerogatives of the Pope:

Art. 9 — The Sovereign Pontiff is entirely free in the performance of all the functions of his spiritual ministry.

Art. 12 — The Sovereign Pontiff corresponds freely with the episcopate and with the whole Catholic World without any interference from the Italian government.[37]

Nevertheless this guarantee was resolutely and constantly rejected,

[35] "Riconoscimento della Repubblica di Estonia," *La Civilta Cattolica,* 1921, IV, 360; Giannini, *I Concordati Postbellici,* p. 44 note 1.

[36] Cf. Micossi, *La Piena Personalità Giuridica Internazionale della Chiesa Cattolica secondo la Dottrina dei Civilisti,* pp. 14-20; 50-59.

[37] Legge delle Guarantigie (13 maggio 1871)—Jemolo, *La Questione Romana,* p. 108; Williamson, *The Treaty of the Lateran,* p. 12.

since its acceptance would have made the Pope the subject of the Italian State, the spiritual recognition therein contained being an *"umbra sine re"* of sovereignty. The predominant idea of the situation was that sovereignty could not exist without a territorial basis. In their protests the Popes upheld the idea that a certain amount of territory, however little, was necessary as a pledge for the independent exercise of spiritual power. Leo XIII writing to Cardinal Rampolla, Secretary of State, on Octiber 5, 1895: "It is vain to have recourse to legislative expedients: no manner of juridical provisions can ever confer independence without territorial jurisdiction. The condition, which they declare to have guaranteed to us, is not that which is due to us and which we need; it is an independence which is not effective, but apparent and ephemeral, because subordinate to the will of another. He who grants this kind of independence can take it away; yesterday they sanctioned it, tomorrow they can abrogate it." [38] The same idea was again answered by Pius XI when commenting on the Lateran Treaty. This treaty, he writes, is "destined to recognize and, as far as is humanly possible, to insure to the Holy See a true and real territorial sovereignty, since no form of true sovereignty has been known, at least until now, other than territorial sovereignty." [39] If these were the just claims of the Pope, of what use was it to assert that spiritual sovereignty was a juridical title sufficient to classify the Holy See as a juridical person in international law? The Theory of spiritual sovereignty did not seek to solve the *"Roman Question"* from the point of view of law. In fact it is unnecessary to state that little or nothing was left to the decision of jurists in the matter. The Theory of spiritual sovereignty did but bring forward an argument to sustain a right inherent in the nature of things and explain the fact that, whether one admitted it or not, the Holy See formed part of the international community and exercised no small influence therein. The basis of this active international personality could not be a principality, of whose hypothetical existence there was no evidence. It could not be the creative or permissive will of other states, since an act of international recog-

[38] Leo XIII Epist. ad Card. Rampolla—*Acta Leonis XIII,* XV, 372.

[39] Discourse to the Lenten preachers (11 February 1929)—*AAS,* XXI (1929) 105.

nition consists merely in the verification of a fact. The true basis of the international personality of the Holy See between 1870 and 1929 was her spiritual sovereignty.

One of the first jurists to approach the problem of the international personality of the Holy See from a point of view not based on territory was Pasquale Fiore. For this author the characteristic requisite for an international personality consists in its individuality and its independence of territorial relations in its own juridical sphere. A religious society can arrive at this position when, on the basis of the principle of liberty of conscience (a principle respected by all civilized people), it voluntarily establishes itself under the authority of a supreme head as the centre of unity of doctrine and worship.[40] Not every religious association, however, can enjoy this right, but only an association which possesses a world-wide character. In this case territorial sovereignty is not required for its personality and its independence.[41] According to this principle: "every church can be a person of international law, provided it can be considered world-wide."[42] As a matter of fact, "the right to be regarded as a universal institution and thus to assume *"iure suo"* the character of an international person has to be attributed to the Roman Catholic Church. The Catholic Church as it is, and as tradition and history have formed it . . . possesses the character of a world-wide institution and . . . no other religious body can claim for itself the same condition."[43]

Fiore next proceeds to discuss the right of autonomy and the freedom of government which the Catholic Church should enjoy, and the duties which She should assume with reference to States. She is in fact a member of the international community for the security of social order.[44]

The argument for the international recognition of the Church, based on the essential demands of her constitution was further de-

[40] Fiore, *Trattato di Diritto Internazionale Pubblica,* I, 462-474.

[41] Fiore, *Il Diritto Internazionale Codificato,* art. 555.

[42] Fiore, *Op. cit.,* art. 72.

[43] Fiore, *Op. cit.,* art. 705.

[44] Fiore, *Op. cit.,* art. 706-732.

veloped by Pillet.[45] The Church like the State, is a sovereign juridical society, independent and perfectly organized, and so to her belongs international personality for the same reasons that it belongs to the State. The acknowledgment of the international personality of States is a necessity of social life. Every State in its relations with other States presents itself as a distinct, independent and organized community, with which it is impossible to have contact except by treating it on terms of equality and recognizing that it has a juridical capacity on a par with their own. These juridical characteristics are found in the Catholic Church. She is distinguished from every State by the universal character of her mission, by her highly-developed organization—the most perfect known to the world—and by the independence which she displays to the point of not permitting any authority to interfere with her dogmas and her moral code.

According to Pillet, for the international recognition of the Catholic Church it is not necessary to have recourse to dogmatic requirements, since the right to recognition arises directly from the principle of liberty of conscience, a principle which has acquired universal value among the civilized peoples. The problem does not admit of discussion from the point of view of Catholic and non-catholic states. The Pope is not, and cannot, be considered an outsider to any country. His mission is spiritual and, by its very nature, (though there is, besides, the divine mandate), is destined to embrace the whole world. The international personality of the Catholic Church, or of the Holy See, emanating as it does from a spiritual principle, is rightly present everywhere. The foundation of this personality is not derivative, but intrinsic to the very nature of the Church. Thus a state may, if it so wishes, ban Catholicism, but it can never call into question the international juridical capacity of the Holy See.

As may be seen, these authors base the arguments which they bring forward both on the natural rights of individuals to form themselves into a religious society, and on the social requirements of such society, provided it possesses the elements to enable it to perform its respective mission in the world.

Since international personality belongs to societies which exist

[45] Sirey, Recueil général des lois et des arrêts (a. 1895, IIe partie): Note, pp. 57-61.

"iure suo," the spiritual sovereignty of the Church forthwith calls for international personality.[46] The Holy See is therefore a necessary person of international law.

There were some who held that the Holy See should be accepted as an international person from point of view of politics above. The Popes wield such power even in the political sphere that States, so far from excluding them from the international community, should cultivate a friendship that would be entirely to their advantage. Besides the Holy See is a political power which by its very independence demands the recognition of governments.[47]

In view of statements such as these and taking the prevailing international practice into account, the almost dogmatic principle of territorial sovereignty gradually lost much of its rigidity, and the way was opened to unanimous agreement in favor of the international personality of the Holy See. The idea of a Spiritual Sovereignty gained little by little, such consistency in the doctrinal treatises,[48] as to appear as a logical consesuence when it was later inserted in Art. 2 of the Lateran Treaty. Here the sovereignty of the Holy See in international affairs is recognized as an attribute inherent in its nature and as necessary for the discharge of its spiritual mission in the world.

Article III: The Holy See and the Vatican City

On February 11, 1929 the Holy See and Italy reached an irrevocable and definite settlement of the *"Roman Question" by* means of the Lateran Treaty. In this agreement reciprocal recognition was given to the Kingdom of Italy under the dynasty of the House of Savoy with Rome as capital of the Italian state, and to the Vatican City State under the sovereignty of the Pope.

Now what becomes of all the controversies regarding the international position of the Holy See? Can it be said that the Lateran

[46] Flaischlen, "La situation juridique du Pape comme Chef suprême de la religion catholique," *RDILC,* XXXVI (1904), 89-95; Vergnes, *La condition internationale de la Papauté,* pp. 187-223.

[47] H. Donnedieu de Vabres, "La souvraineté du Pape et la separation des Eglises et de l'Etat, *"RGDIP,* XXI (1914), 351-354.

[48] Cfr. Le Fur, *Etat fédéral et Confederation d'Etats,* pp. 418-443.

Treaty, recognizing a territorial sovereignty and restoring a situation substantially the same as that which existed before 1870, has placed the fact that the Holy See belongs to the international community beyond doubt. To settle this point it remains to be seen what juridical condition the Treaty has established within the small enclosure of 108.7 acres which marks the territorial limits Vatican City.

The principal questions arising out of the conditions created by the Lateran Treaty may be summed up in the following queries: (1) Is the Vatican City a state? (2) What is the juridical connexion between the Vatican City and the Holy See? (3) What consequences may be deducted from the existence of a Vatican State so far as the international position of the Holy See is concerned?

In the text of the Lateran Treaty we read as follows:

"Preamble. To assure absolute and visible independence to the Holy See and to guarantee its undisputed sovereignty also in the international sphere, it has been deemed necessary to constitute, by special modalities or provisions, the Vatican City, acknowledging the full ownership and the exclusive and absolute power and sovereign jurisdiction of the Holy See over the same.

Art. 2 — Italy recognizes the sovereignty of the Holy See in the international sphere as an attribute inherent in its nature, in conformity with its tradition and the requirements of its mission in the world.

Art. 3 — Italy recognizes in the Holy See full ownership and exclusive and absolute power and sovereign jurisdiction over the Vatican as it is actually constituted, together with all its appurtenences and endowments, thus creating the Vatican City for the special ends and in the manner described in the present Treaty.

Art. 4 — The exclusive sovereignty and jurisdiction acknowledged by Italy as belonging to the Holy See over the Vatican City implies that the Italian government may in no manner interfere therein, and that no authority exists there except that of the Holy See.

Art. 26 — The Holy See acknowledges that with the agreements signed today adequate provision has been made for the exercise of the pastoral government of the diocese of Rome and of the Catholic Church in Italy and in the world with due liberty and independence.

It declares that the *"Roman Question"* is definitely and irrevocably settled and consequently eliminated, and recognizes the Kingdom of Italy under the dynasty of the House of Savoy with Rome as the capital of the Italian state.

In its turn Italy recognizes the Vatican City State under the sovereignty of the Pope." [1]

These articles constitute the juridical foundation of the origin of Vatican City. Some authors, however, raise the question whether by these articles Vatican City has been constituted a State in the true and proper sense of the term.

First of all it seems certain that a state cannot result directly from a treaty: a treaty can determine the elements of a new State, but a State, as such, does not materialize until effectively organized.[2] On the other hand it is also certain that a treaty to establish a new state is not conceivable unless the elements which form the object of the agreement be present.

With reference to Vatican City it is alleged that, whatever may be said to be the value and import of the expression sused, it cannot be said that a State is realized until its constitutive elements are evidenced. Now, as is well known, the elements commonly required for the establishment of a state are territory, a people and an independent political organization. As a matter of fact these elements, as Charles Rousseau observes,[3] are not found in a sufficient measure in the Vatican City to justify its being designated as a State. Its territory is too small and is divided into a multiplicity of moral entities; its population is insignificant and consists of functionaries; and its organization is reduced to a hierarchy of offices. Besides, the specific juridical character of a State, namely sovereignty, is lacking. The sovereignty attaching to the Head of a State is essentially different from that attaching to the Pope. The sovereignty of the former is based on Territory elements while that of the latter is based on the separation of the temporal from the spiritual power.

[1] Trattato fra la Santa Sede e l'Italia (11 febbraio 1929,—*AAS*, XXI (1929), 209-211; Perugini, *Concordata Vigentia*, pp. 96-110.

[2] Fedozzi, *Trattato di Diritto Internazionale*: *vol. I, Introduzione e Parte Generale*, p. 109.

[3] "L'Etat de la Cité du Vatican" *RGDIP*, XXXVII (1930), 145-153.

The Holy See, continues this author, remains in the position in which it was before the Lateran Treaty, that is, excluded from international law. The Treaty did not establish a juridical basis sufficient for the existence of a State and did not even confer on the Pope that sovereignty which is a prerequisite of international personality.

Other authors go so far as to deny to the Vatican City the character of a State because of the juridical relation which binds the Vatican City to the Holy See. In the Treaty no mention is made of the creation of a distinct State, but merely of territory placed at the free disposition of the Holy See. This territory is not the subject of rights but has been formed and exists for the one purpose of serving as an attribute of the independence of the Holy See. Therefore the Vatican City becomes by its constitution the *object* of the rights of the Holy See: this amounts to saying that this territory is not endowed with any distinct juridical capacity, since nothing can be at the same time the subject and object of international rights.[4] "The Holy See and the Vatican City—adds D. Donati [5] are two institutions of which one is coordinated or subordinated to the other, but the Holy See assumes the civil functions of the State and identifies itself with one of its elements, namely, with the person of the State. Hence the person of the State and of the Holy See are identical, that is, they are one person. A more or less similar opinion is held by some French authors who consider the Vatican City not as a state but as an extra-state territory, separated from any other power, that is, as an *enclave* created for the Holy See's aims and submitted to her spiritual sovereignty.[6]

[4] Checchini, "La natura giuridica della Città del Vaticano e del 'Trattato' Lateranense," *RDI,* IX (1930), 200-202. It seems to Checchini (*Op. cit.,* p. 203) that A. C. Jemolo also arrived at this conclusion. In fact Jemolo, "Carattere dello Stato della Città del Vaticano," *RDI* VIII (1929), 188-196, holds that the Vatican City is a *non-sovereign state* and is so necessarily bound to the Holy See that if by an hypothesis it wished to establish itself independently, that portion of territory would return to the Italian State. A *non-sovereign state* is equivalent to *no state.*

[5] *La Città del Vaticano nella teoria generale dello Stato,* p. 54.

[6] Renard, "L'Eglise et la souveraine té," *La Vie Intellectuelle,* XIV, 20-30. Jarrige, *La Condition international du S.Siège,* p. 75; Rivet, *La question romaine et le traité du Latran,* p. 216.

Arguing from the element of sovereignty Bracci[7] also denies the character of a State to Vatican City. Being merely Vatican territory under the sovereignty of the Holy See, it is not possible to predicate of it that original or native sovereignty which is necessary to the very nature of a state.

Finally, according to others, Vatican City is nothing more than a collection of proprietary rights and persons with special features designed for the service of the Holy See. Had the Holy See become a state it would have changed its nature by ceasing to be the central organ in charge of the government of the Church: in the Lateran Treaty no double personality can be detected ([7] bis).

All these authors when faced with the difficulty arising out of article 26 of the Treaty, ("Italy recognizes the *State of the Vatican City* under the sovereignty of the Pope,") answer unanimously with the gratuitous statement that this article should be interpreted and identified with article 2 where mention is made of the personality of the Holy See but not of the Vatican City.

To reasonings of this kind the upholders of the theory which acknowledges in the Vatican City the characteristics of a real State reply by rightly observing as follows.

First, with reference to *territory,* as essential to sovereignty, one recalls the noble words of a discourse of Pius XI: " . . . . no worldly desires moves the Vicar of Jesus Christ, but only the conscientious necessity of demanding that which it is impossible not to demand. Territorial sovereignty is universally recognized as a condition indispensable to all true jurisdictional sovereignty. Therefore it is, that we demand at least *such amount of territory as is required to supply a basis for sovereignty;* that amount of territory without which this sovereignty would be impossible, as it would lack that on which it could rest. It will be clear we trust, that the Pope has only that amount of material territory as is indispensable for the exercise of the spiritual power entrusted to men for the welfare of men. We do not hesitate to say that we are pleased that things should be so.

[7] *Italia, S.Sede e Città del Vaticano,* p. 69; lf. Petroncelli, "La Santa Sede e lo Stato della Città del Vaticano," *RISS* XL (1932), 181-185.

[7] bis) Siotto-Pintor, "Les sujets du droit international autres que les Etats," *Recueil des cours,* XLI (1932-III) 327-332.

We are pleased to see the material territory reduced to such small proportions that it can and should be considered spiritualized by the immeasurable, exalted and truly divine spirituality which it is destined to support and to serve." [8]

The area of the territory of Vatican City is about one square kilometre; but there is no rule in the international juridical order prescribing the extent required for the existence of a State. The only thing necessary, and also sufficient, is that the authority therein exercised be not subject to outside control; and that obtains in the case of Vatican City.[9] Besides, the conditions in which the Holy See found herself with respect to the unification of Italy showed that it would have been enormously difficult to secure a solution which would have granted more territory. In any case the territory obtainable would have been very small. The reduction of it to a minimum is evidence of great wisdom. On the one hand, a great principle is saved, on the other, difficulties of a political, economic and administrative order are eliminated. The smallness of the territory becomes a protection, since the government of the universal Church is then not worried by problems of a material nature. A State, a political power, is the stronger in the measure that its resources are the greater and its territory the more extended but the opposite may be said to be true in the case of the Pope, who is a spiritual power.[10]

Secondly, with reference to *population*. The population of Vatican City certainly exhibits a juridical aspect which may be said to be altogether singular. Though the *"ius sanguinis"* and the *"ius soli"* are here fundamentally respected, these do not, of themselves, constitute an exclusive right to *"civitas."* In its ultimate analysis Vatican citizenship depends on the authorization of the Pope. This is due to the narrow limits of Vatican City and to its special functions for in the service of the Church. This, however, does not mean that the inhabitants of the Vatican City have a citizenship that is juridically defective. The citizenship of all States is regulated

[8] Discourse to the Lenten preachers 11 february 1929)—*AAS,* XXI (1929), 108; cf. Cammeo, *Ordinamento Giuridico dello Stato della Città del Vaticano,* pp. 37-49.

[9] Brazzola, *La Cité du Vatican est-elle un Etat?* p. 141.

[10] Cf. Le Fur, *Le Saint-Siège et le Droit des gens,* pp. 30-33.

by their internal laws, and is entirely independent of all regulations of an international character. Limitation in numbers in no way affects the nature of citizenship.[11]

It does not appear, then, how an argument to deny that Vatican City is a State can be deduced from the fact that the majority of its citizens are officials. Vatican citizens enjoy a greater amount of civic benefits than are enjoyed by members of other states.

Thirdly, with reference to *organization*. The Vatican City has its own special juridical life. "The Pope, the sovereign of the Vatican City State, enjoys the fulness of legislative, executive and judicial power."[12] The Vatican City has its administrative laws, its tribunals, its economic service and its own police force. The Pope as a territorial sovereign has taken part in international transactions and agreements relating to commercial and monetary questions, means of transport and postal services.[13]

What must be specially stressed here is the fundamental statute governing Vatican City. This enactment does not emanate from the Holy See as the supreme organ of authority in the Catholic Church, but from the Holy See as the supreme organ of a State. The Pope is a temporal sovereign in the same sense as earthly princes are. The two sovereignties are found united in the same person, but this does not prevent their being considered separately. So true is this, that the temporal sovereignty might cease (as actually happened in the period 1870-1929) and the spiritual sovereignty still continue to exist. Though Vatican City is intimately bound up with the Holy See, it is evident that the ends intended and pursued by Vatican City are not those of the Holy See. The pursuit of the common temporal good of the citizens and right administration are the proper ends of the State and can in no way be identified with the ends of the Church. In this respect it may be said that the relation between the Holy See and the Vatican City is not sub-

[11] Cf. Legge sulla cittadinanza (June 7, 1929) — *AAS*, XXI (1929): Supplemento, pp. 14-16; Brazzola, *Op. cit.*, pp. 175-200; Cammeo, *Op. cit.*, pp. 49-60.

[12] Legge fondamentale della Città del Vaticano, art. 1 — *AAS*, XXI (1929): Supplemento, p. 1; Cammeo, *Op. cit.*, 60.

[13] Cf. Brazzola, *Op. cit.*, pp. 202-216.

stantially different from that obtaining between the Holy See and other States.[14]

In the Vatican City, therefore, all elements are found that are essential to the constitution of a state. There are special features present and it appears that these can be explained by considering the ends and the juridical relation which exists between Vatican City and the Holy See. In the Treaty itself there occurs an explicit declaration to the effect that Vatican City is a State and that there exists a double international personality. Article 2 recognizes the ***personality of the Holy See*** as an attribute inherent in its nature, and altogether in conformity with its tradition and the requirements of its mission in the world. Article 26 recognizes the ***State of the Vatican City.*** To say that the two articles mean the same thing and refer to the single personality of the Holy See is arbitrary and contrary to the clear and unequivocal meaning of the terms.

Due to the absolute power of the Pope as Supreme Head of the Church and as Sovereign of the Papal State, the Holy See, the common organ, represents two subjects which are distinct in international law. Hence it has to be seen what juridical relation exists between the two personalities. Some authors favor the juridical form which is called a personal union,[15] but the generality advocate a real union.[16] The union of two or more States is said to be personal when two States so maintain their independence that the bond of union is the common sovereign. Real union is present when two or more States have a common representative body in international juridical life.[17] The union known as real seems better to correspond to the link which necessarily binds Vatican City to the Holy See. Here again we

[14] Pennisi, "La personalità internazionale della Chiesa Cattolica ed il rapporto giuridico tra la Chiesa Cattolica e lo Stato della Città del Vaticano" *ACII,* V (1937) 10-11.

[15] Morelli, "Il Trattato fra l'Italia e la Santa Sede," *RDI* VIII (1929), 223.

[16] Piola, *La questione romana nella storia e nel diritto.* Da Cavour al Trattato del Laterano, p. 222; "Per una bibliografia ragionata dei patti del Laterano," *DE,* XLV (1934), 479-484; Pennisi, *Op. cit.,* pp. 12-13; Wagnon, *Concordats et Droit International,* pp. 59-60.

[17] Le Fur, *Précis de droit international public,* pp. 74-75. Güenechea, *Principia Iuris politici,* I, 38-39.

are dealing with an analogy rather than a state of affairs which has a parallel in political life in general. In fact a union occurs here between an international person which is a state, and another international person which is not a state. Since Vatican City has been established in order to serve the spiritual mission of the Holy See, the link between them does not arise from an international treaty but from the relation of two elements, such as of body and soul; it is a union which is stronger and more intimate than any formed by an international agreement.[18]

The Lateran agreement has an international value not only because of the solution of the *"Roman Question"* but also for the changes it effected in the teaching of jurists. Those who require territorial sovereignty as a condition necessary for international personality hold that the Holy See has again taken its place among the members of the international community. According to the supporters of this theory, the international person in question is the Vatican City State, since the latter constitutes an order of things substantially the same as that existing before 1870.[19] Likewise the Holy See, as personifying the Vatican City State, has acquired an international personality which it did not previously possess.[20]

It is, however, certain that both before and after the Lateran agreements the Pope was and is the representative person in international law, namely the Catholic Church; and, as a result of these agreements, he has also become the organ of a new subject of international law, namely the Vatican City State.

It cannot be said that the Lateran Treaty has not further enhanced the Holy See from the point of view of the different nations

[18] Fedozzi, *Trattato di Diritto Internazionale*: vol. I, *Introduzione e Parte Generale,* p. 156; cf. Jemolo, "Carattere dello Stato della Città del Vaticano" *RDI,* VIII (1929), 193-195. Brazzola, *Op. cit.,* p. 239; Balladore-Pallieri, "Il Rapporto fra Chiesa Cattolina e Stato Vaticano secondo il Diritto Ecclesiastico e il diritto Internazonale," *RISS,* XXXVIII (1930), 200-203; Cammeo, *Op. cit.,* pp. 67-72.

[19] Cavaglieri, Corso di Diritto Internazionale, p. 115; Ottolenghi, "Sulla condizione giuridica della Cità del Vaticano," *RDI,* IX (1930), 180-195.

[20] Donati, *La Città del Vaticano nella teoria generale dello Stato,* pp. 72-74.

apart from making peace with Italy. On the contrary it is evident to all the nations that the Holy See is now in possession of a territory, however small, over which it exercises sovereign powers, as a symbol of the independence and the liberty necessary for the carrying out of its mission in the world. On the other hand the Treaty is a political agreement, concluded by the Holy See before she was in possession of territory—a fact which demonstrates once more that the international juridical capacity of the Holy See has its foundation on its spiritual powers. If this were not true, it should be said that the Treaty, like the Law of Guaarntees, was merely an agreement unilateral on the part of Italy; or, at most, a Concordat, as Checchini would have it.[21] The Treaty is, however, a true political instrument for matters therein dealt with, namely the recognition of a sovereignty and of a juridical personality in international affairs, the settlement of a question arising out of an act of war and partly territorial in nature, the exchange of diplomatic relations, etc. If the Holy See is juridically pledged in an act which has an international value, it is also in possession of a juridical title which places it among the subjects of Jus Gentium.

Article IV: The Basis of the International Personality of The Holy See

The controversy regarding the international personality of the Holy See originated with the events of September 20, 1870, but linked with it is the juridical question, namely, what quality is required that an institution could demand to be numbered among the members of the international community. The prevalent doctrine held that territory was an element indispensable to international recognition. The opinions based on this supposition are reduced to two, according as the territorial jurisdiction of the Holy See is either affirmed or denied. The majority of authors held that this jurisdiction over territory did not exist. Some forthwith dismissed the question of the international personality of the Holy See as one not to be entertained. Others, not being able honestly to deny this per-

21 "La natura giuridica della Città del Vaticano e del Trattato Lateranense," *RDI*, IX (1930), 204-211.

sonality, had recourse to a juridical order altogether *sui generis,* adducing a "personality of attribution." These latter acknowledged the fact and also the right proceeding from a peculiar state of things, though perhaps not admitting the fundamental right inherent in the very constitution of the Church. The few who still maintained the continuity of the temporal power based their theory on the fact that the Vatican itself was never occupied, and accordingly contended that the fundamental element of juridical recogntion, namely territory, was not absent. This plea was offered as an argument against the extremists who absolutely denied the international personality of the Holy See, but they always maintained that this personality was a postulate of the juridical perfection of the Church, whose territorial rights were not subject to prescription. Finally there were some who considered the question entirely apart from the existence of territorial dominion and who drew an apodictic argument from the independent existence of the Holy See, which is accordingly in possession of a legitimate juridical title enabling it to be numbered among persons of international law.

It may be noted that while the majority of authors looked on territory as an indispensable element for the recognition of persons in the Law of Nations, the Supreme Authority of the Church, while proclaiming the necessity of that territory, regarded it merely as a means of guaranteeing and protecting the liberty of the spiritual power. Here international personality was not considered from the point of view of territory. The right of the Holy See to this guarantee, "adequately assuring it such measure of liberty and independence as is required for the pastoral government of the diocese of Rome and of the Catholic Church in Italy and in the world," [1] was recognized by the Agreements of 1929. In the meantime, as has been often stated, the Holy See belonged to the international community and took therein an active part. But it may be asked, by what juridical title? Before laying down and re-affirming directly the international position of the Holy See, it is necessary to make some observations on the suject which has been the stumbling-block in the whole of this

[1] Lateran Treaty, art. 26—Perugini, *Concordata Vigentia,* p. 110. The quotations from the concordats, unless otherwise stated, are from this collection of Perugini.

long controversy. The question is: What part does territory play in the classification of subjects of international law?

From the positive point of view, territory is indispensable to the State,[2] but it is not indispensable for international law. "The liberty which belongs to states in international law is exercised, on the one hand, in the power of issuing orders to citizens no matter where they may be, and, on the other hand, in the power of issuing orders within certain territorial limits to all persons and with respect to all matters connected therewith. Hence according to international law the territory is nothing more than the space in which the power of the State is exercised, having due regard for the limits imposed by the general or particular rules of international law."[3] Furthermore the internal order of a state is quite distinct from the international order, and the fact that Law of Nations permits a state to pass its territorial limits shows that territory is not the constitutive element of international personality.

There are territorial powers, such as Colonies, Vassal States and Protectorates, which are not persons in international law. The element required for personality is not so much territory, as sufficient political autonomy. Article I of the Covenant of the League of Nations expressly declares that all States, Dominions and Colonies may become members of the League provided that they are freely governed.[4] The right of territorial powers to international recognition is therefore based on the independence of their political organi-

[2] Cathrein states: "Territorium non pertinet stricte ad essentiam Status; patet ex eo quod supposita unione plurimum familiarum sub aliqua auctoritate suprema cui competant, iura essentialia potestatis civilis, omnia ad essentiam societatis civilis requisita adsunt, sed haec omnia adesse possunt sine territorio."—*Phlosophia Moralis in usum Scholarum* (7th ed., Friburgi Brisgoviae, 1911), p. 422. However it does not appear that this opinion can be held since in the absence of its own special territory there is no way in which a group of families can exercise independence and consequently no real political organization is possible. Cf. Ottaviani, *Institutiones Iuris Publici Ecclesastici*, II, 5-6; Güenechea, *Principia Iuris Politici*, I, 20.

[3] Fedozzi, *Trattato di Diritto Internazionale*, vol. I: *Introduzione e Parte Generale*, p. 349.

[4] Covenant de la Société des Nations, art. I, (2).

zation. That such an organization, in order to be independent, requires territory is explained by the fact that, since the end of all States is identical, namely, the attainment of the common good in the temporal order, States cannot exist together while operating in the same territory, without encroaching on and destroying one another. Also in the case of the state, a relation exists between territorial dominion and a sovereignty which, though not material, is none the less real: territory becomes a means of guaranteeing liberty and independence of action which is of necessity in a civilized community. In ultimate analysis territory is but the material element and support of sovereignty, constituting nothing more than the negative element of power, in as much as it determines and places the limits beyond which the sovereignty of the state cannot extend.[5] The power of the State is necessarily confined to certain limits, but it is clear that sovereignty as such is not subject to limits. International action is thus explained, for it is precisely the power of acting outside the confines of one's own territory.

Now, since it is held that sovereignty constitutes the basis of international personality, it is necessary to consider this aspect of it in its application to the Holy See. The notion of sovereignty seems to be one of the subjects most discussed by international jurists. Authors go to great pains in order to define it. They describe it as the right of commanding, the right of saying the last word, the union of all power, the *"competence des competences,"* the right of being ruled only by one's own will, etc.[6] The fact most worthy of note, in this connexion, is, as Le Fur observes,[7] that all the definitions, though framed to explain the sovereignty of the State, are conveniently and easily adapted to the idea of the sovereignty of the Holy See. The only difference consists in the different ends which the State and the Church have in view. The notion of sovereignty in the two institutions is identical and not infrequently it suits the latter better than the former.

1) Sovereignty is above all a right to command individuals. That this right of ruling men belongs to the Holy See is clear from the

[5] Le Fur, Le Saint-Siège et le Droit des Gens, p. 47.
[6] Cf. Le Fur, *Etat fédéral et Confédération d'Etats,* pp. 418-443.
[7] *Le Saint-Siège et le Droit des Gens,* p. 53.

divine mandate charging the Church to lead all nations into the ecclesiastical fold.[8] In fact the sovereignty of the Holy See over the faithful is more complete than that of the State over its citizens. The Holy See exercises its rule over the intellects and will of its subjects and orders their moral life. The unity of the faith professed and the teaching power of the Church constitute a moral link between superiors and inferiors which is all the stronger because freely accepted by individuals ever ready to submit themselves to the supreme authority.

From the point of view of temporal sovereignty, that is, dominion over territory as well as over individuals, the Holy See makes use of it as a power adaptable to its ends and as necessary to life on earth;[9] this dominion, however, always remains an accessory element of a sovereignty which is altogether spiirtual.

2) For the welfare of the community in its relations with the supreme power it is necessary that the exercise of the sovereignty of the State should be limited by the decision of an authority which cannot be appealed. Transcending from this limitation the authority of the State is regarded as practically infallible, so that every complaint should be considered as practically finished as a result of the decision of the sovereignty whose duty it is to say the last word.[10]

In the case of the Catholic Church infallibility is a reality;[11] consequently the right to the last word does not exist simply for practical reasons, but is a doctrinal question concerning which Catholics have no doubt. Even those who do not believe in papal infallibility as defined by the Vatican Council are obliged to admit that there should exist an authority in religious matters, from whose decision there is no appeal.[12]

3) "The *competence des competences,*" as it is called, undoubtedly belongs to the Holy See so far as the sphere of her exclusive

[8] Mt. XXI, 31; XXVIII, 19; Jn. X, 16; XII, 32; Acts II, 38; 40; IV, 11.

[9] Cavagnis, *Institutiones Iuris Publici Ecclesiastici,* I, 24.

[10] Le Fur, *Op. cit.,* p. 50.

[11] *Conc. Vaticanum,* Sess. IV, cap. 4—Denzinger-Bannwart, *Enchiridion Symbolorum et Definitionum,* nn. 1832-1840.

[12] Le Fur, *Op. cit.,* p. 51.

dominion in spiritual matters is concerned, that is in matters of faith and morals and in questions of ecclesiastical discipline.[13]

4) Lastly, if sovereignty is considered as the right of being ruled only by one's own will, sovereignty again belongs to the Holy See for the reason that for the juridical effects of the acts of the Pope their confirmation by the faithful is in no way required.[14] This power, as also infallibility, do not mean that the authority of the Pope can be used arbitrarily. Papal sovereignty, as also that of the State, does not depend on any other human authority, but proceeds from moral and positive law. In this respect the difference between the two sovereignties consists in the fact that too often the State does not take account of either morality or of positive law.

In accordance with the current interpretation of the Law of Nations it is clear that territory is not the basis of the personality of States. The ultimate reason why States belong to the international community is sought in the sovereignty of the powers they exercise and in the independence of their organization. Thus the international position of the Holy See conforms to the notions of modern terminology. Institutions enjoying independent organization are normal persons in the Law of Nations. If such a quality is found in the Church, it should be concluded that she is in possession of the ordinary requisites of international personality. It will no longer be necessary to have recourse to conceptions *sui generis* or to classifications of a juridical order distinct from the ordinary international order. The personality of the Church should forthwith be accepted with all the characteristics which accompany it.

The elements of the international personality of the Holy See are summed up in a positive and systematic form in article 2 of the Lateran Treaty;

"Italy recognizes the sovereignty of the Holy See in the international sphere as an attribute inherent in its nature, in conformity to its tradition and the requirements of its mission to the world."

In this emphatic affirmation of principle and of fact is to be found the solution of every controversy regarding the juridical basis of the international personality of the Holy See.

[13] Can. 218; 1431; 1518; 1557.

[14] Can. 227; 228; § 2; 2332.

The above article supplies three arguments which in a brief and clear way can serve as a guide for a systematic exposition of the thesis.

A. Sovereignty in the international sphere is an attribute inherent in the nature of the Holy See. The catholic Church is a society of individuals far exceeding in number that of any organization of individuals in the world. Membership of this society is acquired by means of a solemn act of initiation which confers rights and duties. The members are united together in the communion of one faith.[15] But there are essential differences between the members: Some are invested with characteristics of a juridical kind and are deputed to the exercise of the sacred ministry. The vast majority, known as the body of the faithful, may be said to be the object of the sacred ministry. The first are distinguished by the name of *clerics* (persons set apart); the rest are known as the *laity* (people). This distinction is fundamental in the constitution of the Catholic Church and is required by the end for which she was established, namely, the sanctification of souls. The communication of spiritual benefits is entrusted to the clerics for the good of the people.[16]

Again, clerics are also divided into a two-fold hierarchy: the "*hierarchia ordinis*," and the "*hierarchia iurisdictionis*," which denote that they are not all placed on the same level, but that some are subordinated to others, either by reason of the different grades of sacred ordination, or because of the different powers conferred on them in the government of the faithful. The "*hierarchia ordinis*" sub-divides clerics, as deputed to divine worship, into the three categories of bishops, priests and inferior ministers. The "*hierarchia iurisdictionis*" is invested in the Supreme Pontiff, the Pope of Rome, and in the body of Bishops the latter being subordinate to the former in the exercise of their power.[17] The Pope with the Bishops constitutes the "*Ecclesia docens;* the faithful form the "*Ecclesia discens*," and the aggregate of all members constitutes a social body with its own independent organization. A simple glance at the hierarchical organization of the Church shows a central power invested in the Roman Pontiff, and a local power commited to the Bishops, to whom

[15] Can. 87.

[16] Can. 107; 108, § 1; 682.

[17] Can. 108, §§ 2-3; 329.

is entrusted the spiritual care of the faithful who live within a definite territory. It is scarcely necessary to mention that since the erection of dioceses and ecclesiastical provinces,[18] is reserved to the Supreme authority in the Church, the appointment and transfer of the members of the hierarchy, who are sent to govern the different parts of the Catholic fold, appertains to the same Supreme Authority.[19] Likewise the organization of the Church in the various countries does not depend either on the jurisdiction of the body of Bishops or on the authority of the State, but remains subject to the sovereign right of the Roman Pontiff.

The Head and Centre of the Catholic Church is the Pope with supreme and universal power of orders and of jurisdiction over each and all the faithful and over all the churches in matters of faith, morals, and ecclesiastical discipline.[20] Surrounding the Pontiff is the Senate of Cardinals, his chief counsellors and assistants in the government of the Church.[21] Various duties of the pastoral ministry are committed to the Sacred Congregations, each of which is constituted and organized with special powers to deal with the various branches of dogmatic, sacramental, administrative, economic or scholastic discipline.[22] Then there are the Supreme Tribunals of the Holy See: the Sacred Roman Rota to deal with certain appeals with some causes in the first instance, and with all matters which the Pope wishes to submit to its decision,[23] and the Signatura Apostolica which is in charge of the general revision of procedure and of the different powers of the inferior tribunals.[24]

What has been said goes to show the Holy See enjoys sovereignty in the internal administration of the Church. What is of special interest here is to see how the same sovereignty is displayed in relation to the State. The basis of the autonomy of the Church with reference to the State is established by the distinction between the

[18] Can. 215, § 1.

[19] Can. 293; § 1; 312; 329; 332, § 1; 350, § 1; 430, § 1.

[20] Can. 218.

[21] Can. 230.

[22] Can. 242 seqq.

[23] Can. 1598-1601. cf. 1557 § 2.

[24] Can. 1602-1605.

temporal and the spiritual. The sphere of action of the Church is the spiritual order. She exercises her activity in this respect by employing due and adequate means, such as her Divine Founder has provided.[25] Since she turns to all men without distinction of race, nation or class, she is truly said to be supernational and universal. The relative values of the two orders of Society—the civil and the ecclesiastical—are thus set forth by Leo XIII:

"Itaque Deus humani generis procurationem inter duas potestates partitūs est, scilicet ecclesiasticam et civilem, alteram quidem divinis, alteram humanis rebus praepositam. Utraque est in suo genere maxima: habet utraque certos, quibus contineatur, terminos, eosque sua cuiusque natura causaque proxima definitos: unde aliquis velut orbis circumscribitur, in quo sua cuiusque actio iure proprio versetur." [26] The same distinction with reference to the two orders is made by Pius XI when he writes: "If there are not two States, certainly there are two sovereignties, each of which is perfect in its own order, the order which is necessarily determined by its respective end; while it is scarcely necessary to remark that the objective dignity of the ends determines objectively and necessarily the absolute superiority of the Church." [27]

The civil and ecclesiastical societies, though distinct and on a different plane with regard to their respective ends, are on the same plane in respect of the quality of sovereignty. Each of them is directed towards a good which is in itself complete and each possesses the means necessary to attain this good: each is juridically perfect and consequently sovereign and independent.[28] This juridical parity places the Catholic Church in the position required to act as a member of the international community. The relations between juridically in-

[25] Cf. Mt. XXIV, 14; Lk. XXIV, 47; Jn. VI, 40; X, 10; XVII, 3; XX, 21.

[26] Leo XIII, Enc. *"Immortale Dei"* (Inov. 1885), Fontes, n. 592.

[27] Pius XI, Chirogr. ad Card. P. Gasparri (30 maji 1229)—*AAS*, XXI (1929), 300; Lo Grasso, *Ecclesia et Status*, p. 326.

[28] Cf. Cavagnis, *Institutiones Iuris Publici Ecclesiastici*, I, 31-34; Solieri, *Institutiones Iuris Ecclesiastici*, pp. 89-96; Ottaviani, *Institutiones Iuris Publici Ecclesiastici*, I, 57-69.

dependent persons are not subject to their respective internal legislation, but are determined by international law.[29]

The personality attributed to the Catholic Church in international affairs is inherent in her nature in as much as she is a religious society existing *"iure divino seu iure proprio,"* so that her position is fundamentally different from that of any other religious association. Precisely because personality in the international sphere is "an attribute inherent in the nature of the Holy See"—and the Holy See being the personification of the Catholic Church[30] — it is a right which belongs to her even abstracting from any act of formal recognition. An act of recognition constitutes and attributes rights only in the case of religious societies which exist merely by a concession of the State.[31]

The Pope, because of his sovereignty over the Catholic Church, is a sovereign in the international order even abstracting from the consideration of his temporal power (which is nothing more than an external expression). It is his spiritual sovereignty which gives him his international position, in accordance with the Law of Nations.[32]

B. *Sovereignty in the international sphere is in conformity with the requirements of the mission of the Holy See in the world.* The recognition of international personality as a requirement of the mission of the Holy See in the world follows logically from its nature. The Holy See is in charge of the government of the Church in its work of spreading the kingdom of God on earth. Its mission is therefore that of ruling, teaching and governing the faithful in order to lead them towards eternal life. This mission of a spiritual and supernatural order is in itself free and independent, and is confined to strictly religious matters. The Pope appeals only to the conscience of Catholics, without reference to any civil authority, when there is question of propounding revealed truths or framing dogmatic definitions.[33] In fact the civil authorities do not concern themselves

29 Pasquazi, *Ius Internationale Publicum,* pp. 81-82.

30 Le Fur, *Le Saint-Siège et le Droit des Gens,* p. 157.

31 PaPsquazi, *Op. cit.,* pp. 83-84; Brazzola, *LaCité du Vatican,* Est-Elle un Etat? pp. 27-28.

32 Ottaviani, *Op. cit.,* I, 446-447.

33 Can. 1322.

with such matters. There are, however, some matters in which the civil authority claims to have a right on account of their connection with the internal order of the State. It is evident that to the ecclesiastical authority belong all matters purely spiritual, such as the sacraments, ecclesiastical jurisdiction, indulgences, etc.; as also things inseparably connected with these, for example, benefices and the right of patronage (*ius patronatus*). Likewise to the exclusive judgment of the Church appertains the moral guilt in the violation of ecclesiastical laws and the punishment incurred, as also matters which have reference to the persons who enjoy the *privilegium fori.*[34] Moreover, it not infrequently happens that matters, over which the Church has exclusive power, are of vital interest to the State. Thus problems arise connected with the legal position of the clergy, the appointment of bishops, matrimonial legislation, the question of education, church property and in general all questions which become the matter of concordats. Here conflicts can and often do occur and compromise enters in; but only on the lines of juridical equality between the Church and the State, since the two societies are juridically perfect and equally sovereign in their own spheres.

Since in the relations between Church and State there arise for settlement questions different from those which are generally dealt with between one civil State and an other, some hold that such questions should not be dealt with in international law. Pursuing the theory previously elaborated by Baron de Taube, Le Fur[35] argues from the difference of the ends, due necessarily to the nature of the two societies, and maintains that the relations between Church and State should be regulated by *"ius inter potestates"* or to use the French expression, by *"droit intersouvrain"* or *"droit intergroupal."* In the event of competition or aggression the heads of States seek to safeguard their independence by seeing to the security of their territorial boundaries. On the other hand the Pope and the head of a State do not aim to ensure their mutual independence by means of territorial barriers, but by protecting their respective interests in regard to their common subjects. The Pope is not an outsider to any territory or State; he is rather of all States. This is necessarily

[34] Can. 1553; cf. can. 727; Ottaviani, *Op. cit.,* I, 287-294.
[35] *Le Saint-Siège et le Droit des Gens,* pp. 92-96; 190-212.

the case, since no State could permit an outside spiritual power to deal at will with its citizens. The relations therefore between the Holy See and States belong to a juridical order which extends beyond the politico-international one. In fact international law does not go beyond the limits defined by its own terms (*inter nationes, between states*), while the juridical order (*inter potestates*) embraces the relations between social groups of a kindred nature. Thus there are political relations which are international strictly so called, and relations between groups of a different competence, such as the relations between the spiritual and temporal power.[36]

It must certainly be admitted that the relations between the Holy See and different States are of a character *sui generis,* but papal documents, nevertheless, seem to refer them to the rules of international law. The right of active and passive legation follows the general rules of international law,[37] and concordats claim for themselves the solemnity of international pacts.[38] Further, the Church by reason of the immutability of her moral principles and her traditional respect for law proclaims herself the custodian of the Law of Nation.[39] There are those who see no advantage in having recourse to a new terminology,[40] but this is perhaps merely a matter of agreeing on the terms. No matter what language we use, it is paramount to maintain that the mission of the Holy See demands that the State should meet it on terms of equality, since otherwise, the hierarchy of values would be upset. Further, it should not be forgotten that the spiritual is, by its very nature, superior to the temporal. While the end of the Church is nobler than that of the State, the recognition which she demands in international affairs accords her place which is due to her among sovereignties, that is, among moral persons not subject to the internal legislation of States. This condition is,

[36] Cf. Chklaver, *Le droit international dans ses rapports avec la philosophie du droit,* pp. 166-167.

[37] *Tract. Lateran.,* art. 12; *Conc. cum Polonia,* art. 3; *Conc. cum Lithuania,* art. 3; *Conc. cum Germania,* art. 3.

[38] Pius XI, Discorso agli Alumni dell' Università del SS. Cuore di Milano (February 13, 1929) *AAS,* XXI (1929), 114; Enc. "Mit brennender Sorge," (March 14, 1937—*AAS,* XXIX (1937), 146-148; 168-171.

[39] Pius XI, Enc. *"Ubi arcano"* (23 dec. 1922)—*AAS,* XIV (1922) 689.

[40] Wagnon, *Concordats et Droit International,* pp. 73-76.

on the one hand, necessary to the unity of the Church in order that she may safeguard her constitution as against the formation of national religious associations, and, on the other, to guarantee her liberty in her benevolent activity.

C. *The sovereignty of the Holy See in the international sphere is in conformity with her traditions.* To prove from tradition the international position occupied through the ages by the Holy See it would be necessary to retrace the whole history of the Church. A general survey, besides, not being feasible, would also seem superfluous in as much as the problem of the personality of the Holy See did not arise, in an acute form, until after 1870. Let it suffice to give here some references to the earlier manifestations of the juridical personality of the Holy See and recall how it continued to assert itself normally even during the period 1870-1929.

The idea of attributing juridical personality to the Catholic Church comes from the conception vividly portrayed by St. Paul who describes her as a living unity constituting the mystical body of Christ.[41] This idea of St. Paul is, however, nothing more than a development of the words of Our Lord who in order to express the same mystical reality compares Himself to the vine and his disciples to the branches,[42] teaching and praying that the bond of faith and charity would unite His followers[43] and declaring that He would remain with them even to the consummation of the world.[44]

This doctrine found its realization in the first Christian community grouped around the apostles and united in the bond of faith, in the practice of the worship and the exercise of works of charity.[45] Such harmony of thought and affection reigned among the faithful that St. Luke could write: "Multitudinis autem credentium erat cor unum et anima una."[46]

The proscription of the Catholic Church during the three centuries of persecution made impossible the recognition of her juridical

[41] I Cor. XII, 12; 27; Eph. I, 22-23; IV, 16; Gal. III, 16.
[42] Jn. XV, 1-7.
[43] Jn. XVII, 11.
[44] Mt. XXVIII, 20.
[45] Acts II, 42-47; IV, 31-37.
[46] Acts IV, 32.

capacity: the inherent right of the Church was violently repressed. But no sooner had the Christian emperors officially granted her the free exercise of her rights,[47] than she began to assert her position as sovereign power among the nations. This assertion of the Church's sovereignty is enshrined in a historical tradition which is more ancient than that of any civil power.

After the fall of the Empire of the West (476), the political disorganization and the continual incursions of the barbarians seriously endangered the progress previously made by the Catholic Church. Owing to the neglect of the authorities at Byzantium and Ravenna the Popes had often, single-handed, striven to stem the onslaught of the invaders, while never losing sight of their conversion to *Catholicism* and establishing a policy of peace.[48] Deprived of guidance and protection, the people of Rome naturally turned to the Pope. Nothwithstanding the presence of the Commissaries of the Emperor, a command was established in Rome under the title *"Sancta Dei Ecclesiae Respublica"* [49] with a government in the hands of the Pope. His authority is the authority of Peter: "an authority which is present and active like that of a living man; the authority of the Apostle Peter: his tomb is his throne. St. Peter it is who possesses, St. Peter who receives donations, St. Peter who writes, disposes, entreats, commands."[50] Pepin declares that he is fighting not on behalf of any man, but only for the sovereignty of the blessed Peter and the rights of the Roman Church and the Apostolic See.[51] The principal champions of this sovereignty and of the autonomy of the Catholic Church during the middle ages were Gregory VII, Innocent III and Boniface VIII, and in more recent times Innocent XI, Pius VII and Pius IX. To what cause is to be attributed the importance of the Holy See in the life of the world, and the tremendous struggles often under-

[47] Edict of Milan (313)—Kirch, *Enchiridion Fontium Hist. Eccl. Antiquae*, n. 314; cf. *C.Th.* (16,2); (16,5); *C.* (1.1) 8 §§ 7; 11; *N.* (132, 2).

[48] St. Gregorius Magnus, *Epistolae*, VIII, 18; IX, 4—*MPL*, LXXVII, 921; 941. Montini, *Note Scolastiche per la Storia della Diplomazia Ecclesiastica*, pp. 54-61.

[49] *Liber Pontificalis*, I, 449.

[50] Montini, *Op. cit.*, p. 76.

[51] *Liber Pontificalis*, I, 452-453.

taken by her against most formidable and deadly opponents in defence of the rights of the Church? It is certainly not to secure the prestige of a small State, it is to maintain the sovereignty of the Supreme Head of a society which counts its members in every State and which is bound by no earthly limits. For this reason even after 1870, when the Pope was deprived of all territorial dominion, the participation of the Holy See in international life did not on this account suffer serious injury. Governments continued to regard the Holy See as a moral power superior to their own armed forces and they maintained their traditional relations by acts which had full value in Law of Nations. We have already seen what distinction of place was gradually given by jurists to manifestations of the sovereignty of the Holy See, such as the right of active and passive legation, the right of recognition and the concordats. These acts furnish a confirmation of no small value. There is no code in international law, and arguments derived from tradition and custom are often the only terms of comparison in ordinary relations and for juridical results.

Since the right of legation is discussed in the present work a brief reference to the juridical value of the other two elements will suffice at present.

One does not speak of international recognition unless between those who are already members of the international community.

Abstracting from the different theories regarding the juridical nature of concordats, it is certain that the Holy See claims for them a juridical value in the Law of Nations. The object of these pacts is not affected by internal ecclesiastical legislation, but it is regulated directly in conformity with the agreements themselves and by arrangement with governments.[52] In reality concordats are made between two moral persons who have expressed the will to contract a bilateral pact. The different nature of the contracting parties, such as the superiority of the Church over the State on account of its end, does not affect the obligation contracted by the common agreement of the two parties. Concordats are positive agreements made to regulate matters of common interest. Hence the nature of the obligation depends on the will of those who contract it, a fact which the Popes

[52] Can. 3; 255.

have so often and explicitly asserted as to exclude all possible doubt.[53]

In studying the concordats we find solemnities and declarations of such a nature as to render them meaningless unless the Holy See had a place in the Law of Nations. Besides, the acceptance of the rules of Canon Law, even with regard to the theological principles of the constitution of the Church, is so general that it can fully justify the assertion that in each of these agreements the spiritual sovereignty of the Holy See is affirmed.[54]

The concordat creates rights and duties for both parties and establishes juridical rules which have value in both ecclesiastical and civil law. The reciprocal responsibility of the obligations assumed prevents one from ocnsidering it as an internal law of the state which contracts it. It concerns the citizens of one State but is not liimted to particular laws. On the contrary it proposes and defends universal principles which interest the whole of society. For these reasons the concordat belongs to the class of relations which have their basis in Law of Nations.[55] One cannot speak of rights and duties in the international community without presupposing that the institutions which thus bind themselves are persons of that community. Hence the history of concordats supplies a good argument for saying that the international position of the Holy See is in conformity with its tradition.

In conclusion, the necessity of enumerating the Holy See among

[53] Leo X, Const. "*Sacro approbante Concilio*" (1 oct. 1516)—Mercati, *Raccolta di Concordati*, p. 246; Pius VI, *Responsio ad Metropolitanos* cap. VI, n. 34; Pius VII, *Conc. cum Gallia* (a. 1817)—Wernz, *Ius Decretalium*, I, 223, note 27; Leo XIII, Enc. "*Nobilissima Gallorum Gens*" (8 feb. 1884)—Fontes, n. 590; Enc. *Aux milieu des sollecitudes*" (16 feb. 1892)—*Acta Leonis XIII*, XII, 37; Pius X, Enc. "*Vehementer*" (11 feb. 1906)—*Fontes*, n. 671; Benedictus XV, Alloc. "*In hac quidem*" (21 nov. 1921)—*AAS*, XIII (1921), 521; Pius XI, Discourse to the Students of the Sacred Heart University of Milan (February 13, 1929)—*AAS*, XXI (1929), 114; Enc. "*Mit brennender Sorge*" (March 14, 1937))—*AAS*, XXIX (1937), 146-148, 168-171.

[54] Wagnon, *Concordats et Droit International*, pp. 33-37.

[55] Poletti, *La natura giuridica dei concordati postbellici nella dottrina canonica e nel Diritto Pubblico Internazionale*, pp. 75-143; Wagnon, *op. cit.*, pp. 86-111.

the persons of international law arises from the very nature of the constitution of the Church. This right, which is fundamental in a society like the Catholic Church has been recognized, in spite of the suppression of the temporal power, if not by all States, at least by the vast mapority of them. The situation created in the small territory of the Vatican enclosure is simply not sufficient to explain the position occupied by the Holy See in international life and, with respect to Italy, in the conclusion of the Lateran Treaty, if we abstract from the consideration of the spiritual sovereignty of the Roman Pontiff. And this spiritual sovereignty, absolute and exclusive by reason of its origin,[56] not only makes the Holy See a person to whom the rules of international law may be applied, but also bestows on it the title of maker of these laws—with what advantage to the community of nations is readily perceived, if one considers its mission of justice and peace.

[56] Can. 100, § 1.

PART TWO

THE RIGHT OF PAPAL LEGATION

CHAPTER II

PRELIMINARY NOTIONS

Article I: Terms and Definitions

Etymologically, the word *"legation"* is derived from the Latin verb *"legare,"* i.e., *to send on some business.* Accordingly, the term *"legatus"* originally meant, and in general denotes, a person who is sent on some mission. In modern usage the word *"legate"* is generally reserved to the extraordinary envoys of the Pope. One of the higher and more important class of diplomatic representatives is called *"nuncio"* or *"orator"* corresponding to *"ambassador,"* while a representatives of lower grade is called "minister, envoy, chargé d'affaires."[1] The term of widest meaning in use is that of *diplomatic agent,* which signifies anyone who represents a sovereign abroad. On the basis of this terminology the interchange of legates, nuncios, ambassadors, ministers, chargés d'affaires, etc. is called *diplomatic relations,* while the art or science governing these representatives is called *civil* or *ecclesiastical diplomacy.*[2] The words "legate," "nuncio," "ambassador," etc. denote a person who takes the place of another and acts in his name. The legate then, is an intermediary between two persons—the person from whom he receives his mission and the person to whom he is sent. This mission can be concerned with matters of various kinds, from those connected with private people and their affairs to matters of public importance.

On such considerations is based the principal classification of legations:

a) *free legation,* so called for one of two reasons: 1) because

[1] Cf. Satow, *A Guide to Diplomatic Practice,* I, 237-238.

[2] Cf. Pinchetti-Sammarchi, *Guida Diplomatica Ecclesiastica,* I, 17-34.

the ambassador has discretionary powers and is not restricted to definite method of procedure; 2) because the business of the legation is in the interests of a private individual although it is carried out by an ambassador.[3]

b) *public legation,* when it deals with a matter connected with the interests of the community. This public legation may be either 1) a *war legation;* or 2) a *peace legation,* with which we are here concerned.

c) *peace legation.* This term can in general be applied to a mission relating to anything that tends to foster good relations along the ordinary lines of human progress. Here therefore there can be as many distinctions as there are special purposes for which an ambassador may be deputed. Usually the following kinds of legations are distinguished (using the Latin terminology: 1) the *legatio negotiorum gestiens,* for the transaction of business; 2) the *legatio caerimonialis,* or *officiosa,* for offering congratulations, condolence, etc.[4]

A division of sepcial importance, based on time limits, is that of:

d) *temporary legations,* which are those dealing with only one affair, and

e) *permanent legations,* which deal with more than one affair.[5] This last distinction constitutes the principal difference between legations in ancient and modern times. Before the Italian Renaissance each legation was sent to deal with a single matter, but since that period it has been found necessary to entrust to ambassadors the charge of all matters of interest to the countries they represent. As we shall see later, on this distinction of temporary and permanent legations is based tht historical development of Papal representative bodies.[6]

3 "Libera legatio est eius, qui publico legati nomine commendatus ornatusque re ipsa ob privatam exiit occasionem"—Gentili, *De Legationibus,* I, 8.

4 "mittuntur officii qui gratulari, dolere, atque id generis reliqua peragere debent."—Gentili, *Op. cit.,* I, 7.

5 Gentili, *Op. cit.,* I, 5.

6 Biaudet, *Les Nonciatures Apostoliques permanentes jusqu'en* 1648, pp. 2-3.

Article II: The Right of Legation

In international law sovereigns have the power of sending and receiving diplomatic agents. The power of sending diplomatic agents is called the "right of active legation," the power of receiving them is called the "right of passive legation."

The right of legation is one of the essential attributes of sovereignty and independence of the members of the international community. Indeed the idea of sovereignty necessarily implies that the sovereign, either personally or through his envoys, can represent his people with other nations: so much so that to contest the right of a sovereign of being represented abroad is equivalent to contesting his very sovereignty.[7] All this becomes clearer by reference to actual practice. Not infrequently the occupation of new territory by a country is not recognized immediately as legitimate. Before the formal act of recognition, diplomatic relations are not set up, either in protest, or in order to contest the right of sovereignty over the occupied territory. The right of legation constitutes, therefore, a prerogative inherent in the nature of sovereign institutions and is one of the manifestations of their independence.

Only by recognizing the right of legation as appertaining to sovereigns can the privileges and favors enjoyed by diplomatic agents be explained. Like the sovereigns they represent, they are not subject to the internal legislation of other countries. Furthermore, these privileges are necessary to the ends of the right of legation. Indeed, it would be impossible for the envoys to carry out their duties if they were not exempted from the jurisdiction of the state to which they are accredited. Their rights and privileges are based on very ancient historical traditions and upheld by international custom.[8] They enjoy personal inviolability, both civil and penal; and by virtue of the immunity accorded them their residences are not subject to the juridiction of the local authority, and state officials cannot enter the premises of the legation without permission. These privileges are shared by the personnel of the legation, who are regarded as forming one legal person with the head of the legation.[9]

[7] Calvo, *Le droit international, théorique et pratique,* III, 132.

[8] Cfr. Gentili, *Op. cit.,* II, 6.

[9] Pasquazi, *Ius Internationale Publicum,* pp. 137-140.

With reference to the exercise of the right of legation, the following general principles may be laid down:

I. The exercise of the right of legation does not, in itself, constitute an obligation in the strict acceptation of the term. No doubt, the purpose of all states, individually and collectively, is to procure the welfare of their peoples. But while diplomatic missions can do much in this respect, they are not a necessary means. Their employment is not demanded by the laws of social justice and hence is not a matter of strict, or juridical, obligation.

II. We could say, however, that there is an obligation in the wide, or moral, sense to exercise the right of legation. For nations, like individuals, are bound to foster co-operation and good-will, and render mutual assistance when needed. Now, towards the achievement of this end, diplomatic relations can make an important contribution. For there is no better means of co-operation than the bringing of whole peoples together through their representatives, no better good-will than the friendship thus engendered, and no better help than the well-being arising from concord. By means of international relations collective confidence is increased, many difficulties are forestalled, and not a few disputes amicably adjusted. Through them the best interests of individual states and of the comity of nations are admirably served, and therefore good administration requires them, unless grave reasons stand in the way, e.g., the lack of sufficient means for their suitable upkeep. Any sovereign who is alive to his responsibilities as head of the state cannot neglect the exercise of a right which, through the mere fact of its being in use among all peoples should certainly have its own advantages.[10]

III. No international law imposes on states the exercise of either active or passive legation. There exist however laws, in part written and in part arising out of custom, which regulate the exchange of diplomatic missions, and there exist besides pacts by which two or more nations bind themselves to this form of recognition.[11] It may be mentioned here that this way of maintaining diplomatic relations is found in the practice of the Holy See. Not infrequently, in con-

[10] Pasquazi, *Op. cit.*, p. 133.
[11] Satow, *Op. cit.*, I, 190-191.

cordats, the Holy See and the states concerned pledge themselves to the exchange of diplomatic agents with a view to maintaining good relations.[12] The considerations set forth above are of a general character and to a large extent are applicable to Papal representatives sent on diplomatic missions to various governments, or on purely ecclesiastical missions to the hierarchy and faithful of particular countries. The right of papal legation, however, assumes special characteristics that have a tradition connected with the very origin of the Church. So before proceeding to study the right of papal legation in its present statutes, we have to consider its historical development.

[12] *Conc. cum Polonia,* art. 3. *Conc. cum Lithuania,* art. 3; *Tract. Latern.* art. 12; *Conc. cum Germania,* art. 3.

CHAPTER III

HISTORICO-JURIDICAL NOTES ON THE ORIGINS OF PONTIFICAL REPRESENTATIVE BODIES

ARTICLE I: THE FIRST PONTIFICAL REPRESENTATIVES

The Councils were the earliest occasions in which the Popes used the right of legation.[1] It is certain that pontifical envoys were present at the Council of Arles (314), where, *"missi ex urbe Roma a Silvestro Episcopo,"* [2] the priests Claudian and Vitus, were present, with the deacons Eugene and Cyriacus, but we have nothing more than this simple historical reference. In order to see the juridical position of the first papal representatives it is necessary to go to the Councils in the East, and more particularly to the ecumenical councils. In this regard the right of legation is linked up with the right of presiding, both having a common dogmatic origin and historical development.

Among the few representatives of the West at the Council of Nicaea three personages are worthy of special note: Hosius, Bishop of Cordova, and Vitus and Vincentius, Roman priests. This small group instead of being lost in the large assembly of Eastern bishops, enjoyed a position of special importance which, while not overlooked by historical documents had not yet been sufficiently clarified. Were they sent to preside at the Council in the name of the Roman Pontiff? The question has been keenly discussed.

The opinion that Hosius presided at the Council in the name of

[1] Cardinal Baronius writing about the Council of Palestine, held at the end of the second century by Theophilus of Caesarea on the authority of Pope Victor, observes: "Vide ex his antiquum Ecclesiae morem: per legatos Romani Pontifices cogi concilia et dirimi controversies."—*Annales eccl.*, ad a. 198, n. 7, II, 452; Cf. Plati, *De Cardinalis dignitate et officio*, p. 344.

[2] Hardouin, I, 266; Mansi, II, 476; Hefele-Leclercq, *Histoire des Conciles*, I, 202-204.

the Pope is supported by solid arguments,[3] and authors generally regard it as safely tenable[4] but there are many who, arguing from the general attitude of Constantine towards the papacy, do not admit it.[5] Neither opinion is quite certain and therefore the whole matter remains an open question.[6]

Nevertheless the fact remains that the Roman priests, Vitus and Vincentius, sent by Pope Sylvester on the invitation of the Emperor, were present at the Council. And though, in the absence of official acts of the Council we do not know for certain what was the nature of their mandate, and what part they took in the discussions and decisions, the very fact that they sat in the front bench among the presidential body,[7] along with, or more probably preceding, the Bishops of Alexandria and Antioch, leads one to believe that their presence like that of Hosius had a special importance, and it seems reasonable to conclude with Schroeder:[8] "The position these held at the council indicates clearly that they were recognized by the bishops as the representatives of the supreme head of the Church."

The definitions of the Council of Nice asserted the doctrine that Christ was the Son of God, but that did not put an end to all con-

[3] *"Ipse etiam Hosius ex Hispanis nomine et famae celebritate* insignis, qui Silvestri Episcopi maximae *Romae locum obtinebat una cum Romanis presbyteris Vitone et Vincentio . . . "* — Gelasius, *Volumen actorum Concilii Nicaeni,* II, 5 — Hardouin, I, 375; Mansi, II, 806; cfr. Socrates, *Historia Eccl.* I, 8 — *MPG.,* LXVII, 60; Rufinus, *Historia Eccl.,* I, 1 — *MPL,* XXI, 467.

[4] Baronius, *Annales eccl.,* ed. A. 325, n. 20, IV, 113; C. A. Kneller, "Das Papsttum auf dem ersten Konzil zu Nicaea," *Simmen aus Maria-Laach,* LXXVII (1909), 503-522; F. X. Wernz, *Ius Decretalium,* II, 465, note 20; K. Ruess, *Die rechtliche Stellung der paepstlichen Legaten bis Bonifaz VIII,* pp. 5 and 15; H. J. Schroeder, *Disciplinary decrees of the General Councils,* pp. 8-14.

[5] N. H. Baynes, "Alexandria and Constantinople: A Study in Ecclesiastical Diplomacy," *Journal of Egyptian Archaelogy,* XII (1926), 149-158; A. A. Vasiliev, *History of the Byzantine Empire,* I, 70.

[6] Hefele-Leclercq, *Histoire des Conciles,* I, 40-43; 292-302.

[7] Cfr. Hardouin, I, 311; Mansi, II, 692; 697; *"Deinceps concilii praesidibus sermonem concessit* (Imperator) . . . ." — Eusebius, *Vita Constantini,* III, 13 — *MPG,* XX, 1069; Hefele-Leclercq, *Op. cit.,* I, 42.

[8] Disciplinary decrees of the General Councils, p. 11, note 4.

troversy. Arians and the supporters of the Council of Nicaea continued their discussions for long and bitterly sometimes to the point of open blows, violence, depositions and banishments. The life of Athanasius is well known. To this period belongs the Council of Sardica (343-344), the canons of which are of supreme importance to the scope of this dissertation. Here there was established the principle which regulated, defended, and gave to councils juridical form and concrete value. Local synods had only too often given way to action that was violent and harmful. There were depositions and excommunications which frequently took on all the aspect of personal revenge.[9] The Council of Sardica, wishing to prevent such unfortunate occurrences, provided for them in a form which, be it noted, was more than disciplinary when it affirmed: "—Quod si aliquis episcoporum iudicatus fuerit in aliqua causa, et putat se bonam causam habere, ut iterum concilium renovetur, si vobis placet, sancti *Petri Apostoli memoriam honoremus,* ut scribatur ab his, qui causam examinarunt, *Julio Romano Episcopo,* et si iudicaverit removandum esse iudicium, renovetur et det iudices" [10] and immediately afterwards: " . . . Quod si is qui rogat causam suam iterum audiri, deprecatione sua moverit Episcopum Romanum, ut *de latere suo* presbyterum mittat, erit in potestate episcopi; et si is decreverit mittendos esse, qui praesentes cum episcopis iudicent, *habentes eius auctoritatem a quo destinati sunt, erit in suo arbitrio."* [11] In spite of the discussions which centre around these canons, their meaning seems clear and certain conclusions can be logically drawn.[12] The expression: *"Sancti Petri Apostoli memoriam honoremus"* does not mean to attribute to St. Peter and to his successors some new prerogative that did not pertain to them, but simply to recognize the Supreme Pastor of the Church and the prerogatives conferred on him by the Divine Founder: that is, to acknowledge the direct and immediate fulness of his power over all the members of the Church. Since in virtue of his primacy the Bishop of Rome has jurisdiction over all the faith-

[9] e.g., Council of Tyre (355) and Council of Antioch (341)—Mansi, II, 1123, 1306.

[10] Can. 3—Hardouin, I, 639; Mansi, III, 7.

[11] Can. 5—Hardouin, I, 641; Mansi, III, 10.

[12] Hefele-Leclercq, *Histoire des Conciles,* I, 561-577.

ful, any one of them can appeal to him. In such a case the controversy is referred to the supreme judge, the execution of the sentence imposed is suspended; and the Pope can proceed to nominate the members of the tribunal which will pass judgment in the second instance chosen from among the bishops of the neighboring province; or, if he thinks necessary, he can send his legates vested with his own authority.

Abstracting from particular circumstances and considering the Council of Sardica in its true light, it must be agreed that the principle and right of legation were here set forth in precise form. There had convened at Sardica many bishops of the most celebrated sees of West and East. Pope Julius *"corpore separatus, mente concordi ac voluntate,"* [13] was prevented by special circumstances from intervening but he sent his representatives in the persons of the priests, Archidamus and Filossenus and the deacon Leo.[14] In the absence of the Pope, and very probably by his express delegation, the Council had as president Hosius, Bishop of Cordova, as we are clearly told by St. Athanasius [15] and Theodoretus.[16] It is he who directed the discussions, proposed the canons and who, with the Roman priests, was the first to sign the acts.

To preside at the Council of Ephesus (431) Pope Celestine nominated Cyril, Patriarch of Alexandria, who was always the first voice of the Council, the echo of the Bishop of Rome.[17] The Pope sent as his Legates the Bishops Arcadius and Projectus, and the priest Philip: "Coelestinus episcopus *nos ipsius praesentiam supplentes* ad hanc sanctam synodum misit." [18] The powers conceded to them extend over all the members of the Council and allow them if necessary even to rescind the acts: "Ad disputationem si fuerit ventum, vos de

[13] Hardouin, I, 63; Mansi, III, 40.

[14] Hardouin, I, 670; Mansi, III, 66; St. Athanasius, *Apologia*, L.—*MPG*, XXV, 337.

[15] " . . . *Sacra synodus cuius praeses erat magnus Hosius."* . . . *Historia Arianorum*, XVI—*MPG*, XXV, 712.

[16] *Historia Eccl.*, II, 6—*MPG*, LXXXII, 1001.

[17] Hardouin, I, 1523; III, 10; Mansi, IV, 1019; IX, 53;—62; 892; Evaprius, *Historia Eccl.* I.4—*MPG*, LXXXVI, 2428.

[18] Mansi, IV, 1295; cfr. Hardouin, I, 1347; Mansi, IV, 555.

eorum sententia iudicare debeatis, non subire certamen." [19] It is their presence and authority which give legal force to the sentence against Nestorius, of which they definitively approve.[20]

The circumstances regarding the presidency at the Council of Chalcedon (451) throw further light on the juridical position of the papal representatives at the Councils.

The Emperor Marcian *"Petri Apostoli iure atque honore servato"* seems to have wished that Pope Leo would have come perosnally to preside at the Council; circumstances did not permit this, [21] and so the Pope sent a mission of five Legates with the Bishop Pascasinus at their head: " . . . fratrem et coepiscopum meum *vice mea synodo convenit praesidere.*[22] He therefore wrote to the Emperor that his Representatives were the same as his own person, and to the Fathers of the Council he added more specifically:

" . . . in his fratribus . . . qui ab apostolica sede directi sunt, *me synodo,* vestra fraternitas aestimet *praesidere,* non abiuncta a vobis praesentia mea qui nunc in vicariis meis adsum."[23]

The faculties conceded to the Legates were expressed in one single word but everyone sees what and how great is the extension of the term *"praesidere."* Such fulness of powers was not a singular occurrence; a careful examination of the documents by which the presidency of the Councils was assigned to the Legates demonstrates a representation of the Pope which is entire and personal and consequently endowed with the same faculties which he possesses. Only one limitation is placed, that which is opposed to the very nature of

[19] *MPL,* L, 503.

[20] Mansi, IV, 1302; 1338.

[21] St. Leo Magnus, *epist.,* 31; 37; 93;—*MPL,* LIV, 789; 811; 937. The Pope insists a great deal on these circumstances. The invasions of Attila were taking place; the bishops of the West could not participate at the Council in the required number; but what exactly does he mean by the phrase *"nec antiqua hoc tenuit consuetudo, sc. permittere (meam praesentiam)?* Does it not seem to allude to a tradition which already existed of the Roman Pontiffs making use of Legates for similar missions? In such a supposition a new and strong argument favors the antiquity of the practice of using the right of papal legation.

[22] St. Leo Magnus, *epist.* 89—*MPL,* LIV, 930.

[23] *Epist.* 93—*MPL,* LIV, 937.

the Council itself. In fact the sole reason that justifies the convocation of a Council is a matter pertaining to the Faith, and anything that goes beyond the limits thus imposed must be considered as not done and not approved by the Pope.[24]

It would certainly be useful to proceed to consider the other Councils examine the relations of the Roman Pontiffs to them in matters of faith by means of their representatives, regard to, but for the purposes of this dissertation let it suffice to have dealt with the Councils of the early centuries. As to those of a later period there can be no serious doubt regarding the part played by Papal legates.[25] Besides, at that time there already existed in ecclesiastical history other institutions of a character more closely linked up with the actual legislation of the Code. However, before passing to a consideration of these, a brief reference to the mission which Pope Zosimus sent to Africa in the year 418 will not be out of place.

The priest Apiarius of Sicca had been excommunicated and deposed by his bishop. According to a canon of the sixteenth Council of Africa (a. 418),[26] he could not appeal to Rome. However, the Pope admitted his appeal and gave a judgment in his favor. Thereupon there arose some disorder. The Pope then sent a mission composed of the Bishop of Potenza, Faustinus, and the two Roman priests, Philip and Asellus, to discuss in a council the question of appeals to Rome. The legates brought with them a written document, the *Commonitorium,* containing the main points of the controversy and the powers which had been granted to them: other powers had already been granted to them verbally. Their juridical position was thus defined; "Vos ita ut nostra, immo quia nostra ibi in vobis praesentia est, cuncta peragite. . ."[27]

With regard to this mission the following points may be observed:

[24] *Epist.* 114; 119, v — *MPL,* LIV, 1029; 1045; cfr. K. Ruses, *Die recrtliche der papestlichen Legaten bis Bonifaz VIII,* pp. 6-7.

[25] For a complete treatment of the subject cfr. K. Ruess, *Op. cit.,* pp. 4-41.

[26] *Codex canonum Ecclesiae Africanae,* can. 125: "Presbyteri . . . non provocent nisi ad Africana Concilia, vel ad primates provinciarum suarum; *ad transmarina autem qui putaverit appellandum, a nullo intra Africam in communionem suscipiatur."*—Hardouin, I 934; Mansi, III, 822.

[27] Hardouin, I, 942; Mansi, IV, 403.

1) The stay of the Legates in Africa is prolonged for some years (418-424): their activities in this period must have been of varied kinds, and at any rate assume an aspect of higher consequence than those of representatives sent simply to preside at Councils.[28]

2) At the death of Pope Zosimus (26th December 418), the Legates continued in their office (cfr. can. 268 § 1).

3) Bishop Faustinus acts as one having full powers: he interrupts the Council, calls the members to observe its procedure, settles doubts and asks for union.[29] From what has been said we are justified in drawing the conclusion that the Popes readily made use of the right of legation as soon as the Church found herself able to act freely and publicly. There is a special importance in this intervention of Papal Representatives at Councils, not only from the dogmatic point of view on account of apostolic sanction which the acts receive, but also because we find here a very important argument in favor of the historical development of the Roman Primacy.

The frequency with which the Supreme Pontiffs made use of Legates for matters of such supreme importance as were those first Councils, from which cthe doctrine of the Church always emerged with increased splendor, not only assures the legitimacy of their mode of procedure, but is besides a sign of the authority they exercised in defence of Christian legislation.

Besides, the recognition given to the person and voice of the Papal representatives, the need that the Fathers of the Councils feel of their approbation, and the confident assurance of their mode of acting when they have their consent,[30] show that, from the first centuries, Christian tradition saw in them Rome's constant solicitude for the custody of the *depositum fidei.*

Delegation to the Councils had naturally a definite character.

28 Cfr. Hardouin, I, 947; Mansi, IV, 515.

29 Mansi, IV, 405.

30 " . . . fuerunt enim in consensu nostro et illi quoque qui a sanctitate tua missi sunt, . . . qui sua praesentia tuam nobis exhibuerunt apostolicaeque sedis locum suppleverunt."—Mansi, IV, 1338; " . . . non singillatim faciente in occulto unoquoque doctrinam, sed uno spiritu, una conspiratione atque concordia confessionem fidei declarantes; . . . *Quibus tu quidem, sicut membris caput, praeeras in his qui tuum tenebant ordinem benevolentiam praeferens."*—Mansi, IV, 147.

The Papal representatives were not allowed to interfere in matters not strictly relevant to the issue, nor does it appear that they ever did so. Their powers—as the juridical nature of the institution requires (cfr. can. 267, § 1, 3°)—were therefore delegated.

The case of the mission sent to Africa by Pope Zosimus was very probably not unique in its details; here are met signs characteristic of stability of office and of jurisdiction. On the one hand it indicates once aagin that the Pope did not believe himself bound by previous forms or by limitations in his powers; and on the other hand, it shows that the authority of the Papal Legates prevailed over that of the local bishops.

Article II: The Apocrisiarii

The term *"Aprocrisiarius,"* Greek equivalent of the Latin "Responsalis," was used to denote various officials from a simple messenger of the imperial chancellery,[1] or a military judge,[2] to an ecclesiastical envoy: but it is in this last mentioned sense it is most commonly used. The envoy in question could be of a bishop to a metropolitan,[3] or of a metropolitan to the patriarch,[4] or of the metropolitans and Popes to the court of Constantinople and Ravenna: "Responsales non tam Romanae Sedis quam et aliarum praecipuarum Sedium in palatio pro ecclesiasticis negotiis excubabant."[5]

The distinction and the competence of the various kinds of *apocrisiarii* can be determined only by consideration of the authority and prestige of the see they represented.

It is not easy to say when exactly the *apocrisiarii* of the Pope commenced to reside permanently at Constantinople. The opinion of Hincmar of Rheims that they go back to the time of Constantine is

1 Isidorus Pelusiota, *Epistolae,* IV, 144—*MPG,* LXXVIII, 1225.

2 *C.* (12 35) 18.

3 *C.* (1, 3) 42.

4 "Dioscorus . . . elegit Anatolium quemdam, qui tunc Constantinopoli *apocrisiarius erat ecclesiae Alexandrinae."*—Theodorus Lector, *Fragmenta—MPG,* LXXXVI, 217.

5 Hincmarus Rhemensis, *De ordine palatii,* 13—*MPL,* CXXV, 998; cfr. Pargoire, "Apocrisiare," *Dictionnaire d'Archeologie Chretienne et de Liturgie,* I, 2537-2555.

no longer accepted, and it is held that the institution of these Papal Representatives dates from the first half of the fifth century.

The first Papal *apocrisiarius* of whose existence we are certain is Julian of Chio. It is not absolutely certain that Leo the Great sent him to the imperial court before the Council of Chalcedon,[6] but there exist the letters of the year 453 with which he was presented to the Emperor Marcian with these words: *"Vicem ipsi meam contra temporis haereticos delegavi atque propter Ecclesiam pacisque custodiam ut a comitatu vestro non abesset, exegi";*[7] and to the Empress Pulcheria: "Cum in causa fidei . . . vicem ipsi meam delegarim, ut ab ea, quae vobis debetur observantia non recedens, pietati me vestrae praesentare non desinat, *exequens in custodia fidei et in ecclesiasticis disciplinis* per omia sollicitudinem, et opportunis suggestionibus, quod universali Tcclesiae prosit, insinuans, ut in ipso, nec catholicis vestrum praesidium, nec vobis meum desit obsequium."[8] In the year 458 Pope Leo acceded to the request of the Emperor Leo I, and sent as apocrisiarii the bishops Domitian and Geminian.[9]

The sending of Roman *apocrisiarii* to Constantinople thus initiated, continued for a period of two centuries and a half. There were however not infrequent interruptions. During the Acacian schism (484-519) the permanent office of *apocrisiarius* ceased but relations were resumed by Pope Hormisdas (514-523), and during the whole of the sixth century there was a constant succession of apocrisiarii vested with all the characteristics of papal legates. The following *apocrisiarii* are mentioned as persons of first-rate importance, Vigilius* (535-537); Pelagius* (538-545); Gregory* (578-587); Sabinian* (593-596); Anatole (597-601); Boniface* (603-) and some others.[10]

The seventh century opened with omens of disaster; the West

[6] G. B. Montini, *La "Responsio super Nunciaturis" di Papa Pio* VI, pp. 168-169 and note 8; Cerretti, "Legate," *The Catholic Encyclopedia,* IX, 118.

[7] *Epist.* III—*MPL,* LIV, 1022.

[8] *Epist.* 112—*MPL,* LIV, 1024; cfr. *epist.* 116—*MPL,* LIV, 1035.

[9] Mansi, VI, 339; 343; *epist.* 164—*MPL,* LIV, 1148.

[10] J. Pargoire, "Apocrisiare"—*Dictionnaire d'Archeologie* Chretienne et de Liturgie, I, 2544-2545.

* Later elected Pope.

was in constant fear of barbaric invasions; the East was torn by civil discords and religious controversies. What added to the difficulties of the Popes in maintaining *aprocrisiarii* at Constantinople was their preoccupations with the religious and civil defence of the West. Still, when necessity called for them there were extraordinary missions to the East, some of them noteworthy, like the mission performed by the *apocrisiarii* of Pope Severinus (a. 640), who "firmae revera et immobilis *petrae ministri*"[11] ably resisting the violence of the Byzantines, defended the Catholic faith against the heresy of the Monothelites.[12]

In 680 Constantine IV petitioned Pope Agatho "ut aliquot mitteret, qui eius personam obtinerent,"[13] and a group of ecclesiastical dignitiaries was sent on an extraordinary mission. But two years later the same emperor asked Leo II to send a permanent *apocrisiarius* who *"in emergentibus sive dogmaticis sive canonibus, ac prorsus in omnibus ecclesiasticis negotiis"* would take the place of the person of the Pontiff.[14] It does not appear however that the emissary sent had a permanent position.[15]

The office of *apocrisiarius* gradually declined; References to the *apocrisiarii* are found in later times,[16] but the name alone does not necessarily indicate the special ecclesiastical mission as heretofore understood. It may well be held that by the beginning of the iconoclastic heresy the permanent office of the Papal emissaries at the court of Constantinople had definitely ceased.[17]

The juridical position of the *apocrisiarius* has a double aspect: one in regard to civil, and the other in regard to ecclesiastical law.

The legislation of Justinian regards the *apocrisiarii* in a generic way as the representatives of the bishops, and prescribes that recourse to the court whether to solve disputes or to ask favors should be made

[11] Mansi, X, 677.

[12] Cfr. G. B. Montini, Note: *Scholastichi per la Storia, Storia della Diplomazia Pontificia,* p. 32-33.

[13] Mansi, XI, 714.

[14] Mansi, XI, 718.

[15] Mansi, XI, 735; J. Pargoire, *Op. cit.,* I, 2546.

[16] Theophanes, *Chronographia,* a. 6207—*MPG,* CVIII, 779; *Liber Pontificalis,* I, 432.

[17] G. B. Montini, *Op. cit.,* p. 89-90.

through their mediation.[18] The *apocrisiarii*, however, cannot take up cases in the name of their bishops either in civil or in religious matters without a special delegation for each particular case. But they are allowed to complete the cases for which they have taken responsibility during their term of office.[19]

Though the Roman See has first place among all the episcopal sees, no reference of preeminence is made regarding the *apocrisiarii* sent by the Popes. In practice, however, the concern which the emperors show to have the Roman *apocrisiarius* at court [20] and the weight they give to their judgment in the settling of disputes [21] are a sure indication of the recognition given to the overruling authority of those who come and act in the name of the Popes.

The presence of the *apocrisiarii* at Constantinople assumes a diplomatic rôle. The emperors look upon them as a sign of their good relations with the Popes; the recall of the *apocrisiarius*, when his place is not immediately filled, indicates a breaking off of diplomatic relations.[22] The Popes, to a great extent, adopt the same line of conduct. Some writers assert that St. Gregory the Great made use of a protest of this kind to destroy the arrogant pretensions to the title of "*oecumenicus*" which the Patriarch John, strongly supported by the Emperor Mauritius, attributed to himself.[23] It is certain that he not only made bitter protests to the patriarch and to the emperor, but also forbade the *apocrisiarius* Sabinian to take part in the official acts of worship.[24]

It is well known how great was the interference of the Byzantine emperors in ecclesiastical affairs and legislation. Now since the

18 *N.* (6, 2) 3.

19 *N.* 123, 25.

20 St. Gregorius Magnus, *Epistolae*, XIII, 38—*MPL*, LXXVII, 1287; Thomassin, *Vetus et Nova Ecclesiae Disciplina*, P. I. Lib. II, c. 108, n. 25.

21 Cfr. Liberatus, *Breviarium*, 23—*MPL*, LXVIII, 1044; Duchesne, *L'Eglise au VI siecle*, p. 170; Batiffol, *St. Gregoire Le Grand*, p. 36.

22 K. Ruess, *Die rechtliche Stellung der paepstlichen Legaten bis Bonifaz VIII*, p. 44.

23 A. A. Vasiliev, *History of the Byzantine Empire*, I, 210; Batiffol, *Op. cit.*, p. 50; 205 n. 1.

24 *Epistolae*, V, 18-20—*MPL*, LXXVII, 738-744.

apocrisiarii were at court to back up *"apostolicae sedis responsa,"* [25] it would seem natural that they would have some part in the *"consilium principis"* which in practice made the laws. But this can only be said—and then with some reserve—of perhaps one or other apocrisiarius.[26]

From the ecclesiastical point of view the *apocrisiarii* were generally deacons,[27] ordained expressly for that office, that is, for the purpose of taking the place of the Pope at Constantinople in the defence of the faith amid the rise of the many heresies, and by maintaining contact with the centre that had the greatest religious influence, of favouring in every way the unity of the Church. In regard to the Christian East they were to observe and regulate the development of theological doctrines.[28] The fact that they were *apocrisiarii* did not mean that they should take part in the ecumenical or local councils, much less that they should preside over them. Their powers depended for the most part on the particular circumstances. While they were entrusted with the interests of religion in general, to act in any case of importance they probably had to receive special instructions from Rome. Thomassin referring to a citation from St. Gregory the Great,[29]

[25] St. Gregorius Magnus, *Epistola ad Leandrum in Moralium* Libri *MPL;* LXXV, 510; *Dialogi,* III, 36—*MPL,* LXX VII, 304.

[26] Victor Tun., *Chronicon* (a. 558)—*MPL* LXVIII, 961; 1053; "Quanta autem auctoritate ministerium sui apocrisiariatus impleverit, quantae reverentiae apud Augustos extiterit, quantoque sollicitudine afflictae Italiae succurri saepius fecerit . . ." Johannes Diac., *Vita Gregorii,* I, 31—*MPL,* LXXV, 75.

[27] St. Gregorius Magnus, *Epistolae,* XIII, 38—*MPL,* LXXVII, 12.

[28] K. Ruess, *Op. cit.,* p. 43.

[29] " . . . si qua causa vel *fidei,* vel *criminis,* vel *pecuniaria* . . . potuerit evenire, vel per eos qui nostri sunt, vel fuerint in urbe regia responsales, si mediocris est quaestio, cognoscatur; vel huc ad apostolicam sedem, si ardua est, deducatur, quatenus nostrae audientiae sententia decidatur."—*Epistolae* III, 7.—*MPL,* LXXVII, 611; Thomassin, *Vetus et Nova Ecclesiae Disciplina,* P. I, Lib. II, c. 107, n. 12.

A Keen consciousness of the sublime mission of the primacy, and zeal for the salvation of souls had led St. Gregory the Great to create a great number of representatives, especially on temporary missions, in Italy, Sicily, Sardinia, Gaul, Africa and Illyria; and his voluminous correspondence (*Epistolarum libri XIV — MPL,* LXXVII) shows us his immense activity also in this field. With regard to this Thomassin (*Op. cit.,* affirms that the regard the holy Pontiff had for such a dignity was so great and so manifest that he put before the judgment of the *apocrisiarius* all questions that could arise between the metropolitan and the bishop. The citation from St. Gregory in question refers to the dispute which arose between the Metropolitan of Larissa and the Bishop of Thebes. In this case the Bishop of Thebes was taken from the jurisdiction of the Vicar Apostolic of Illyria and placed under that of the *apocrisiarius* of Constantinople. This however was an exceptional remedy, since ordinarily the powers of the *apocrisiarii* were not extensive, nor can we say that they had jurisdiction in the strict sense of the term, that is, that they had power to govern. "The jurisdiction of the papal emissaries, both temporary and permanent, in the East is directed rather towards affairs than to persons, places and things. One could more correctly speak of commissions than of jurisdiction. These commissions are however of such a nature as to show that the *apocrisiarii* had plenary powers, a hierarchical superiority, and a spiritual sovereignty not unknown to the first centuries of the Church." [30]

Having seen the position of the *apocrisiarius* at Constantinople, it now remains to consider briefly the positions of the ecclesiastical dignitaries at the Carolingian court.

Here again the term "*apocrisiarius*" had several meanings: more commonly it was used to indicate the official to whom was entrusted the care of the imperial seal. Honorius of Autun explains it in this sense:[31] "*Apocrisiarius,* i.e., *segretorum sigillator,*" and like the term "*Referendarius*" it denoted a purely civil office.

In our case, according to what Hincmar of Rheims says,[32] it signifies "*Responsalis negotiorum ecclesiasticorum*" and could perhaps

n. 17) makes the following appreciation: "Erant ergo nuntii Gregorii velut pervigiles oculi infatigatae eius vigilantiae inspectoresque universales et censores Episcoporum vitae et regiminis, excessum cleri, monachorum defectionis a sanctitate regulae, laicorum violentiae; . . . ut summa potestas et invicta dominatio esset penes Ecclesiae leges sanctissimas, utque earum transgressoribus impune nunquam esset."

[30] Cfr. G. B. Montini, *La "Reponsio super Nunciaturis" di Papa Pio VI,* p. 171.

[31] *Gemma animae,* I, 185—*MPL,* LCXXII, 602.

[32] *De ordine palatii,* 13—*MPL,* CXXV, 998.

be translated in the sense of the modern "Minister of ecclesiastical affairs," but Hincmar immediately adds:[33] "Apocrisiarius autem, quem nostrates *Capellanum* vel palatii custodem appellant, omnem clerum palatii sub cura et dispositione sua regebat." From this it seems possible to deduce that the office of the ecclesiastical dignitary at the Carolingian court is very different from that of the *apocrisiarii* at the court of Constantinople. The *apocrinarii* at Constantinople never were, and never could be, *court chaplains.*

With regard to their influence in ecclesiastical affairs Pargoire maintains:[34]

" . . . une question religieuse ne s'agite, une affaire ecclesiastique ne se regle dans le palais ou dans le royaume sans que l'apocrisiaire n'y intervienne pour dire son mot." That should have been the case not only on account of the fact that they were at court and therefore in contact with members of the government, but also because they represented, or it was understood that they represented, the Pope in the West in the same way as the Roman deacon at Constantinople.

Other authors,[35] however, see in the *apocrisiarii* at the Carolingian court mere functionaries using the name; they had neither the importance nor the permanence of papal legates; their office is completely different. The use of the term is so varied that apart from the Byzantine court, *"apocrisiarius"* very probably means nothing more than an envoy in general.

With reference to the Grand Chaplain of the court, apart from his high position and the influence he could there exercise for the advantage of the Church, it would be diffcult to determine if, and in what measure, he represented the Holy See.

Article III: Vicars Apostolic

Vicars Apostolic form a new class of pontifical representatives. They date from the fourth century. In the first instance Pope Damasus (366-384) assigned this office to Acolius, Bishop of Thes-

[33] *Op. cit.*, 16—*MPL,* CXXV, 999.

[34] "Apocrisiaire," *Dictionnaire d'Archeologie Chretienne et de Liturgie,* I, 2552.

[35] K. Ruess, *Die rechtliche Stellung der paepstlichen* Legaten bis Bonifaz VIII, p. 45-46; G. B. Montini, *Op. cit.,* p. 168, n. 3.

salonica.[1] The documents are of the year 380, but they presuppose that relations had previously been established and writers believe that the *Vicariate Apostolic of Illyria* goes back to the time when the Emperor Gratian divided the territory of the Balkan peninsula giving the two provinces of Macedonia and Dacia to the Emperor of the East. These two porvinces, called Eastern Illyria, passed under the civil jurisdiction of the Eastern Empire, but ecclesiastically speaking they remained in the Western Empire in subjection to the Bishop of Rome. The office of the Vicar Apostolic became permanent despite the attempt of Theodosius II to unite Illyria to Constantinople,[2] and the difficulties created by the schism of Acacius, it lasted until the separation caused by the Iconoclasts.[3]

In setting up the Vicariate Apostolic of Illyria the Popes base their right not only on their quality of Patriarchs of the West but especially on their authority as universal pastors of the Church.[4]

The Vicar Apostolic of Illyria is a papal representative in the full sense of the word. This is indicated by the expressions used by the Popes: *"Te . . . omnis cura respectat . . . vice sedis apostolicae"*;[5] *"Quanta fraternitati tuae a beatissimi Petri Apostoli auctoritate sint commissa et qualia etiam nostro favore sint credita . . ."*[6] It is also shown clearly by their very comprehensive powers, by the exten-

[1] *Epist.* 5 et 6—*MPL,* XIII, 365; 369: " . . . praedecessores mei . . . Damasus, Siricius atque supra memoratus vir (Anastasius) ita detulerunt *ut omnia quae in illis partibus gerentur, sanctitati tuae,* quae plena iustitia est, *tradere cognoscenda,* meam quoque paritatem hoc tenere iudicium eamdemque habere voluntatem, te (Anysium) decet recognoscere"—Inno centius I, *epist.* I—*MPL,* XX, 465; Baronius, *Annales eccl.,* ad a. 380, n. 6, V, 453; Thomassin, *Vetus et Nova Ecclesiae Disciplina,* P. I, Lib. I, c. 18, n. 7.

[2] *C.* (1, 2) 6; *C.Th.* (16, 2) 45.

[3] G. B. Montini, *La "Responsio super Nunciaturis" di Papa Pio VI,* p. 173-175; K. Ruess, *Die rechtliche Stellung der paepstlichen Legaten bis Bonifaz VIII,* p. 49-50; Hinschius, *Kirchenrecht,* I, 579.

[4] Pius VI, *Responsio ad Metropolitanos,* cap. VIII, n. 47-50.

[5] Bonifacius I, *Epist.* 5—*MPL,* XX, 762.

[6] St. Leo M., *Epist.* 14—*MPL,* LIV, 668; ibid., 615; 617.

sion of their territory and especially by the diversified matters with which they deal.[7]

It is the duty of the Vicar Apostolic to visit the diocese and watch over the Christian communities, and hence to correct abuses and maintain peace; to grant permission for candidates to be promoted to the episcopacy, and hence to investigate the suitability of those elected:[8] "Ipsum maior cura respectat eorum qui ad Episcopatum vocantur, discutiendi sollicitius et probandi";[9] to select and consecrate the metropolitans: " . . . Metropolitanos a te (Anastasio) volumus ordinari *maturo tamen et decocto iudicio.*"[10] Besides, he can convoke a council when he considers it necessary,[11] or permit the bishops to meet on their own authority.[12] The metropolitans cannot absent themselves from their sees without his permission.[13] Furthermore, *"Ad eum (antistitem Thessalonicensem) quidquid a singulis sacerdotibus agitur, referatur;*[14] and he should report to the Holy See all appeals.[15] Finally, he should give an account of the state of the churches and he is held responsible for the lack of observance of the directions emanating from the Apostolic See.[16] In the early times he had power to deal with *causae maiores*: "Ad Thessalonicensem maiores causae referantur Antistitem,"[17] and he gave judgment in disputes between bishops.[18] It seems, however, that at the time of St. Leo the Great some restrictions were made in this matter: for, while the more serious matters should be dealt with in the council convoked and presided

[7] Innocentius I, *Epist.* 13—*MPL,* XX, 515; Bonifacius I, *Epist.* 4, *ibid.,* 760.

[8] " . . . litteras dederamus, ut nulla licentia esset sine consensu tuo (Anysio) in Illyrico episcopo ordinare praesumere"—Siricius, *Epist.* 4—*MPL,* XIII, 1148; "sine eius consilio nullus ordinetur"—Coelestinus I, *Epist.* 3,—*MPL,* L, 429.

[9] Xystus III, *Epist.* 8—*MPL,* L, 611.

[10] St. Leo M., *Epist.* 6—*MPL,* LIV, 619.

[11] Xystus III, *Epist.* 10—*MPL,* L, 616.

[12] Coelestinus I, *Epist.* 3—*MPL,* L, 417.

[13] Xystus III, *Epist.* 9—*MPL,* L, 612.

[14] Xystus III, *Epist.* 10—*MPL,* L, 617.

[15] Innocentius I, *Epist.* 13—*MPL,* XX, 515.

[16] St. Leo M., *Epist.* 5—*MPL,* LIV, 616.

[17] Xystus III, *Epist.* 8—*MPL,* L, 611.

[18] Bonifacius I, *Epist.* 5 et 13—*MPL,* XX, 761; 774.

over by the Vicar, he should not forget that there always remains the right of appeal to the Holy See: "ut enim auctoritatem tuam vice nostra te (Anastasium) exercere volumus; ita nobis quae illic componi non potuerint, vel qui vocem appellationis emerserit, reservamus."[19]

From all this it is not difficult to understand the words of Pius VI when he says:[20] " . . . hae facultates cum voluntariae tum contentiosae iurisdictionis quemadmodum omnes causas et negotia ecclesiastica comprehendebant, ita etiam fideles omnes, omnesque Episcopos et Metropolitanos . . . "

But if matters were so in early times the Vicariate Apostolic of Illyria began to lose some of its prestige when Justinian divided its territory and raised to primatial dignity the episcopal see of Justiniana Prima, his native land, "secundum ea quae definita sunt a sanctissimo Papa Vigilio."[21]

The Archbishop of Justiniana Prima thus begins to enjoy the privileges in administrative and judiciary matters already granted to the Archbishop of Thessalonica; besides, "nulla communione . . . Thessalonicensi episcopo servanda," [22] the Archbishops of Justiniana Prima have powers to settle disputes, create metropolitans and the very election of the new archbishop will be made without recourse to Thessalonica.

A new partition of the Vicariate of Illyria was made with the erection of the metropolitan see of Corinth which was given primatial rights over Greece,[23] and thus, "the title, which was still held at Thessalonica, tended to become purely honorary.[24]

In the seventh century the Popes resumed their direct government of Illyria. In his correspondence with the East, St. Gregory the Great does not seem to attribute more authority to the Metropolitan

[19] St. Leo M., *Epist.* 6—*MPL,* LIV, 619.

[20] Pius VI, *Responsio ad Metropolitanos,* cap. VIII, n. 66.

[21] *N.* 131, 3 (a. 545).

[22] *N.* 11; St. Gregory the Great acknowledges that the Bishop of Justiniana Prima has wide powers: *Epistolae* II, 22; 23; III, 6; XII, 31—*MPL,* LXXVII, 557; 558; 607; 1241.

[23] St. Gregorius Magnus, *Epistolae* V, 57; 58—*MPL,* LXXVII, 790; 792; Thomassin, *Op. cit.,* P. I, Lib. I, c. 32, n. 6.

[24] Cfr. G. B. Montini, *La "Responsio super Nunciaturis," di Papa Pio VI,* p. 174.

of Thessalonica than he does to other metropolitans.[25] With the advent of the Iconoclastic heresy Illyria ceased to depend on Rome in ecclesiastical matters, and so ended the title of Vicar Apostolic attributed to the Metropolitan of Thessalonica.[26]

Similar to the Vicariate of Thessalonica was that of Arles. Its origin was probably derived from the importance that the city began to assume when about the year 400 it was made the seat of the *praefectus praetorio.*[27] Arles became, in consequence, a centre of catholicism also. In 417 Pope Zosimus conferred on Patroclus, Bishop of Arles, *"sicuti semper habuit"* the power to approve and ordain bishops for the provinces of Vienne and Narbonne I and II, and appointed him vicar for all the ecclesiastical affairs between the Holy See and the bishops of Gaul. Furthermore anyone who came to Rome should have letters of recommendation (*litterae formatae*) from the Bishop of Arles.[28]

Such concessions aroused discontent among the neighboring bishops and Boniface I (418-422) brought matters back to their original condition.[29] "The primacy had hardly been inaugurated when it vanished from the scene"—observes Duchesne.[30] Celestine I[31] and St. Leo the Great[32] confirmed the revocation of the privilege. However, towards the middle of the fifth century the same neighbor-

[25] St. Gregorius Magnus, *Epistilae,* VIII, 5; IX, 68; X, 42; XI, 74—*MPL,* LXXVII, 909; 1003; 1100; 1212.

[26] Cfr. L. Duchesne, "L'Illyrium Ecclesiastique"—*Byzantinische Zeitschrift, I* (1892), 531-550.

[27] Originally the *praefectus praetorio* was the head of the imperial guard established by Augustus. He then became the chief representative of the ruler, especially in matters of civil and criminal jurisdiction. After Diocletian, for example, when the empire was divided into four prefectures (*Oriens, Illyricum, Italia, Galliae*), a *praefectus praetorio* was set over each of these (G. Gigli, *Brevi cenni di Storia del Diritto Romano,* p. 37).

[28] Zosimus, *Epist.* I et 7—*MPL,* XX, 652; 668.

[29] *Epist.* 12—*MPL,* XX, 772.

[30] *Fastes episcopaux de l'ancienne Gaule,* I, 85.

[31] *Epist.* 4—*MPL,* L, 430.

[32] *Epist.* 10—*MPL, LIV,* FBR. The ruling of St. Leo the Great was conlrmed by a constitution of Valentinien III—*Nov. Valent.* III, tit. XVII, ed. Meyer, p. 101.

ing bishops resolved to claim for Arles the right of a metropolitan see and they asked that the bishop should be restored to his position of "*Vicar Apostolic of the Gauls*."[33] Pope Leo the Great then granted some generic concessions, dividing practically the same powers between the Bishops of Vienne and Arles, but he made use of Ravennius, Bishop of Arles, to obtain more easily the adhesion of the Gauls to the Council of Chalcedon.[34]

There followed in the vicarial see of Arles a period of inactivity, and consequently we find Pope Hilary (461-468) reproving Leontius of Arles and reminding him of his duty to correct or report "*iniqua et contra patrum nostrorum statuta in provincia quae ad tuam monarchiam pertinet*."[35] He gave power to deal, by virtue of his apostolic authority, with matters regarding the bishops, to convoke a council and to watch over the following provinces: "Viennensis, Lugdunensis, Narbonnensis utriusque et Alpiniae" (Martime Alps). Thus all the privileges granted by Pope Zosimus were restored.[36]

This tradition continued with Pope Gelasius (492-496), Anastasius (496-498), and Simmachus (498-514).[37] The last-mentioned Pontiff enlarged the domain entrusted to the care of the Vicar, and St. Caesarius by investing him with the use of the pallium "per omnes gallicanas regiones,"[38] gave a guarantee of the permanence of the privileges conferred on Arles. Shortly afterwards the interests of religion "tam in Gallia quam in Hispania provinciis" were entrusted to him, together with the power to convene councils and possibly to settle all disputes, at least when the "*existentis negotii qualitas*" did not call for the judgment of Rome.[39] No special regulations determined what matters should be referred to Rome; in practice this depended on the Vicar Apostolic or was probably regulated by custom.

33 *Epist.* 65—*MPL,* LIV, 879.

34 *Epist.* 67, *MPL,* LIV, 886.

35 *Epist.* 7—Thiel, *Epistolae Romanorum Pontificum genuinae,* I, 140.

36 *Epist.* 8; 9; 12—Thiel, *Op. cit.,* I; 146; 148; 152. Cfr. Duchesne, *Op. cit.,* I, 129.

37 *Epist. ad episcopum Arelatensem*—Thiel, *Op. cit.,* I, 385; 634; 655.

38 *Epist.* 15—Thiel, *Op. cit.,* I, 727.

39 *Epist.* 16—Thiel, *Op. cit.,* I, 728.

40 *Epist. ad Auxanium*—*MPL,* LXIX, 26; 27; 29.

Pope Vigilius (537-555) and Pope Pelagius (555-560) [41] acknowledged and continued the privileges of Arles. Pope Gregory the Great appointed Vigilius as Vicar Apostolic but it seems that with Vigilius came a change in vicarial law. To Vigilius were made warm recommendations in the struggle against simoniacal consecrations, but it appears that he had nothing more to do with the approval of the nomination of bishops. There was besides a change in juridical procedure: "Si qua vero inquisitio de fide vel fortasse aliarum rerum inter Episcopos causa emerserit quae discerni difficilius possit, collectis duodecim Episcopis ventiletur atque decidatur." [42]

Vicariates apostolic multiplied on the pattern of those of Thessalonica and Arles.

In Spain were created the Vicariates of Seville, [43] of Tarracona [44] and of Toledo.[45]

In France the Vicariate of Vienne,[46] was established by Popes Celestine I and Leo the Great; at the time of Pope Hormisdas (514-528) the see of Rheims was raised to the same dignity.[47]

In England the see of Canterbury had held from the time of St. Augustine a position of preeminence, all the churches of Britain and in 731—"omnes Ecclesiae Britanniae"—were made subject to Archbishop Tatwin who was constituted Vicar Apostolic.[48]

During the Monothelite controversy Stephen of Dor [49] and John of Philadelphia held the office of Vicar Apostolic. To the latter Pope

[41] Jaffe, nn. 941; 942; 945.

[42] St. Gregorius Magnus, *Epistolae* V, 53; cfr. 54; 55—*MPL*, LXXVII, 782-789; and also in *MGH*. *Epistolae* VII, 92; 109.

[43] Simplicius, *Epist.* I—*MPL*, LVIII, 35; Hormisdas, *Epist.* 26—*MPL*, LXIII, 425.

[44] Hormisdas, *Epist.* 24—*MPL*, LXIII, 420.

[45] The Twelfth Council of Toledo (a. 681) can. 6: " . . . licitum maneat deinceps Toletano pontifici, quoscumque regalis potestas elegerit et iam dicti Toletani episcopi dignos esse probaverit, in quibuslibet provinciis in praecedentium sedibus praeficere praesules et decedentibus episcopis eligere successores"—Mansi, XI, 1033. Cfr. Mansi, X, 513.

[46] Coelestinus, *Epist.* 4—*MPL*, L, 434; St. Leo Magnus, *Epist.* 10—*MPL*, LIV, 635.

[47] Hormisdas, *Epist.* I (a. 514)—*MPL*, LXIII, 367.

[48] *Epist.* 17—*MPL*, LXXXIX, 527.

[49] Martinus I, *Epist.* 9—*MPL*, LXXXVII, 169.

Martin I writes: " . . . charitatem tuam exhortamur, *nostram illic vicem implere, i.e., in Orientis partibus in omnibus ecclesiasticis functionibus et officiis . . .*" [50]

The papal representative constituted in Sicily by St. Gregory the Great assumed a special character.[51] There the Holy See held a patrimony; the "*Rector patrimonii*" was an official sent from Rome, and so here a departure was made from the ordinary rule followed in the creation of vicars apostolic, who were selected from among residential bishops. Besides, the origin and the scope of the Rectorate of the ecclesiastical patrimony seem to have nothing in common with the institution of the vicars. However, the Rector was not solely a financier but also took charge of spiritual matters, such as the supervision of the Christian communities and monasteries, and above all he had the office of selecting candidates for the episcopacy and sending them to Rome for consecration.[52] The Rector of the patrimony had also the power to establish an inquiry into the worthiness and suitability of the newly elected.

Later Maximian, Bishop of Syracuse, was constituted Vicar Apostolic: "super cunctas Siciliae ecclesias." His powers were not very well determined and were, perhaps, more restricted than those granted to the Vicars who were more distant from Italy.[53]

As regards vicars apostolic it is worth while noting that they are not to be confused with the present-day vicars apostolic who are placed to rule missionary countries not yet divided into dioceses.[54] The vicar apostolic in missionary lands holds the position of an *Ordinarius loci.* He rules a definite territory *in spiritualibus et temporalibus* in the name of the Pope,[55] but he has no jurisdiction over other *Ordinarii loci* nor does he supervise any district entrusted to their care.[56]

The juridical position of the vicar apostolic of the early centuries

[50] Martinus I, *Epist.* 5—*MPL,* LXXXVII, 154.

[51] St. Gregorius Magnus, *Epistolae,* I, 1-3—*MPL,* LXXVII, 442-446.

[52] St. Gregorius Magnus, *Epistolae,* I, 18—*MPL,* LXXVII, 463.

[53] St. Gregorius Magnus, *Epistolae,* II, 7—*MPL,* LXXVII, 543.

[54] Cfr. Can. 293-311.

[55] Cfr. Can. 1350, § 2.

[56] S.C. de Prop. Fide, 14th. February 1702—Coll. n. 253; Fanning, "Vicar Apostolic," *The Catholic Encyclopedia,* XV, 401; Winslow, *Vicars and Prefects Apostolic,* pp. 4; 15-16.

of the Church was that of a papal representative with special duties exercised directly in the name of the Roman Pontiff and referring to matters pertaining to the supreme ecclesiastical authority. Such a form of papal representation was the most complete known in those centuries, for the vicar apostolic held a number of offices and exercised acts of jurisdiction which in the aggregate were not ordinarily entrusted to other representatives.

The title and office of vicar apostolic were permanent with regard to him who held them but with the exception of the Vicariate of Thessalonica it does not appear that they were necessarily connected with any see. In practice, the Popes often refer to custom. Sometimes, however, they do not renew the privilege to a successor, or if they do, they change quite informally the limits of the territory assigned. The activities of the vicar apostolic were of an exclusively spiritual character, and his powers were confined to matters of ecclesiastical discipline. He fulfilled his mission by exercising a kind of general supervision and by urging the fulfilment of the Popes' instructions, but above all, he acted through the plenary council which he had the power to convoke and over which he had the right to preside.

Article IV: Missionary Legations

Those who went forth to preach the Gospel to the infidels always did so fortified by the blessing of the Pope, who was in the habit of giving them ample faculties in order to facilitate their work for the rapid extension of the kingdom of Christ. Sometimes these powers were granted in an extraordinary form, for particular ends and with a special mandate, and in this case the missionary really became a papal legate. Thus we have the case of *missionary legations.* Such a mission was entrusted to the priest Ninian for the evangelization of Scotland at the time of Pope Siricius (384-399).[1] In the year 431 *"Ad Scotos (Hiberniae) in Christum credentes ordinatus a Papa Coelestino Palladius primus episcopus mittitur;*[2] St. Palladius was

[1] Beda, *Historia Eccl.,* III, 4—*MPL,* XCV, 121.

[2] St. Prosper Aquitanus, *Chronica—MPL,* LI, 595.

followed in 432 by St. Patrick who with the consent of Pope Leo the Great established the primatial see of Armagh.[3]

St. Augustus of Canterbury received from St. Gregory the Great the mission of evangelizing.[4] Not only was he granted faculties to consecrate bishops for his mission and supremacy over the province of Canterbury, but all the priests of Britain were obliged to give him obedience and to accept his instructions as emanating from the chair of truth, the Apostolic See, to which Augustine professed great devotion and unconditional loyalty.[5]

The most famous of the missionary legations is that of St. Boniface, apostle of Germany. Established by Gregory II (715-731),[6] it flourished under the Pontiffs Gregory III (731-741), St. Zachary (741-752) and Stephen III (752-757). Boniface "ab apostolica sede directus" or "nostram agens vicem" as Gregory III declares,[7] invested with the pallium of jurisdiction, "ex vigore apostolicae sedis" had the duties of ordaining bishops and convoking councils.[8] In virtue of the authority vested in him and of the fulness of the powers conferred on him he could carry on his mission successfully. His labors and devotion to the Holy See not only won for him great praise, but Pope Zachary proclaimed him *"Apostolicae Sedis Legatum"* for Gaul

[3] *The Canon of St. Patrick*: "Moreover, if any case should arise of extreme difficulty, and beyond the knowledge of all the judges of the nation of the Scots, it is to be duly referred to the chair of the archbishop of the Irish, that is to say, of Patrick, and the jurisdiction of the bishop (of Armagh). But if such a case, as aforesaid, of a matter at issue cannot be easily disposed of (by him) with his counsellors in that (investigation), we have decreed that it be sent to the apostolic seat, that is to say, *to the Chair of the Apostle Peter, having the authority of the city of Rome.*"—William B. Morris, *The Life of St. Patrick,* (6th ed. p. 31 note 1). For the Roman mission of St. Patrick, *Op. cit.,* pp. 102-115; 288-290; also Abbe Riguet, *Saint Patrick,* translated by C.W.W., pp. 54-56; 92-99; Eoin McNeill, *St. Patrick,* pp. 50-52.

[4] St. Gregorius Magnus, *Epistolae* VI, 5-59—*MPL,* LXXVII, 836-842; Beda, *Historia Eccl.,* II, 2-3—*MPL,* XCV, 81-86.

[5] St. Gregorius Magnus, *Epistolae,* IX, 65—*MPL,* LXXVII, 1200.

[6] *Epist.* I; 3; 6—*MPL,* LXXIX, 495; 501; 503.

[7] *Epist..* I; 4;—*MPL, ibid.,* 575; 580.

[8] *Ibid.,* 577.

and Germany with the express task of founding churches and spreading the apostolic Teaching.[9]

A missionary legation was also conducted by St. Methodius, apostle of the Slavs, for the evangelization of Pannonia at the time of Adrian II (867-872).[10]

Missionary legations are by their very nature transitory and personal. They are the first step in an evangelical conquest, and are of special importance since this stage the work of the propagation of the faith demands that by unity of direction and combined action all efforts should be concentrated to the attainment of the end.

Artacle V: The Transition Period
(9th century - 11th century)

Throughout the period extending from the ninth to the eleventh centuries the Vicariates Apostolic continued to be erected. Some episcopal sees obtained the title; others, having by degrees risen to a position of special importance by their ecclesiastical administration, gained the special favor of the Holy See, and by way of privilege exercised some jurisdiction in adjacent territory.

Sergius II (844-847) in the year 847 entrusted the duties of Vicar Apostolic to Drogus, Archbishop of Metz, over all the transalpine provinces, "cunctis provinciis trans Alpes constitutis." We note, however, in the instructions of his letters of nomination, a restriction in the exercise of his discretionary powers: some criminal cases had to be submitted to a collegiate tribunal of Bishops; his powers regarding the approval of those elected to the episcopacy were to be used subject to the rights of the Holy See and also with due regard to the Emperor.[1]

Meanwhile in the second half of the ninth century there came about a significant development. There appeared legates more closely and directly dependent on Rome, to whom the Popes entrusted the most varied tasks, both in affairs purely ecclesiastical and those of a

[9] *Epist.* 12—*Ibid.*, 948; Pius VI, *Responsio ad Metropolitanos*, cap. VIII, n. 92-93.

[10] Jaffe, n. 2924; 2973.

[1] *Epist. ad Episcopos Transalpinos—MPL*, CVI, 913.

political complexion.[2] Through the frequency of these extraordinary legations changes were gradually introduced in the office of the Vicars Apostolic effecting a transformation which became complete at the period of the Decretals. It appears that the bishops of the ecclesiastical provinces preferred to be controlled directly by an envoy from Rome than by the Vicar Apostolic. Drogus of Metz had soon to resign his position, so hostile had the bishops become.[3] Nicholas I sending Arsenius, his apocrisiarius and nuncio of the Holy See, to the Bishop of Gaul, thus recalls in a letter their invitation: *"crebrius exegistis, hortatu vestro plurimum invitati . . ."* [4]

However at the time of John VIII (872-882(the position of vicar apostolic was still the most complete form of pontifical representation, so much that so (in reference to the reestablishing of the Vicariate of Arles) it is defined: *"transitoriae potestatis culmen."* [5] This power was also vested in Ansegisus, Archbishop of Sens (a. 876) "sive in vocanda synodo sive in aliis negotiis exercendi per Gallias et Germanias," with the obligation of making a report only occasionally and when the opportunity presented itself.[6] Since Ansegisus was already the intermediary of the Emperor Lothair with the Pope, Lapotre [7] sees in this appointment, and in the concession of such ample powers, an act of that political policy by which John VIII held that

[2] Cfr. e.g., *Liber Pontificalis,* II, 141; 158; 160; 180, etc.; *O. Engelmann*; *Die paepstilichen Legaten in Deutschland bis zur Mitte des* 11 *Jahrhunderts,* p. 52 seqq.; Lapotre, *L'Europe et le Saint-Siege a l'epoque carolingienne,* cap. V, p. 203.

[3] Pius VI, *Responsio ad Metropolitanos,* cap. VIII, n. 127.

[4] Mansi XV, 288. We may recall what Lapotre (*Op. cit.,* p. 37) says of the apocrisiarius at this period: "L'apocrisiaire du Saint-Siège etait alors une sorte de Minstre d'Etat, a qui ressortissaient principalement les relations du Pape avec l'empereur et les autres princes de la chretiente." Hence it seems that the apocrisiarius has now nothing in common with the office of the deacon who resided at the court of Constantinople. The Papal officials were designated by various names at this time; for example Cardinal Humbert of Selva Candida, legate at Constantinople is called: *"comes et consiliarius Papae."* Cfr. David J. Hill, *A History of Diplomacy in the International Development of Europe,* I, 206, n. 1.

[5] *MGH, Epistolae* VII, 109.

[6] *Epist.* 15—*MPL,* CXXVI, 660.

[7] *Op. cit.;* p. 259.

Empire and Papacy should put their authority and co-operation at each other's disposal.

The Carolingian policy of John VIII—"the one force which tried to prevent the dissolution of the empire" [8] was put into execution chiefly by legates in extraordinary mission.[9]

Among the variety of terms used at this age to denote papal legates one often meets that of *"legatus a latere."* [10] But it did not yet denote any specific kind of legate with exclusive, clearly-defined competency, but rather an envoy in general specially delegated by the Holy See, and thus distinct from the Vicar Apostolic. It seems that a more exact classification can be deduced from what John XIII (965-972) and Benedict VII (974-983) say in relation to the privileges granted to the Archbishop of Trier. They speak of *"vicarius constitutus"* and *"legatus ordinarius,"* [11] and so they leave it to be supposed that there exists a third category of pontifical representatives, that of extraordinary legates who will henceforth be the true *legati a latere.*

It may also be noted that at the end of the tenth century and the beginning of the eleventh century special privileges, in addition to those of Trier already mentioned, were granted to the sees of Mainz and Salzburg.[12] The privileges chiefly consisted in certain rights of precedence and the use of pontifical insignia, but there were added some powers concerning the consecration of the bishops of some neighboring cities and duties of supervision with the obligation of furnishing a report periodically to the Holy See.[13]

It does not appear that much can be said regarding the jurisdiction exercised by the *legati missi* over the local bishops. Ordinarily powers of this kind were conferred on the vicars apostolic:[14] they were granted

[8] Cfr. G. B. Picotti, "Giovanni VIII," *Enciclopedia Italiana,* XVII, 252.

[9] *Epist.* 20-23—*MPL,* CXXVI, 664-675.

[10] Bouquet, *Recueil des Historiens des Gaules,* VII, 386; 389; *Epist.* 209—*MPL,* CXXVI, 919.

[11] Privilege 13, *MPL,* CXXV, 974; Privilege 4—*MPL,* CXXXVII, 320.

[12] Pius VI, *Responsio ad Metropolitanos,* cap. VIII, n. 110-116.

[13] Jaffe, n. 3729; 4074; *MPL,* CXLIII, 594.

[14] "Te ergo frater carissime omnis cura respectat earum Ecclesiarum quas tibi vice sedis apostolicae a nobis creditas recognosces ut et patrata corrigas et dissipatas componas"—Bonifacius I, *Epist.* 5—*MPL,* XX, 762; Thiel, *Epistolae genuinae Rom. Pontificum,* I, 140.

to the *legati missi* only as an exception and for each particular case. The cases which best illustrate this point are the mission entrusted by John VIII to Paul, Bishop of Ancona, in the year 873, and the other entrusted by Sylvester II, to the Cardinal-priest Frederick in the year 1001. The first refers to the controversy which arose regarding the mission of Methodius and the bishops of Bavaria. The apostolic legate claimed the right for the Holy See to deal with the *causa maiores,* and the natural right of the Church of Rome to legislate for the provinces converted to Catholicism. The Archbishops of Frisinga and Salzburg had deposed and imprisoned Methodius, who had been previously consecrated archbishop by the Pope himself (Adrian II—867-872) and established in authority as *"legatione apostolicae Sedis ad gentes fungens"*:[15] they had taken advantage of a political situation and usurped the Pope's exclusive right of judging an archibshop. The apostolic legate restored Methodius to the full exercise of his rights and punished the guilty parties.[16] In the other example the Cardinal-priest Frederick was commissioned to hold a council for the settlement of a dispute which had arisen among some German bishops. The Archbishop of Hamburg was excommunicated and deposed by the papal delegate.[17] Noteworthy is the solemnity with which the delegate entered the council; bearing special insignia he proceeded with all the pomp and the honors reserved to the Pope;[18] a custom that from this time became more common and was reserved in a special and quite distinctive fashion in the case of legati a latere.

The instructions given to the legates and the extent of their powers were usually contained in the letters that the Popes addressed to those to whom the legation was directed. But in the time of Nicholas I

[15] Jaffe, n. 2979.

[16] " . . . ad hoc missus sum ut tanto vos tempore a divinis ministeriis separem, quanto vos eundem venerabilem virum a ministerio sacro coegistis"—Jaffe, n. 2976. Cf. *MGH, Epistolae* VII, 280-286; Lapotre, *L'Europe et le Saint-Siéie a l'epoque carolingienne,* pp. 117-23.

[17] Thangmarus, *Vita Bernawardi,* cap. 28-30—*MGH, Scriptores* IV, 771-773.

[18] "Cardinal Presbyter Frithericus, omnibus insigniis apostolicis ac si papa procedat infulatus, equis apostolica sella Romano more ostro instratus—*MGH, Scriptores,* IV, 771.

(858-867) the instructions were more frequently addressed to the legates themselves.[19]

During their mission the legates nearly always find friendly hospitality at the courts of ecclesiastical or secular princes and in this way provision is made for their sustenance. Sometimes they were offered gifts either in grateful recognition of their services or to honor the person of the Pope whom they represented.

In the case of France, especially, the *legati missi* did not come much into contact with the clergy. This is probably explained by the fact that in that country ecclesiastical affairs were generally under the supervision of the vicars apostolic and the tasks entrusted to the *legati missi* were generally of a political nature.[20]

Article VI: The Legates (11th Century - 14th Century)

A. The Reform of Gregory VII

The programme of emancipation from civil interference and of ecclesiastical reform initiated by the abbacy of Cluny and by its dependent communities became in the eleventh century the programme defended and supported by the Holy See.[1]

The vast proportions of the struggle against the simoniacal and

[19] *Epist.* 19; 20; 21—*MPL,* CXIX, 799-803.

[20] Cfr. O. Engelmann, *Die paepatlichen Legaten in Deutschland zur Mitte des 11 Jahrhunderts,* pp. 120-122; 128.

[1] Cfr. A. Fliche, *Etudes sur la polemisue a l'epoque religieuse de Gregoire VII,* pp. 12-30. St. Peter Damien writes enthusiastically of the life of Cluny in the following words: "Vidi siquidem paradisum quattuor Evangeliorum fluentis irriguum, imo totidem spiritualium rives exuberare virtutum; vidi hortum deliciarum diversas rosarum ac liliorum gratias germinantem, et mellifluas aromatumac pigmentorum fragrantias suaviter redolentem, ut de illo valeat Deus Omnipotens dicere: Ecce odor filii mei sicut odor agri pleni, cui benedixit Dominus. Et quid aliud Cluniacense monasterium nisi agrum Domini plenum dixerim ubi velut acervus est coelestium segetum, chorus tot in charitate monachorum? Ager ille quotidiano sanctae praedicationis ligone praescinditur et in eo coelestis eloquii semina consperguntur. Illic spiritualium frugum proventus aggeritur ut horreis postmodum coelestibus inferatur."—*Epistolae* VI, 4—*MPL,* CXLIV, 374.

Nicholaitic heresies demanded unity of direction in the hierarchy and contact of the Head with the members of the Christian world. It therefore became necessary for the Popes to have a vanguard of preachers of reform fortified with the assurance of success which the sanction of papal authority provides. Through this movement and the increasing influence of papal supremacy, the legates developed and attained a definite organization.

The term that occurs almost exclusively to denote papal representatives in this period is that of *legatus* which, however, is followed by the most diverse specifications indicating offices which differ greatly in quality and importance.

Alexander II in a letter to the Archbishops of Gaul gave to the legation of St. Peter Damian (a. 1063) the highest grade of pontifical representation when he says: " . . . talem vobis virum destinare curavimus, quo nimirum *post nos* maior in Romana Ecclesia auctoritas non habetur . . . qui nimirum et noster est oculus et apostolicae Sedis immobile firmamentum. Huic itaque vicem nostram *pleno iure commissimus,* ut quidquid in illis partibus, Deo auxiliante, statuerit, ita ratum teneatur et firmum ac si specialis nostri examinis fuerit, sententia promulgatum."[2]

The expression *"pleno iure"* has a clear meaning from thsi context and later passes into the equivalent expression *"plenae legationis officium committere,"* by which is normally meant the fulness of the power of the *legatus a latere.*

Legati *non pleno iure,* or as they will be called *simpliciter missi,* are those to whom are entrusted offices of lesser importance, or at least those who have not the same full exercise of powers as the *legati pleno iure.*

The development of the right of legation assumes an extraordinary importance at the time of Gregory VII. It is used by him not only as an instrument to carry into effect his plans of reform but also as a means to vindicate the prestige of the Roman primacy.[3]

Gregory VII first of all asserts: " . . . *necessarium valde est ut*

[2] *Epist. ad Archiep. Galliae*—Mansi, XIX, 958; cfr. St. Petrus Damianus, *Epistolae,* VI, 1; 4—*MPL,* CXLIV, 371; 373; *De Gallica Profectione*—*MPL,* CXLV, 865-880; R. Biron, *St. Pierre Damiani,* pp. 134-151.

[3] G. Soranzo, "Gregorio VII"—*Enciclopedia Italiana,* XVII, 933-935.

exigente ratione vel tempore aliquem modo ad has, modo ad illas partes remittere studeamus, per quem commissa nobis secundum voluntatem Dei representetur auctoritas et Dominici gregis salus atque communis provideatur utilitas . . . ," since the absence of the shepherd causes harm to the sheep.[4] The Roman See has always, he says, made use of this means of coming into contact with all nations and while, "apud antecessores nostros"—writes the Pontiff to the King of Denmark—"iuris et consuetudinis erat caritativis legationibus docere viam Domini universas nationes, corripere in his quae arguenda erant omnes reges et principes et ad aeternam beatitudinem cunctas invitare legalibus disciplinis," it is now to be lamented that so little regard is had for these representatives of the supreme ecclesiastical authority. The legations seem to be no longer in use, and through relaxed discipline and want of reverence so many calamities have fallen on the Church.[5] However Gregory VII sends his legates wherever the interests of the papacy seem to require his presence, namely, to civil princes and the Catholic hierarchy.

According to the practice of this Pontiff the permanent and temporary legations are quite distinct. For the first class, the legates are chosen from the clergy of the district, and they are practically the same as the vicars apostolic. Noteworthy examples of this category are Hugo, Bishop of Die in Burgundy,[6] and Amatus, Bishop of Oleron in Gascony (IV, 28). Gregory VII recalls their juridical position to the bishops of the district[7] and names their numerous duties with regard to the disputes in connection with the monasteries;[8] their right of inflicting ecclesiastical censures:[9] in regard to which he says: " . . . volumus vos in omnibus conciliis vestris, vice nostra, omnes illos excommunicare qui de manu alicuius laici investituram Ecclesiarum susceperint";[10] the absolution and redamission of

[4] Caspar, *Registrum Gregorii VII Libri IX, Epistolae selectae,* Lib. V, 2 in the collection *MGH.*

[5] Caspar, *Op. cit.,* lib. II, 75.

[6] Hugues de Flavigny, *Chronicon—MGH, Scriptores,* VIII, 412.

[7] Caspar, *Op. cit.,* Lib. IV, 18; 19; 20.

[8] Caspar, *Op. cit.,* Lib. IV, 16; VI, 24; 25.

[9] Caspar, *Op. cit.,* Lib. III, 10 a; VI; 5 b.

[10] Hugues de Flavigny, *Op. cit.—MGH, Scriptores,* VIII, 421.

penitents to the communion of the Church;[11] the regularization of marriages;[12] the approval of those elected to the episcopacy.[13] But the apostolic legate should above all convoke councils to affirm and spread the doctrine of the Church, particularly with reference to the investitures and the disciplinary laws emanating from the Roman Councils which Gregory VII held at the beginning of each Lent. The activity of the legates in this respect is untiring. In virtue of the general delegation conferred by the Pope, councils follow one another in rapid succession: Autun, Lyons, Clermont and Poitiers are so many centres where the dioceses of France pass under review. The secular and regular clergy are present in strength; the principle of the superiority of the Church over the state is defended, but much more frequently the legislation covers matters of ecclesiastical discipline, and the weeding out of the simoniacal and Nicholaitic heresies proceeds. The guilty are subjected to a vigorous test: they must retract their errors and promise amendment, or suffer inevitable deposition and separation from the Mystical Body.[14] The task of the permanent legates is properly limited to a given nation but they sometimes receive the command to pass outside the confines of their own territory to examine appeals[15] or solemnly enforce disciplinary laws where most needed.[15 bis]

In his frequent correspondence the Pope directs the actions of his legates: he sometimes moderates their zeal ("pro tempore canonicum rigorem vestra sapientia temperet"[16] and even revokes their sentences.[17]

[11] Caspar, *Op. cit.,* Lib. IV, 22; VI, 7; VII, 16.

[12] Caspar, *Op. cit.,* Lib. VI, 20.

[13] Caspar, *Op. cit.,* Lib. VI, 21; VIII, 18.

[14] Hugue de Flavigny, *Op. cit.—MGH, Scriptores,* VIII, 414-422.

[15] Caspar, *Op. cit.,* Lib. IV, 17.

[15 bis] Caspar, *Op. cit.,* Lib. VII, 10.

[16] Caspar, *Op. cit.,* Lib. IX, 5; 33.

[17] Caspar, *Op. cit.,* Lib. VII, 22.

Fliche says of Hugues de Die " . . . imperieux, autoritative, dur pour les autres comme pour lui-même, incapable d'admettre le moindre adoucissement à la règle, Hugues a été la terreur des simoniaques et des nicolaites qu'il a harcelés sans cesse de ses reproches et traduits devant les conciles provinceaux convoqués par ses soins. Son action a été decisive

In connection with the position of the Vicar Apostolic of the Gauls we may note that Gregory claimed for the see of Lyons the primacy over the provinces of Tours, Rouen and Sens, and asked that it should be paid due honour and obedience.[18] When, however, the archbishop died in 1082 and Hugues de Die was translated to Lyons,[19] "l'institution de la primatie se trouve du même coupe denaturée; le primat n'est plus le chef de l'Eglise nationale, mais le répresentant du Saint-Siege qui déjormais peut librement intervenir en toute occasion."[20]

Gregory VII made frequent use of particular legations[21] to expedite purely ecclesiastical affairs or to get into touch with civil princes in the matter of defending the rights of the kingdom of St. Peter. The Pope believed these legations necessary and gives the reason: "Nunquam enim hoc negotium rectius aut diligentius quam in eadem ecclesia pertractari posse videtur."[22] To these emissaries were entrusted tasks of no less importance than those given to the permanent legates. The delegation sometimes embraced a whole series of affairs and faculties, and so was the exercise of the highest papal mandate. In the case of a mission in Bohemia the legate was given plenary powers to correct errors, impose obedience on the seditious, reprove the disloyal and impose ecclesiastical censures on those who refused to maintain order. Thus the chronicler observes: " . . . *missus apostolici tanta auctoritate usus est et potestate ac si idem Summus Pontifex praesens fuisset.*"[23]

The Pope, however, reserved to himself in a general way the *causae maiores*;[24] in these cases the legates were limited to the con-

et, si les effets de la reforme grégorienne se sont fait sentir en France plus rapidement que partout ailleurs, c'est à lui qu'em revient le principale mérite."—*La Chrétienté médiévale*, p. 289.

18 Caspar, *Op. cit.*, Lib. VI, 34.

19 Caspar, *Op. cit.*, Lib. IX, 13; 19.

20 Fliche, *Etudes sur la polemique religieuse à l'epoque de Grégoire VII*, p. 317.

21 Caspar, *Op. cit.*, Lib. I, 6; 8; 17; II, 2; 23; 25; IV, 17; 23; V, 15; VII, 7.

22 Lib. IV, 17.

23 Cosmas, *Chronicon Boemorum*, II, 30—*MGH, Scriptores* IX, 87.

24 Caspar, *Op. cit.*, (*Dictatus Papae*), Lib. II, 55 a, n. 21.

duct of the preliminary procedure, and even then they were allowed act only when their duty was clear and the issue unavoidable: " . . . omnibus modis omnique ingenio usque ad mortem, si oportet, nostra vice, immo B. Petri auctoritate ei (Henrico) resistite." [25]

In the correspondence of Gregory VII mention is also made of the *"nuntii e latere apostolicae sedis"* [26] and of the *"nuntii ex latere nostro."* [27] The context seems to suggest an interpretation in favour of the emissaries being on a mission chiefly diplomatic: for mention is made of the negotiations the legates are to carry on with the Emperor of Germany and in the kingdom of Berengarius. It is also to be noted that in the case of Berengarius the "nuntii ex latere" will be sent only in case the local legates do not reach the desired peace.

The attitude of Gregory VII towards the different categories of legates appears clearly from his practice and letters. The juridical position of the vicar is superior to that of the legate. The vicar apostolic in fact is endowed with general faculties, he has jurisdiction over a vast territory, and no limits of time are imposed on him in the exercise of his office. The legate on the contrary has definite and extraordinary faculties but only *quoad actum suae legationis.*

The two categories of papal legates are sometimes distinguished by a specific term; the *"legatus romanus,"* and the *"Vicarius apos-*

[25] Caspar, *Op. cit.,* Lib. IV, 23; cfr. Lib. VI, 15.

[26] "Et quoniam litis et perturbatio regni in maximum sanctae Ecclesiae periculum et detrimentum cotidie redundare cernimus placet nobis elaborare pro viribus, quatenus idonei tam religione quam etiam scientia pollentes *nuntii e latere apostolicae sedis* ad partes illas mittantur qui omnes religiosos et iustitiae amatores in Teutonici regni partibus commorantes clericalis et laicalis ordinis viros et ad hoc opus idoneos convocent cum quibus Domini gratia praeeunte aut finem et pacem iuste componant aut veritate percognita, cui parti magis iustitia faveat ad plenum ediscere valeant, quatenus pars iniusta desipiscat et apostolica auctoritate munita iustitia vigoris et auctoritatis robur obtineat"—Caspar, *Op. cit.,* Lib. V, 14 a.

[27] " . . . ostensis eis praesentibus litteris ad tenendam eos treuvam firmissimam usque ad determinatum tempus ex auctoritate nostra constringite, infra quod nos *tales illuc ex latere nostros nuntios* dirigimus, qui causam litis eorum ita iuste definant ut non se ad gratiam alicuius nec pretio nec favore deflectant"—Caspar, *Op. cit.,* lib. VI, 16.

tolicae sedis." The "*legati romani,*" that is, " . . . *qui vel Romae nati vel in Romana Ecclesia a parvulo educati vel in eaden sint aliqua dignitate promoti,*" are the extraordinary envoys on a temporary and definite mission; the "*Vicarius apostolicae sedis,*" is generally a bishop of the district, "*cui vicem suam Romanus Pontifex indulgeat.*" [28] Such is the general practice, but since the office of legate depends entirely and exclusively on the will of the Pope, the *legatus romanus* could rise to the highest dignity and authority in the Church when, e.g. he was sent as a delegate to an Ecumenical Council.[29]

The legate is a juridical person created by delegation and in virtue of a privilege of the supreme pontifical authority. This privilege could perhaps be acquired, or handed down by custom from bishop to bishop of the same see, but Gregory VII does not seem very favorable to this practice and at any rate he lays down that the Pope is under no limitation in this matter. Thus he writes to the Archbishop of Rheims: "Ad id autem quod de privilegio dicitis,[30] breviter interim respondemus quod possunt quaedam in privilegiis pro se, pro persona, pro tempore, pro loco concedi, quae iterum pro eisdem, si necessitas vel utilitas maior exegerit licenter valent commutari." [31]

The legates are, besides, always under the control of the Pontiff. While he grants them the fullest powers, he does not cease to exercise a strict watch over their work, and he requires them to be faithful in sending reports on its progress, and to make a special report to himself in person at its conclusion.[32]

Gregory VII claimed for his legates the highest jurisdiction and the honour due to the Pope himself: "Quod legatus eius (i.e. Papae) omnibus Episcopis praesit in concilio etiam inferioris gradus, et adversus eos sententiam depositionis posset dare." [33] He defended their authority on historical and juridical grounds, [34] and protected their

[28] Caspar, *Op. cit.*, Lib. VI, 2.
[29] Caspar, *Op. cit.*, lib. VII, 12.
[30] Cfr. Hinschius, *Kirchenrecht,* I, 602, n. 1.
[31] Caspar, *Op. cit.*, Lib. VI, 2.
[32] Caspar, *Op. cit.*, Lib. I, 16; VI, 16.
[33] Caspar, *Op. cit.*, (*Dictatus Papae*), Lib. II, 55a.
[34] Caspar, *Op. cit.*, Lib. VI, 2.

person and office with grave censures: "Quicumque . . . legatis nostris . . . obponere tentaverit, vinculo eum anathematis alligamus et non solum in spiritu, verum etiam in corpore et omni prosperitate huius vitae apostolica potestate innodamus et victoriam eis in armis auferimus ut sic statim confundantur et duplici confusione et contritione conterantur." [35] And so in the sworn adjurations imposed by the Pope on princes or members of the hierarchy, before they were absolved from the censures incurred, one of the articles of the promise of honour and obedience always refers to the legates. Not only this, but he required that they be sustained and provided with the necessaries of life during their mission, since it was but just and fitting that those who enjoy the benefit of the legation should defray its expenses. Thus the Archbishop of Aquileia promised: "Legatum Romanum eundo et redeundo honorifice tractabo et in necessitatibus adiuvabo." [36] And all metropolitans are bound to take the same oath when they receive the pallium.[37] In this connection also we may cite the example of King Demetrius of Dalmatia who in 1076 presented to the Holy See the monastery of Urana with all its treasury of gold, silver, precious gems, moveable and immoveable goods, "ut sancti Petri legatis semper sit ad hospitium et omnino in potestate eorum." [38]

From all this we may rightly conclude with D. J. Hill [39] that Gregory raised the office of the legates to such a position of importance as to make it thenceforth an essential organ of the papal government. Indeed the institution of the papal legates as found in the ecclesiastical and political activity of Gregory VII bears all the characteristic elements it possesses to-day.[40] Later Pontiffs only followed in his footsteps; and in accordance with the laws of natural development, the various kinds of legations gradually became more clearly defined, assuming a kind of hierarchical co-ordination and,

[35] Caspar, *Op. cit.*, Lib. V, 14a.

[36] Caspar, *Op. cit.*, Lib. VI, 17a.

[37] Cfr. *Pontificale Romanum, pars I, de Pallio*: *Forma Iuramenti.* Baronius, *Annales eccl.* ad a. 1002, n. 2, XVIII, 136.

[38] *Concilium Salonitanum* II—Mansi, XX, 474.

[39] *A History of Diplomacy in the International Development of Europe,* I, 225; cfr. A. Fliche, *Etudes sur la polémique religieuse à l'époque de Grégoire VII,* p. 316.

[40] Cfr. A. Flichce, *St. Grégoire VII,* pp. 73-81.

at least to a certain extent, the consequent enumeration of the powers proper to each class.

As has been already mentioned, it frequently happened that the Popes granted privileges to episcopal sees which had attained special prominence on account either of their position as centres of culture and social life, or of the flourishing condition of the faith. While in other times they would have received the powers of Apostolic Vicariates, now they are raised to a rank of honour—perhaps the primatial—of a certain region, and the diocese itself, and sometimes the whole province, are exempted from the supervision of the Vicar and placed in immediate subjection to the Holy See and consequently its Legate.

Already in the time of Gregory VII the Archbishop of Rheims petitioned such an exemption for which he said: "vobis ipsis interpellatus vel non interpellatus respondeam et legatis vestris romanis non ultramontanis." [41]

Sometimes by way of special favour,[42] but more often to provide a remedy for the tyrannical rule of certain metropolitans, of which the bishops complained, such privileges became more frequent in the twelfth century. In a decree of Paschal II (1099-1118) of the year 1115 we find the following provision in favour of Hugo, Bishop of Portugal: " . . . ut nullius Metropolitani nisi Romani Pontificis aut legati, qui ab eius latere missus fuerit, subiectioni teneatur obnoxius." [43] Obedience to him is enjoined on a certain number of churches, and the refractory are threatened with penalties.

In the same form ancient privileges were renewed, for example, those granted by Callixtus II (1119-1124) to the Archbishop of Vienne in the year 1120:

" . . . concedimus et praesentis privilegii pagina confirmamus ut videlicet super septem provincias primatum obtineat . . . et in eis Viennensis Archiepiscopus Romani Pontificis vices agat, synodales conventus indicat et negotia ecclesiastica iuste canoniceque definiat . . . et Viennensem ecclesiam alicui subiacere legato nisi Cardinali vel alii

[41] Bouquet, *Recueil des Historiens des Gaules,* CIV, 611 n. 76.

[42] Hinschius, *Kirchenrecht,* I, 604 n. 7; Cfr. Gwyn, "Papal Legates in Ireland during the Twelfth Century," *IER,* LXIII (1944), 362.

[43] *MPL,* CLXIII, 385.

de Romana provincia qui a Romani Pontificis latere dirigitur, prohibemus." [44]

B. The Decretals and Decretalists

We have now reached a period in which the privileges and missions confided to the legates have become so numerous and complicated that it is extremely difficult to follow in detail the relative legislation. Our best plan would seem to be to confine ourselves to a generic classification of legates, and to treat of their powers as set forth in the Decretals and teaching of the Decretalists. For the sake of clearness, we shall treat sepaartely 1) of *legati nati;* 2) of *legati missi;* and, among the latter, 3) of *legati a latere* in particular; and finally, 4) of the personal privileges of legates.

§ 1. THE LEGATI NATI

Hostiensis says:[45] "officium hoc (i.e., *legati nati*) adnexum est dignitati," that is, to some episcopal see which has attained a position of preeminence over others. Pius VI explained this dignity as a consequence of the office of vicar formerly granted to the bishop of a certain see. After the eleventh century there was an increase in the number of primatial sees, or, of those legations which, having been repeatedly conferred on the metropolitans of a given see, "perinde haberi coeptae sunt ac si ipsis Episcoporum sedibus collatae et affixae fuissent ita ut Legationes natae dictitarentur." [46]

As we have seen, the title and office of apostolic vicar were almost exclusively personal. However, it was ordinarily conferred on the bishop of a certain see, and so we find the Popes often referring in their documents to their predecessors who had made the original grant. In the period under consideration there are still some examples of legations of a personal character. For instance, since the time of Gregory VII, Landulph, Bishop of Pisa, had exercised the office of

[44] Mansi, XXI, 191. For other documents and examples cfr. K. Ruess, *Die rechtliche Stellung der paepstlichen Legatem bis Bonifaz VIII*, p. 111, n. 1.

[45] *Summa aurea,* I, 30.

[46] Pius VI, *Responsio ad Metropolitanos,* cap. VIII, n. 108; Cfr. Cerretti, "Legate," *The Catholic Encyclopedia, IX,* 119.

supervising Corsica;[47] Urban II extended the legation to Sardinia,[48] and it had already seemed to have become permanently united to the see together with some further concessions of succeeding Popes who had uninterruptedly renewed the privilege of the use of Papal insignia, the cross and pallium, to the Archbishop of that see.[49] But, with Innocent IV this legation seems to have been transferred definitely to the Archbishop of Sassari who was constituted Primate for Sardinia and vested with the powers which the Pope grants to *legati a latere*.[50]

The most celebrated episcopal sees for which the title and office of *legatus natus* were claimed are those of Canterbury, York, Rheims and Salzburg. In the year 1117 Paschal II was petitioned to honour the ancient privilege by which the see of Canterbury had since the time of Gregory the Great the right of supervision, and the Archbishop had bee nlegate for all England. The Pope replied: " . . . in eo statu esse Cantuariensem Ecclesiam volumus ut authentica eius privilegia iuxta canonum sanctiones nullis perturbationibus violentur." [51] Alexander II renewed for this see the office of legation over all England except the province of York, the Archbishop of which enjoyed similar privilege. These two sees become the type of the *legationis natae*. The Gloss illustrating by examples the legates who become such by privilege cities the Archbishops of York and Canterbury.[52]

The special feature of legations pertaining to a see seems, however, to have begun with the pontificate of Gregory IX. This Pontiff determined those limits which would thenceforth be constantly put into practice. Thus, he entrusted the office of legate to the Patriarch of

[47] Caspar, *Op. cit.*, Lib. V, 2.

[48] Mansi, XX, 717.

[49] Jaffe, n. 7890; 8929; 10286; 10693; 14514; 15658; 16809.

[50] "Cum tibi in Sardinia et Corsica concesserimus plenae legationis officium eiusdem plenitudine officii in omnibus fungi te volumus qua praedicti noscuntur apostolicae sedis legati qui de latere nostro transmittuntur praerogativa gaudentes prae aliis potiori."—Berger, *Reg. d'Innoc. IV*, n. 5964.

[51] Baronius, *Annales eccl.*, ad a. 1117, n. 9, XVIII, 274.

[52] *Glossa*, ad c. 6, X, *de officio legati*, I, 30; c. I, *de officio legati*, I, 15, in VI°.

Jerusalem but with the express condition that if a *legatus a latere* should ever pass through the territory under his jurisdiction he should cease to function during the time that the legate was performing his mission.[53] Only by way of rescript was granted to the Patriarch of Antioch the privilege of absolving from the excommunication "pro iniectione manuum in clericos violenta" even those who are not subject to him;[54] while the *legati a latere* could absolve anyone, even though he did not belong to the province assigned to them. Still, Uurban IV alone expressly states the connection of the title of legate with the see to which it is annexed when writing to the Patriarch of Jerusalem, he says: "... *tibi hoc ex legationis officio Patriarchatus annexo competere declaramus.*"[55]

What then were the powers of these legates? According to Wernz[56] they were very dubious and uncertain. It must first of all be remembered that these bishops were metropolitans "*ex iure communi*" and as such were entitled to exercise authority over their suffragans by means of canonical visitation, their duty being to correct abuses and punish more serious and notorious offences,[57] and they were also allowed to inflict censures on anyone who dared to impede these acts of jurisdiction.[58] As *legati nati* they could sometimes receive appeals from episcopal courts and give judgment on the merits of the case,[59] but they could not, for example, absolve from excommunications incurred "pro violenta manuum iniectione in clericos."[60] In practice it appears that they had rights simply to a title of honour, precedence, and some liturgical privileges.[61] If provision had to be made for particular situations, or urgent cases,[62] the Pope naturally made use of them, and thus maintained the ancient privileges whilst

[53] C. 8, X, *de officio legati,* I, 30.
[54] Auvray, *Reg. de Gregoire IX,* n. 4523.
[55] Guiraud—Dorez, *Reg. d'Urbain IV,* n. 243.
[56] *Ius Decretalium,* II, n. 690-V.
[57] C. I, 5, *de censibus, exactionibus et procurationibus,* III, 20 in VI°.
[58] C. I, *de poenis,* V, 9, in VI°.
[59] C. I, X, *de officio legati,* I, 30.
[60] C. 9, X, *de officio legati,* I, 30.
[61] Pius VI, *Reponsio ad Metropolitanos,* cap. VIII, n. 127-128.
[62] Ruess, *Die rechtliche Stellung der paepstlichen Legaten bis Bonifaz VIII,* p. 222, note 3.

reserving for himself the right to intervene more directly by means of the *legati a latere*. It also seems that these archbishops performed to some extent the functions of ordinary legates; to them was entrusted the spiritual welfare of a given province together with the necessary powers. At any rate whatever their activities, powers and privileges, the exercise of these was completely suspended in the case of the intervention of the *legatus a latere*. Thus, Alexander III in 1175 in a letter to the bishops of Gaul orders the Metropolitans of Lyons and Bourges, both legates of the Apostolic See, to go without delay to the meeting convoked by the *legatus a latere* and to pay him honour and obedience.[63]

On the other hand the *legati nati* were not infrequently granted their office "*cum potestate legati* a latere." In 1272 Gregory X gave the Patriarch of Jerusalem the power of the *legati a latere* over all the East,[64] but it seems that such a legation did not fundamentally change its nature. In this connection, there is a certain significance attached to a document sent only two years later by the same Gregory X to a Cardinal legate in France, to whom was entrusted the task of inducing the King to join a crusade. If the legation were successful and the king decided to set out, *ipso facto* the Cardinal was deputed to take part in the expedition as *legatus a latere* of the Pope for all the East;

" . . . Tunc demum in eisdem terra et partibus legationis ven. fratri nostro Patriarchae Jerosolomitano commissae, vel ratione patriarchatus forsitan competentis et cuiuslibet alterius legati . . . omnino cessat officium et eadem ipsorum legatio finiatur cum terras vel partes ipsas attigeris." [65]

While this is admittedly an extraordinary case the distinction between the *legatus a latere,* properly so-called, and the *legatus natus* is clearly indicated here. Such legations (of the *legatus natus cum*

[63] Jaffe, n. 11314; Bouquet, *Recueil des Historiens des Gaules,* XV, 850; 950.

[64] Guirand, *Reg. de Gregoire* X, n. 10.

[65] Guirand, *Op. cit.*, n. 532.

potestate legati a latere) had a rather chequered history and development, but they were fairly common.[66]

According to Montini[67] we have in the fourteenth century a system of stable representation attached to particular sees, but its life was short. The system of personal representation was soon retored, mainly owing to the changes in civil law and the consequent rise of the apostolic nunciatures.

§ 2. THE LEGATI MISSI

The term "*legatus missus,*" can be used in a general sense to indicate any pontifical representative sent for the purpose of performing a certain task in a given province, and who is distinct from residential legates, vicars and *legati nati.* In particular, as regards the period we are considering, it denotes a legate of a rank inferior to that of the *legatus a latere.* The Gloss to the *Liber Sextus* in its triple division of *legati nati, legati a latere,* and *legati missi,* says of these last mentioned: "*Alii sunt . . . legati missi, qui mittuntur ad aliquam provinciam ut in ea reformanda reforment, tamen non sunt Cardinales.*"[68] Hostiensis[69] and Durandus[70] *legati constituti;* others, again, call them *legati "simpliciter missi.*"[71]

These denominations are introduced to distinguish this class of legates from the much more important one of *legati a latere.* During the eleventh and twelfth centuries the terms "*legati Apostolicae Sedis*"

[66] Guirand, *op. cit.,* n. 835; 838; 840; Berger, *Reg. d'Innocent IV,* n. 32; 1106; 4391; 6676; Langlois, *Reg. de Nicholas IV,* n. 219; 224; Pius VI; *Responsio ad Metropolitanos,* cap. VIII, n. 119.

[67] *La "Responsio super Nunciaturis" di Papa Pio VI,* p. 199. At this point of the history of papal right of legation, writers discuss the question of civil legations, like those of Urban II and Paschal II to Robert Count of Sicily (Jaffe, n. 6562; Mercati, *Raccolta di Concordati,* pp. 1-10; Cavagnis, *Institutiones Iuris Publici Ecclesiastici,* II, 168-186; Sentis, *Die Monarchia Sicula,* passim), and that of Sylvester II to St. Stephen, King of Hungary (Hinschius, Kirchenrecht, I, 518, nota 3; Jaffe, n. 3909; Auvray, Reg. de Gregoire IX, n. 4482); these are purely historical questions and have no connection with the actual legislation.

[68] Ad c. I, de officio legati, I, 15, in VI°.

[69] *Summa aurea,* I, 30.

[70] *Speculum iuris,* Lib. I, Pars I, de Legato, § 3.

[71] Cfr. Ruess, *Op. cit.,* pp. 112-113.

and *"legati sanctae Romanae Ecclesiae"* were used to indicate holders of different offices of varying importance but all derived from the duty of representing the Pope. It would be rather difficult to determine the various characteristics of these legates, for their powers varied from mission to mission. The title of *legatus Apostolicae Sedis* sometimes brought with it duties of such importance as one would associate with *legati a latere,* while at other times it connoted matters of ordinary ecclesiastical administration. For practical purposes it now seems opportune to consider the subject from a double point of view: the *legati missi* were either sent with the powers of *legati a latere* (and we shall presently see the importance of these), or they were sent to a special province with duties of a general nature but without the powers ordinarily conferred on the more important legates. Under the influence of particular circumstances and of the changes introduced in international law, the *legati missi* gradually assume a special juridical character, i.e., that of apostolic nuncios, as we shall see later on when dealing with Apostolic Nuncios.

§ 3. THE LEGATI A LATERE

The title of *"legatus a latere"* is of very ancient usage. It is found in the fifth canon of the Council of Sardica, and sometimes in the letters of Boniface I (418-423) [72] and Leo the Great (440-461) [73] to indicate in general an emissary of the Holy See; Nicholas I (858-867) prefers to use it in relation to temporary legates [74] but only at this period does it acquire a proper and specific meaning.

The name is derived from the idea that the Pope and the Cardinals constitute, as it were, a single body, after the manner of the Roman senators, of whom the Emperors Arcadius and Honorius say *"ipsi pars corporis nostri sunt."* [75] In the same sense the Gloss comments on the text of the Decretals and stresses the bond of unity

[72] *Epist.* 13—*MPL,* XX, 774.

[73] *Epist.* 32; 34—*MPL,* LIV, 795; 801.

[74] *Epist. Ad Universos Catholicos*—Mansi, XV, 160; Bouquet, *Recueil des Historiens des Gaules,* VII, 386; 389.

[75] *C.* (9, 8) 5; *C.Th.* (9, 14) 3; c. 22, *C.* 6, q. 1.

that binds the Pope and Cardinals, referring to the latter as members that remain united and receive life from the head.[76]

From this we see that the title "legatus a latere" is naturally applicable to the cardinals, to whom it is generally reserved, but—as Hostiensis observes:[77] "intelligi potest de latere Papae missus etiam si non sit Cardinalis, sed et si de familia vel etiam sit extraneus, dum tamen mandatum ab eo recipiat viva voce ut si tetigerit fimbriam vestimenti eius quo ad hoc salvus sit et privilegiatus." Moreover Durandus,[78] while admitting that the *"legatus a latere"* can be an intimate of the Pope or an official of the Roman Curia, adds: " . . . proprie dicuntur missi de latere Domini Papae Cardinales." In relation to the term *"a latere,"* such legates are also called by canonists *"legati laterales,"* or, on account of their lofty duties, *"legati specialissimi."* [79]

The *legatus a latere* now holds the first place among papal representatives: " . . . maius omnibus post Romanum Pontificem in provincia sibi decreta imperium censetur habere . . ." [80] and in virtue of his office he enjoys very great powers expressed in the words of the prophet usually quoted in the letters of appointment: "Ecce constitui te hodie . . . ut evellas, et destruas, et disperdas, et dissipes, et edifices, et plantes." [81] Faculties of the widest extension and without reservation of any sort are conceded to the legate in everything pertaining to the good government of the Church and the religious interests of the province confided to his care. For this reason he is compared to the Roman consuls and procunsuls to whom was committed the gov-

[76] *"mittuntur de latere Domini Papae, quia et ipsi pars corporis eius esse intelliguntur"—Glossa* ad c. 9, X, *de officio legati,* I, 30; *"Ita similiter Papa et Cardinales faciunt unum Corpus, cuius Papa est Caput et Cardinales sunt membra"—Glossa* ad c. 1, *de officio legati,* I, 15, in VI°.

[77] *Summa aurea,* I, 30.

[78] *Speculum Iuris,* Lib. I, Pars I, *de Legato* § 3.

[79] Ruess, *Die rechtliche Stellung der paepstlichen Legaten bis Bonifaz VIII,* p. 112.

[80] C. 36, *de electione et electi potestate,* I, 6, in VI°.

[81] Jerem. I, 10; cfr. Ruess, *Op. cit.,* pp. 67-69.

ernment of the provinces outside Italy;[82] and canonists [83] sometimes introduce another distinction applying the title of *legati a latere ordinarii* to those who receive such a mission and that of *legati a latere extraordinarii* to those sent to deal with questions of urgent necessity and of interest to the universal Church.

Since the legate takes the place of the person who appoints him, his powers, generally speaking, are measured by the competency of the delegating authority. However, there are special exceptions, and for these a special delegation is required.[84] They are enumerated in the following verses of the Glossa:[85]

"Restituit papa solus, deponit et ipse,
Articulos solvit synodumque facit generalem.
Transfert et mutat, appellat nullus ab ipso,
Dividit ac unit: eximit atque probat."

The *legatus a latere* therefore does not enjoy *ex officio* such powers as that of translating bishops from one see to another, uniting or dividing dioceses, ordering a general council, granting exemptions, "quae omnia in signum privilegii sunt tantum Summo Pontifici reservata." [86]

It seems that such restrictions are regularly understood even when the Popes grant the "*officium plenae legationis.*" Innocent III (1198-1216) while entrusting the "officium plenae legationis" immediately adds:

"Ut autem tibi nihil desit ex illis quae ad plenitudinem legationis pertinent exsequenda, plenariam tibi auctoritate praesentium concedimus facultatem, ut cum necesse fuerit, vice nostra illa etiam exsequaris quae nostro sunt speciali privilegio reservata . . . ";[87] and Urban IV

[82] C. 2, *de officio legati*, I, 15, in VI°; cf. *C.* (I, 35); *D.* (I, 16); (1, 18).

[83] Ferraris, *Prompta Bibliotheca*, "Legatus" n. 4-6; Plati, *De Cardinalis dignitate et officio*, p. 360.

[84] Bernardus Papiensis, *Summa Decretalium*, I, 22.

[85] Ad c. I, X, *de translatione episcopi*, I, 7; ad c. 4, X, *de officio legati*, I, 30.

[86] *C.* 4, X, *de officio legati*, I, 30; cfr. Wernz, *Ius Decretalium*, II, 690.

[87] *Epist.* 235—*MPL*, CCXIV, 794.

(1261-1264) also makes express mention with regard to the matters reserved to the Holy See:

"Ut eadem negotia eo utilius et efficacius prosequaris, quo maiori per nos fueris auctoritate munitus, si aliqua tibi circa ipsorum negotiorum prosecutionem occurrant, quae directionem seu promotionem eorumdem respiciant et *ad quae ipsius legationis officium se forsitan non extendat,* in his fraternitati tuae . . . *committimus auctoritate* praesentium vices nostras." [88]

These two documents enumerate the reserved matters. But perhaps the best illustration of the principle that the *ius plenae legationis* does not extend to them is found in particular examples. At first sight it may seem contradictory to have limitations imposed on the *officium plenae legationis.* However, the examples are clear: a special mandate is required for such cases. And so we find Innocent III thus reproving one of his legates who had deposed a bishop: " . . . ad id sine nostro speciali mandato procedere non debueris, cum hoc sit unum ex illis quod sibi sedes apostolica specialiter reservavit." [89] Such a faculty to remove a bishop is conferred only in exceptional circumstances, when there is an abuse of power,[90] but examples are found frequently enough during the pontificate of Innocent IV. Thus, to the legate for Germany "concedit potestatem amovendi perpetuo tam Archiepiscopos et Tpiscopos quam alios Ecclesiarum prelatos qui fuerint inobedientes Ecclesiae," and similar power is granted to the legates for the March of Ancona, for Sardinia and for Sicily.[91]

In relation to the establishment of new dioceses we meet with some examples of the annexation of new territories to dioceses already existing, or the constitution of dioceses in territories newly conquered for Catholicism.[92]

Similarly, in exceptional circumstances when a legate saw that a bishopric could not continue to exist on account of insufficiency of means and the poverty of the faithful, he had power to divide or unite dioceses, change bishops from one see to another and consecrate

[88] Guiraud-Dorez, *Reg. d'Urb.* IV, n. 588.

[89] *Epist.* 138—*MPL,* CCXVI, 650.

[90] Paschal II to the Archbishop of Toledo—Mansi, XX, 117.

[91] Berger, *Reg. d'Innoc. IV,* n. 2974; 3007; 4713; 4736; 8318.

[92] Berger, *Op. cit.,* n. 115; 6592.

new bishops as necessity arose.[93] But only in very rare cases were the legates given power to convoke a general council at their own discretion.[94]

Of special interest are the legations granted for the Crusades. The initiative for one of these holy undertakings always came from the Pope, and he took care of its spiritual welfare through his *legatus a latere* to whom were granted the most ample powers. At the time of the first crusade Urban II (1088-1099) approved the advice of the Archbishop of Lyons, and, encouraging him to take part in the expedition, authorised him to take his place in Asia. What particular powers were granted, however, do not appear.[95] So also Paschal II (1100),[96] Eugene III (1147),[97] and Celestine III (1195)[98] sent legates with the expeditionary armies to attend to the spiritual needs of the soldiers, to maintain concord among the leaders of the crusades, to provide for the needs of churches regained for the faith, to remedy irregularities in canonical discipline and to restore to its full purity the practice of the Christian life. Even more detailed and more extensive powers can be perceived in the legation for the sixth crusade of 1248. Pope Innocent IV sent the Cardinal Bishop of Tusculum to take part in the expedition as "magni consilii angelus" of the King of France with the position of legate for the army and crusaders, for the provinces and lands of the Christians, for the kingdoms or nations of the East and for all the islands beyond Sicily.[99] In all these territories the legate could absolve from the irregularities in-

[93] Auvray, *Reg. de Greg.* IX, n. 1814; 2945.

[94] "Facultatem concedit convocandi etiam concilium generale"—Guirand-Dorez, *Reg. d'Urb. IV*, n. 820.

[95] Hugues de Flavigny, *Chronicon—MGH, Scriptores* VIII, 487.

[96] " . . . ex apostolicae sedis *gremio* . . . episcopum destinamus; ut qui per B. Petri Vicarium . . . predecessorem nostrum Urbanum tanti peregrinationem itineris assumpsistis, B. Petri solatiis semper abundetis... cui (episcopo) nimirum in paeceptis dedimus ut ecclesiae quam per vos Dominis liberavit, sed liberaturus est, ordinationi vigilantes immineat, quae si minus canonicis regulis apta repererit, corrigat et eidem cum vestro auxilio plantando plantet . . ."—Mansi, XX, 980.

[97] *Epist.* 204—*MPL*, CLXXX, 1251.

[99] Jace, n. 17226.

[99] Berger, *Reg. d'Innoc. IV*, n. 4662.

curred by simony or by the administration and reception of sacred orders from excommunicated prelates, he could punish with censures all those who dared to obstruct his mission, grant dispensations "super defectu natalium" for the reception of sacred orders or for plurality of benefices, grant prebends and ecclesiastical dignities, raise to the episcopacy, "duabus vicibus," clerics in minor orders, erect cathedral churches and dispense from matrimonial impediments.[100]

Sometimes the faculties and graces conceded for the Holy Land were extended in a certain measure to other places where the enemies of Christianity were being fought: thus, for example, for the war with the Saracens in Spain (1121-24) under Pope Callixtus II (1119-1124).[101]

In the matter of dispensation *legati a latere* had ample faculties. In the first place they could dispense from various impediments for the reception and exercise of sacred orders. Thus, within the limits of their respective territories they could dispense from the irregularity arising from *defectus natalium* clerics who were otherwise of good repute, so that these could "in susceptis ministrare ordinibus et promoveri ad superiores," except in the case of children of adultery, incest or sacrilege. The faculties for such dispensations are sometimes granted in a generic form as almost forming a part of the very office of legate, and are sometimes granted in specific cases. Besides, the documents often make no distinction with regard to the quality of the orders to which the persons in question can be promoted;[102] it is expressly forbidden however, that they be elevated to the episcopal dignity and this prohibition seems to have been consistently urged.[103] The following words of Honorius IV have in fact all the quality of a general rule: " . . . huiusmodi non obstante defectu (natalium)

100 Berger, *op. cit.*, nn. 4668-4679.

101 *Epist.* 38—Mansi, XXI, 217; cf. Ruess, *Die rechtliche Stellung der paepstlichen Legaten bis Bonifaz VIII*, pp. 80-84.

102 Auvray, *Reg. de Greg. IX*, n. 4889; Berger, *Reg d'Innoc. IV*, 2929; 2949; Guiraud-Dorez, *Reg. d'Urb. IV*, n. 642; 825; Auvray, *Reg. de Greg. X*, n. 531; 568; Digard-Faucon-Thomas, *Reg. de Bonif. VIII*, n. 711; 749; 3379.

103 Berger, *Reg. d'Innoc. IV*, n. 2984; 4733; 8323; Guiraud-Dorez, *Reg. d'Urb. IV*, n. 615.

in susceptis ministrare ordinibus, ***promoveri ad omnes ordines, pontificali dignitate excepta, obtinere valeant.*"** [104]

We also meet, though less frequently, the faculty of dispensing from "*defectus ordinum*" and "*defectus aetatis.*" [105]

The legates could also dispense from or commute vows, but this, naturally, only in virtue of a special delegation, since the Holy See alone can declare when the divine law no longer binds in this matter.[106] The power of the legates had reference to vows in general, but certain restrictions were imposed. Thus the vow of becoming a crusader could only be commuted at a time when urgent reasons required a campaign for the defence of Christianity on the continent and then the commutation could be given only to those who were willing to take part in such an undertaking.[108] Ordinarily the commutation o fthe Crusader's vow was reserved to the Pope and a dispensation was very difficult to obtain.[109] This strict reservation was extended by Nicholas IV (1288-1292) and Boniface VIII (1294-1303) to the two vows of entering the religious life and of chastity.[110]

Sometimes the legates were also deputed to grant favours of protection for monasteries [111] or confirm the liberty and privileges of churches.[112]

Particular mention of all these matters, which in themselves would pertain to the Holy See, is made in the documents by which the office of a legation is assigned. This shows that even the "*officium*

104 Prou, *Reg. d'Honor. IV,* n. 780. It seems that the faculty granted by Urban, by means of which the irregular persons so dispensed could also be raised to the episcopal dignity, is an unique exception; besides this dispensation covered only three cases and these it seems, in very special circumstances—Guiraud-Dorez, ***Reg. d'Urb. IV,*** n. 614.

105 Berger, *Reg. d'Innoc. IV,* n. 2976; 8344.

106 G. 9, X, *de voto,* III, 34.

107 Guiraud-Dorez, *Reg. d'Urbain IV,* n. 596.

108 Avray, *Reg. de Greg. IX,* n. 2959; Guiraud-Dorez, *Op. cit.,* n. 813.

109 Berger, *Op. cit.,* n. 4065.

110 " . . . facultas dispensandi super votis et convertendi ea in alia pietatis opera, ***transmarino, religionis et continentiae votis exceptis***"—Langlois, *Reg. de Nicholas IV,* n. 4276; 4354; Digard-Faucon-Thomas, *Reg. de Boniface VIII,* n. 725.

111 Alexander III (a. 1176) *Epist.* 12—Mansi, XXI, 968.

112 Auvray, *Reg. de Greg. IX,* n. 771; 772; 4371.

plenae legationis" required at least further specifications in the cases recognized as reserved to the Holy See. To quote yet another example, Innocent IV (1243-1254) places a clear limitation in the force of the expression "*Plenae legationis officium*" *with regard to* ecclesiastical benefices, and while cardinals can "*iure legationis*" reserve and confer such benefices, all other legates are excluded: "*quantumcumque plenae legationis officium obtineant.*"[113]

Other faculties of a more general nature show even more clearly the great importance of the legates. They can freely issue disciplinary regulations and statutes for the province entrusted to their spiritual care. Such regulations are real laws and remain in force even when the legates have completed their mission.[114] By reason of the pastoral charge confided to them by the Holy See they have full legislative powers as regards clergy and people.[115]

The *legati a latere* furthermore enjoy the faculties of absolving from the excommunications "pro violenta manuum in clericos iniectione" everywhere and in the case of anyone who presents himself, while the *legati missi* can only absolve their own subjects and within the limits of their province, and the *legati nati* have no power in this matter.[116]

113 C. I, *de officio legati,* I, 15, in VI°.

114 C. 10, X, *de officio legati,* I, 30.

115 Cfr. Mansi, XXIII, 763; *Constitutiones*—Mansi, XXIV, 247.

116 C. 9, X, *de officio legati,* I, 30; c. 13, 20, X, *de sententia excommunicationis,* V, 39.

A practical example of the action of the legates is afforded by a document of Innocent III with reference to the mission performed by his legates for the reconciliation of the Duke of Suabia with the Church.

"*Processus legationum apostolicae sedis.* Primo receperunt publice iuramentum a Philippo duce Sueiae quod pareret universis mandatis Domini Papae super omnibus super quibus erat excommunicatus, et sic eum secundum formam Ecclesiae solemniter absolverunt. Secundo iniunxerunt eidem ut dimitteret Brunonem Coloniensem Archiepiscopum, quem in captione tenebat; quem libere absolutum assignavit eisdem ad sedem apostolicam perducendum. Tertio indulerunt illum ad hoc quod ipse recepit regalia, licet invitus, a Luipuldo Maguntino intruso, et idem intrusus spiritualia resignavit in manibus legatorum. Quarto apud ipsum obtinuerunt cum difficultate non parva ut permitteret Siffridum Maguntinum Archiepiscopum per procuratorem suum in spiritualibus ministrare. Quinto fecerunt

The whole collection of faculties granted to the *legati a latere*, and, in particular, the delegation in matters reserved to the Pope, leave no doubt as to the ever increasing development of the right of papal legation during the period of the Decretals.

§ 4. PERSONAL PRIVILEGES OF "LEGATI"

Already in the Decretum of Gratian there is a solemn declaration of the law of inviolability of legates. Their work is primarily directed towards the common welfare; those who impede it therefore, do injury not only to themselves but to the community at large. They disturb the peace of the Church and merit expulsion by the punishment of excommunication.[117] This punishment was the chief protection of Papal legates in those turbulent times.

The Popes recommend in the first instance that their legate be received with the honours and the obedience due to their own person on account of the primacy conferred by Our Lord. They remind faithful that they should see in the work of the legates a sign of the sollicitude of the Popes for the welfare of the universal Church. But since men are not always disposed to appreciate this work at its true value, the Sovereign Pontiffs find themselves constrained to protect their representatives by endowing them with the faculty of making use of ecclesiastical censures. Generally the use of this power is left to the judgment of the legates themselves; and the legates can use it against those who dare to use violence or inflict injuries on them or on the other members of the legation.[118] The Popes not only ratify their decisions but solemnly proclaim the sentences already inflicted by the legates: thus acted Pope Anastasius IV in 1153 in regard to some sentences of deposition, interdict and excommunication.[119]

ipsum dimittere magnum exercitum quem congregaverat adversus regem Ottonem. Sexto bis eos ad colloquium perduxerunt tractantes cum ipsis de pace, quam cum consummare non possent, Septimo statuerunt inter eos treguas unius anni; et sic tractatum pacis redigentes in scriptis, ad sedem apostolicam redierunt cum nuntiis utriusque"—*MPL,* CCXVI, 1142.

[117] C. 2, D. XCIV.

[118] Guiraud-Dorez, *Reg. d'Urb. IV,* n. 601; Prou, *Reg. d'Honor, IV,* n. 789; Langlois, *Reg. de Nic. IV,* n. 2129; Digard-Faucon-Thomas, *Reg. de Bonif. VIII,* n. 704; 756; 3375; 3895.

[119] *Epist.* 16—*MPL,* CLXXXVIII, 1008.

Furthermore they propose to enforce everywhere the sentences passed by the legates against the factious and rebellious.[120]

Another prerogative of legates is the right to the *procurationes,* that is, lodging, food and travelling expenses due to them on account of their office. This right of legates was not an innovation but rather a custom common to the period and acknowledged also by lay princes.[121] Some writers of the middle of the twelfth century condemn abuses in this matter;[122] they quote examples but they do not describe these as representing the general practice; besides, they do not deny the right in question. If abuses existed the matters were examined by the Holy See and suitable remedies applied.[123] At all events the right is not prejudiced for this reason and Innocent III declares: " . . . omnes ecclesiae legatis et nuntiis sedis apostolicae procurationes impendere tenentur";[124] and since such *procurationes* are due to the Holy See as a help for the progress of the universal Church, no legal prescription can arise against them.[125] However, generally speaking, it is not necessary to insist on this matter here: the generosity of hierarchy and princes supplied the legates with abundant gifts.[126]

The legate always proceeded with the solemnity suited to his lofty office and therefore used papal insignia. This was especially the case when, for example, a *legatus a latere* went overseas.[127]

The most distinctive privilege of the *legatus a latere* was the absolute nature of his office. The legates of lower grade, "propter reverentiam Apostolicae Sedis," had to suspend their functions and

[120] Berger, *Reg. d'Innoc. IV,* 4663; Digard-Faucon-Thomas, *Reg. de Bonif. VIII,* n. 3887. "L'oeuvre de ceux-ci (les legats romains) avait consisté principalement a briser les Archevêques hostiles à la reforme"—observes A. Luchaire, Innocent III, vol. VI: *Le Concile du Latran,* p. 150.

[121] Pius VI, *"Responsio ad Metropolitanos,"* cap. VIII, nn. 101-106.

[122] St. Bernard, *epist.* 290—*MPL,* CLXXXII, 496; John of Salisbury, *Polycraticus,* V, 16;—*MPL,* CXCIX, 580; Ive de Chartres, *epist.* 109—*MPL,* CLXII, 127.

[123] Pius VI, *"Responsio ad Metropolitanos,"* cap. VIII, n. 103.

[124] C. 17, X, *de censibus,* III, 39.

[125] C. II, X, *de praescriptionibus,* II, 26; Ruess, *Op. cit.,* p. 188.

[126] Cfr. Mansi, XXIII, 442.

[127] C. 23, X, *de privilegiis,* V, 33; Ruess, *Op. cit.,* p. 205.

leave perfect freedom of action to him who was the principal representative.[128]

In conclusion it can be said that the juridical position of the papal legate had by this time reached its complete development. The institution had become one of the principal instruments of the Roman Curia in the government of the Church and one of the most powerful weapons in putting into effect the policy of unification that the Holy See was pursuing in the Christian world.[129]

Article VII: The Apostolic Collectors

Simultaneously with the rise of permanent papal representative bodies we find an institution of a financial character, namely, the Collectorate. The Collectorate was an organization which supervised the gathering of the tribute due to the Holy See, the collecting of Peter's Pence, and the exaction of taxes imposed on the goods of the clergy. Its origin is somewhat difficult to trace and goes back to the administration of the first gifts of property given to the Church. The earliest ecclesiastical legislation in administrative matters can probably be attributed to Pope Gelasius (492-496) who had caused to be compiled the *Polyptyci* or list of all the ecclesiastical patrimonies and their revenues.[1] He also left instructions and regulations for administrators.[2]

During the sixth century the lands belonging to the Church were grouped into districts called the patrimonies of St. Peter. This rule was more clearly determined under Gregory the Great who gave unremitting care to the administration of ecclesiastical property, which

[128] C. 8, X, *de officio legati,* I, 30; "Licet olium dilecto filio Huguitioni, dicto *Marchioni,* cappellano nostro in Romaniola et Massa Trabaria legationis officium duxerimus committendum, volentes tamen ut in premissis et aliis provinciis, quas tuae legationi commisimus, *nullus sit alius apostolicae sedis, tua legatione durante, legatus* commissum eidem cappellano officium huiusmodi per quascumque litteras sub quacumque forma verborum auctoritate praesentium revocamus"—Guiraud-Dorez, *Reg. d'Urb. IV,* n. 637.

[129] Cfr. A. Fliche, *La Chrétienté médiévale,* pp. 362-363.

[1] Johanni Diaconi, *Vita Gregorii,* II, 24—*MPL,* LXXV, 93; St. Gregorius Magnus, *Epistolae,* IX, 40—*MPL,* LXXVII, 973.

[2] Jaffe, n. 633.

he called "the property of the poor," and which enabled him to aid the innumerable victims of the barbaric invasions and the Christian missionaries.[3]

From the sixth century onwards we find mention of officials in charge of the papal finances. These are the *Arcarius* (from arca, treasury), the *Saccellarius* (from *saccellum,* a safe, or strong chest) and the *Vestararius* (from vestiarium, wardrobe), names borrowed from those of similar officials of the exchequer and court services of the emperor in the East.[4] In the papal administration, the office which becomes the most important is that of the *Vestararius.*

The tribute due to the Holy See was twofold: the major (*census grossus*) and the minor (*census minor*).

a) The major tribute is the recognition of the proprietary rights of the Holy See over lands let on a long lease or in some other form of possession. Honorius I (625-638) imposes this tribute on papal possessions near the Baths of Diocletian leased to the subdeacon Gratiosus, and on other possessions granted to the notary Servus Dei.[5] This tribute is imposed very frequently from the eighth to the eleventh century, whenever papal lands are granted to monasteries,[6] or churches[7] or even to private individuals.[8]

b) The minor tribute was a token of spiritual subjection and submission to the Apostle St. Peter, and chiefly consisted in the offerings of monasteries placed under the protection of the Holy See. The privilege of protection (or *privilegium libertatis*) had originally been granted by the French kings to monasteries and hospitals, at first against barbaric invasions, and then as an exemption from interference on the part of feudal lords and bishops.[9] But favours of

[3] St. Gregorius Magnus, *Epistolae,* I, 1-3; 20; II, 32; V, 31; VI, 7; XI, 10; 14—*MPL,* LXXVII, 442-446; 565; 756; 799; 1125; 1130.

[4] Lunt, *Papal revenues in the Middle Ages,* I, 3.

[5] Jaffe, n. 2011, 2013.

[6] Jaffe, n. 2435; 2437; 2544; 2653; 3569; 3605; 3796; 3886; 3895; 3999; 4000.

[7] Diploma of Otho I—*MGH, Diplomata,* I, 251; Jaffe, n. 3843; 4129.

[8] Muratori, *Antiquitates,* I, 941; Jaffe, n. 4486.

[9] *Diplomata*—Bouquet, *Recueil des Historiens des Gaules,* V, 751; 762; VI, 549; VIII, 357; Fabre, *Etude sur le Liber Censuum de l'Eglise romaine,* pp. 32-36.

this kind began to lose their value while the Carolingian empire was falling into dissolution and while at the same time, during the reigns of Nicholas I and John VIII, the Roman See was reassuming its prestige over all the west. As a sign of complete subjection and in order to enjoy spiritual and temporal protection at a period when the power of the Holy See was regarded as the surest pledge of security, the founders of religious orders began to offer their institutions to St. Peter.[10] But we notice a new procedure. In conformity with ancient Roman customs a visible sign of the proprietorship now vested in the Apostle is set up; a contract of leasehold is entered into, and there is fixed an annual rent, i.e., the payment of an annual sum by way of tribute.[11] By transferring their property to the Holy See these monasteries acquired *ipso facto* the privilege of exemption, or, what was then called the *"libertas Romana."* [12]

The collection of the major tribute was supervised by certain public officials called *actionarii.* Adrian I in confirming the possession of lands by the monastery of Sant'Apollinare in Classe in the year 782 writes to the abbot: "pensio . . . actionariis publicis . . . persolvatur";[13] and in the *Liber Diurnus* the usual formula employed is: "actionariis sanctae nostrae ecclesiae apto tempore persolvatur (pensio)." [14]

The minor tribute was originally offered spontaneously on the tomb of the apostle and there collected.[15] As time passed on this method of dealing with the offering became very uncertain and during the eleventh century a reorganization of the whole system was commenced. From the year 1017 the office entrusted with the administration of the finances was indicated by the term: *Camera (apos-*

[10] Cfr. Daux, *"La protection apostolique au moyen age," RGH,* LXXII (1902) 5-60.

[11] Fabre, *Op. cit.,* p. 38.

[12] Cfr. *Vitae Adalheidae,* c. 10—*MGH, Scriptores,* IV, 641; *Epist.* 609—*MGH, Epistolae saec.* XIII, I, 498; Jaffe, n. 3857; 4221; 4347; 5068; Fabre, *Op. cit.,* pp. 76-77.

[13] Jaffe, n. 2437.

[14] Rormula XCV, ed. Sickel, p. 125.

[15] Fabre, *Op. cit.,* p. 150. For the formalities of the collection and the security of the offering in the same convents, cfr. Otliebi, *De fundatione monasterii Zwivildensis,* c. 12—*MGH, Scriptores,* X, 79.

tolica);[16] from 1033 no further mention is made of the *Vestararius*;[17] the term *Camerarius*, that is chief of the *Camera Apostolica*, does not appear before the year 1099.[18] It is not clear whether the functions of administrator were in the meantime entrusted to the *Archdiaconus;* and so it remains uncertain whether Hildebrand had, as archdeacon, so dealt with financial matters as to become their reorganiser.[19] At any rate the re-organization of the finances forms part of the general plan of the reforming Popes of the eleventh century, and so the principal part is attributed to Hildebrand.[20]

At this time the Popes insist that the tributaries present themselves at the Lateran Palace and deliver the tribute and the offering "praesentialiter ut certius approbetur."[21] However, the cases of insolvency are frequent and it is found necessary to send special delegates. The Papal legates co-operate by reminding the faithful of their obligation and by transmitting the offerings to the Holy See, but the obligation of exacting the tribute and of collecting the Peter's Pence rests primarily with the bishops of the different ecclesiastical provinces.[22]

At the end of the twelfth century Cencius Camerarius (later Pope Honorius III—1216-1227) placed the fiscal organization of the Holy See on a stable basis. In 1192 he compiled the *Liber Censuum*, divided into two sections, the first containing a list of people bound to pay a fixed tribute to the Roman Church, the second giving the documents on which the claims are based. With such an inventory at hand it must have been easier for the Popes "ab illis qui non persolverunt sine dubitationis scrupulo per suum legatum aut nuntium census ipsos repetere."[23]

16 *Chronicon Farfense*—Muratori, *Scriptores*, II, part II, 521; Jaffe, n. 4348; Felici, *La Reverenda Camera Apostolica*, pp. 1-6.

17 Lunt, *Papal revenues in the Middle Ages*, I, 6.

18 Fabre, *Op. cit.*, p. 155, n. 1.

19 Lunt, *Op. cit.*, II, 7-9; Fliche, *La reforme gregorienne*, I, 379, n. 4.

20 Fabre, *Op. cit.*, pp. 151-152.

21 Alexander II, *Epist. ad Suenonem* (a. 1062-1063)—Mansi, XIX, 943.

22 Hugues de Flavigny, *Chronicon—MGH, Scriptores*, VIII, 412; Muratori, *Antiquitates*, V, 838; Bouquet, *Recueil des Historiens des Gaules*, XIV, 697; Fabre, *Op. cit.*, p. 160.

23 *Liber Censuum*, ed. P. Fabre, pp. 4-5; Cfr. Felici, *Op. cit.*, pp. 6-9.

The organization of the finances of the Holy See underwent a definite development at the period of the crusades. The necessity then arose of a careful administration of the numerous offerings which were pouring in from the whole christian world. As to the tribute, not only was it more vigorously exacted but ecclesiastical goods were expressly taxed in favour of the Holy Land. The *Vigesima Terrae Sanctae* imposed on the revenue of the clergy by Innocent III for the crusade announced in the fourth Lateran Council (1215) is worthy of note. Special agents were sent throughout Europe to collect the taxes.[24] After the death of Innocent III in 1216 the same taxation was enforced by Honorius III, [25] and it appears that the papal tax collectors went everywhere except to the Scandinavian countries where the collection of the offering was entrusted to the local hierarchy, and particularly to the Bishop of Upsala and Westeraes.[26]

The Popes of the thirteenth century demanded the tribute frequently and sent their agents *"pro colligendis censibus et denario B. Petri"* successively into the different countries of Europe.[27] These collections were made in varying amounts and by different methods "in subsidium Terrae Sanctae" or "pro oneribus Ecclesiae Romanae." But sometimes the money never even reached the *Camera Apostolica*. The collection of the offerings of the faithful was frequently left to the kings who were to lead the Crusade. Such was the case with the *"Decima sexennalis"* asked by Clement V (1305-1314) at the Council of Vienne (1312).[28] Philip the Fair and Louis X, putting aside the interests of the Holy Land, spent all the revenue in the

[24] *Constitutio de expeditione pro recuperanda Terra Sancta*—Mansi, XXII, 1058-1067.

[25] Potthast, n. 5906.

[26] Potthast, nn. 6535; 6536; Fabre, *Etude sur le Liber Censuum de l'Eglise romaine*, pp. 163-164.

[27] Potthast, nn. 9069; 18182; 186884; 196447; 20797; 21862; 22198; 22256; - 22258.

[28] Coulon, *Lettres secretes et curiales du Pape Jean XXII*, n. 23; Mollat, *Jean XXII, Lettres communes*, n. 6; Bourgain. *"Contribution du clerge a l'impot sous la monarchie francaise,"* *RQH*, XLVIII (1890) 70.

wars of Flanders, and Benedict XII to put an end to the abuse had to suspend the collection.[29]

The following are some of the principal documents which refer to the vast and complicated pontifical fiscal system of this period: 1) the bull *"Declarationes"* of Boniface VIII of October 1, 1301, with regard to the imposition of tithes and the exemptions from all taxation in favour of goods belonging to leper hospitals, to the houses of God and of the poor, to the mendicant orders and those beneficiaries whose annual income does not exceed seven and a half florins;[30] 2) the bull *"Si Sacrosancta"* of Clement V, of February 1, 1306, regarding the collecting of the *annates*;[31] 3) the bull *"Si gratanter advertitis"* of John XXII, of December 8, 1316, also with regard to annates pertaining to the Holy See;[32] 4) the bull *"Execrabilis"* of John XII, of November 21, 1317, forbidding the multiplication of benefices and reserving incompatible benefices to the Holy See,[33] and 5) the bull *"Vas Electionis"* of Benedict XII, of December, 1336, by which are regulated in a particular manner the *procurationes* due on the occasion of the pastoral visitation.[34]

To put this vast programme into effect, and to place the allocation of the various imposts on a secure basis, it was necessary to know the approximate value of the goods of the clergy. To this end the Camera Apostolica sent special agents throughout the Catholic world with the task of compiling a list of ecclesiastical benefices, of indicating as accurately as possible their importance and efficiency,

29 Vidal, *Bénoit XII. Lettres communes,* nn. 3954; 3998; 3999; 4985; 5139; 5140. Samaran et Mollat, *La fiscalité pontificale en France au XIV siècle,* pp. 15(16.

30 C. un., *de decimis,* III, 7 in Extravag. comm; Lunt, *Papal revenues in the Middle Ages,* II, 162.

31 Lunt, *"The first levy of papal annates" AHR,* XVIII, (1912), 62-64; *Papal revenues in the Middle Ages,* II, 318.

32 Mollat, *Jean XXII, Lettres communes,* nn. 4934-5071; Coulon *Op. cit.,* nn. 82-99; Lunt, *Op. cit.,* II, 324.

33 C. un., *de praebendis et dignitatibus,* III in Extravag. Johannis XXII; Lunt, *Op. cit.,* II, 225.

34 C. un., *de censibus, exactionibus et procurationibus,* III, 10 in Extravag. comm.

and of fixing an equitable tax for each.[35] The institution therefore of the collectors—continue Samaran and Mollat[36] — certainly goes back to the beginning of the thirteenth century, but since the imposts, which it was their duty to collect, were fixed at infrequent intervals, it was not yet necessary that these officials should be permanent. Only in the fourteenth century, as a result of the conditions in which the Papacy found itself at Avignon, was a regular system of taxation devised. To put this system into operation there were appointed permanent collectors, to each of whom a definite territory, or financial district, was assigned. The institution took on a definite form especially in France with Clement VI (1342-1352). The functionaries in charge of the imposts were everywhere called *Collectores Apostolici* and the financial districts were known as *Collectoriae.* The *Collectoriae* varied a great deal in number and extent. A list of the year 1352 during the reign of Innocent VI (1352-1362) gives for France a number of fourteen *Collectoriae* with special papal envoys, while in another nine dioceses the office of collector is entrusted to the local bishop. In 1359-1360 the papal *Collectoriae* are divided as follows: 17 in France, 4 in Italy, 2 in Spain, 1 in Portugal, and 1 in the island of Cyprus.[37]

Ordinarily a *Collectoria* comprised several dioceses. At its head was a collector and in each diocese there was a sub-collector. Each collector had a fixed residence and a determined field of action. They were responsible for the exacting not only the partial imposts for extraordinary occasions but of the tithes, the fruits of reserved benefices and offices, the tribute, the annates, the *jus spolii,* in a word, the working of the whole complicated fiscal system depended in them.[38]

The appointment of the collector was made by the Camerarius. The newly appointed was bound to present himself at the central office in Avignon to take an oath of loyalty and receive suitable instructions. He had to proceed to his collectorate as speedily as possible. His duty mainly consisted in the supervision and trans-

[35] Samaran et Mollat, *La Fiscalite Pontificale en France au XIV siecle,* p. 12.

[36] *Op. cit.,* p. 76; cfr. Lunt, *Op. cit.,* I, 38-41.

[37] Samaran et Mollat, *Op. cit.,* pp. 71; 220.

[38] Cfr. Lunt, *Papal revenues in the Middle Ages,* pp. 71-111.

mission of the money to the Camera. The collection itself was nearly always made *by the sub-collectors* in the different diocese.[39]

The collectors had full powers in matters of finance, but they were bound to give an account of their administration to the Camera Apostolica. Urban IV (1261-1264) had already prescribed for the fiscal agents a general rendering of accounts.[40] With the development of the collectorate in the fourteenth century the obligation of presenting accounts and receipts became a fixed rule and the collectors had to be prepared for any such request.[41] However the effective control of the organization was always a rather difficult problem; the matter itself was fraught with danger, and, apart from the changed conditions of the times it was probably due to some abuse that the collectorates were finally suppressed.[42] For the rest, the integrity of the institution was carefully protected. Failure to answer the invitation to present the accounts meant to incur excommunication, and if the collector became contumacious a warrant was issued for his arrest and when taken prisoner he was brought under escort to Avignon for trial.[43]

The collectors themselves had means of coercing the stubborn to pay their debts. In a commission of John XXII, we read: "Liceat eis suspendere, excommunicare, absolvere et de causis cognoscere." [44] Not only could they inflict ecclesiastical penalties, but when need arose they could call for the assistance of the secular authority.[45]

The money gathered by the collectors was transmitted to the Camera Apostolica by the merchants and money-changers who were then to be found all over Europe. It seems that their services were first utilised for this purpose only at the beginning of the thirteenth century; they were given the name of *"Mercatores Camerae."* [46]

39 Samaran et Mollat, *Op. cit.*, pp. 77-80.

40 Guiraud-Dorez, *Reg. Camerae d'Urb, IV*, nn. 6-14.

41 Vidal, *Benoit XII. Lettres communes*, nn. 2462-2464.

42 Richard, "Origines des Nonciatures permanentes," *RHE*, VII (1906) 325, n. 1.

43 Samaran et Mollat, *Op. cit.*, p. 127.

44 Coulon, *Lettres secretes et curiales du Pape Jean XXII*, n. 794.

45 Samaran et Mollat. *Op. cit.*, p. 225.

46 Cfr. Lunt, *Papal revenues in the Middle Ages*, I, 51-56.

The ordinary functions of the collectors were therefore restricted to financial matters, but by force of circumstances matters of different kinds were soon entrusted to them. We have seen how at the time of St. Gregory the Great the rector of the ecclesiastical patrimony of Sicily had among his other duties that of presenting candidates for the episcopacy. We know that at their most flourishing period the collectors travelled through the different countries of Europe to preach the crusade, the peace and truce of God, the indulgence and the pardons.[47]

From a bull of Innocent IV, of May 1, 1354, it appears that in exceptional circumstances the collectors could be given the care of souls. This happened whenever the beneficiary, rather than collect the money necessary to pay his taxes, resigned his benefice, and the collector practically became the real administrator with all the obligations of beneficiaries with care of souls.[48]

The Collectors had the advantage of local residence and local experience. Their duties placed them in daily contact with all classes of people and in situations enabling them to render services of signal importance to the Church. This was particularly manifest at the time of the Council of Basle and during that part of the fourteenth and fifteenth centuries in which the growth of excessive nationalism and the conciliar theory had become a menace to the very framework of the hierarchical institution. The Apostolic Vicars and *Legati nati* were inclined to favour over-much the governments of their own countries (it is sufficient to refer to the Pragmatic Sanction of Bourges (1438) which marks the beginning of Gallicanism). But the Collectors, even when natives of the territories to which they were assigned, were led by reason of the nature of their mission and their dependence on Rome to promote the interests of the Holy See and thus to open the way for relations of a more comprehensive nature. They prepared, and in most cases, laid the foundations of the Apostolic Nunciatures.[49]

47 Cfr. Lunt, *Op. cit.*, pp. 115.

48 Samaran et Mollat, *La Fiscalite Pontificale en France au XIV siecle*, p. 29, n. 1.

49 Biaudet, *Les Nonciatures Apostoliques permanentes jusqu'en* 1648, pp. 8-9; Richard, "Origines des Nonciatures permanentes" *RHE*, VII (1906), 54-56.

Article VIII: The Apostolic Nuncios

The juridical, diplomatic and ecclesiastical characteristics of the permanent papal representative bodies are connected with the evolution of similar civil representatives already introduced by states for the new international relations arising out of the great discoveries on the seas, the fall of Constantinople (1453) and especially of the political events that prepared the formation of the great European states in the fifteenth century.

The existing system of sending an ambassador for each separate affair showed itself inadequate for new needs calling for greater promptness and liberty of action. Permanent diplomatic representatives, however, came into existence only little by little, by force of the most varied circumstances connected with questions of collective defence, commercial relations and national prestige. The lead was given by what was then the most able European government in matters of political organization, viz. the Republic of Venice. Here although the institution functioned normally when in the other countries of Europe it was still in an undeveloped state, so that it may be said that Venice was "the school and paragon of embassies."[1] The example of Venice was followed in Italy by the Medici of Florence and the Sforza of Milan. The old system had still a loyal supporter in Louis XI, King of France (1461-1482), but this sovereign also contributed decisively to the development of the new law of legation by the confidential nature and importance of the tasks entrusted by him to his ambassadors.[2]

The first contacts of the Holy See with governments in the form most nearly approaching modern diplomatic relations are found when the Apostolic See was re-established after the Western Schism. The Popes had then to agree to a series of *modus vivendi* agreements with the principal powers for the recognition and regularization of reciprocal duties and rights. These agreements were often effected by

[1] Amelot de la Houssaye, *Histoire du Gouvernement de Venise,* I, 164; cfr. Nys, "Les commencements de la diplomatie et le droit d'ambassade jusqu'a Grotius," *RDILC,* XV, (1883), 577-586; XVI (1884), 55-70; 167-189; Nys, *Les Origines du Droit International,* pp. 297-312.

[2] Degert, '(Louis XI et ses Ambassadeurs," *RH,* CLIV (1927), 1-19.

means of legates.[3] Many concessions made by the Holy See to princes, especially in the matter of ecclesiastical benefices, are to be found in these agreements. One such concession of no less importance was the agreement to appoint national legates. These were favourite cardinals or ministers of the sovereign to whom were generally granted for the state in question the ancient privileges of the *legati a latere,* including the conferring of concistorial benefices, the reservation of the rights of the Camera Apostolica and certain judicial powers in ecclesiastical matters. Such national legates were Cardinal Georges d'Amboise (1501-1510) and Cardinal de Boisy (1519-1520) for France;[4] Rudersheim (1467-1474) and Cardinal Szech, Archbishop of Strigonia, for Hungary,[5] and Cardinal Wolsey for England.[6] These, however, in course of time became a source of serious abuses and constituted a danger to the unity of the Church. The Popes were therefore led gradually to limit this office and finally to suppress it.

The political events of the fourteenth and fifteenth centuries obliged the Holy See to multiply the extraordinary legations, but, while there were in Rome representatives of the different countries, the traditions of the curia did not yet permit the new method to be adopted, and resident nuncios had as yet no existence.[7] The development of the institution of permanent apostolic nunciatures was slow and was carefully adapted to various circumstances and local traditions. However, the events throughout which came into being can be traced back to the second half of the fifteenth century.

The great concern of the Popes of this period was the continual menace of the Turks to Christianity and especially to Italy. The danger could only be averted by uniting the Catholic forces in a crusade. To effect this an action of two kinds was necessary: one

[3] Cfr. Mercati, *Raccolta di Concordati,* pp. 168-185.

[4] Richard, "Origines de la Nonciature de France," *RQH,* LXXX (1906), 167-182.

[5] Richard, "Origines des Nonciatures permanentes," *RHE,* VII, (1906), 64-65.

[6] Pollard, *Wolsey,* pp. 115-116; 180.

[7] Richard, "Origines de la Nonciature de France," *RQH,* LXXVIII (1905), 104.

political, for the pacification of the princes of Europe and the establishment of equilibrium among the different rivals in Italy, for the safeguarding of the temporal power; the other, financial, for the collection of funds necessary for the expedition. Nicholas V (1447-1458) and Pius II (1458-1464) worked with extraordinary vigour to organize resistance to the Turks, and apostolic legates travelled throughout the length and breadth of Europe preaching peace and penance and announcing the indulgences. We meet celebrated figures of cardinals *legati a latere* such as Nicola Albergati, Giuliano Cesarini, Bessarione, John Carnajal and Nicholas of Cusa,[8] and all are endowed with the very ample spiritual powers. Side by side with the legates, the apostolic collectors act their parts, and it is of great interest to study at close quarters, as it were, this new phase in the evolution of their office. Thus, for example, Giovanni Castiglione, Bishop of Constance, appointed collector for the crusade in Austria and Hungary in 1453, took part in political activity as papal representative at the Diet of Ratisbon and Frankfurt in 1454 and at the Diet of Neustadt in 1455;[9] and in 1456 Callixtus III appointed Louis Cescases depositary general of the tithes of the crusades for France with plenary powers in financial matters, the equipment of the papal fleet and the enrolment of soldiers. But, as the Pope mentions in the brief of presentation to Charles VII, he is also given discretionary powers and entrusted with some purely diplomatic business.[10]

Thus the *oratores et nuntii* and the *commissarii decimarum cruciatae* now find themselves in circumstances particularly favourable to the exercise of their influence; they see their powers increased; each one enters into the life of the nation which is the sphere of

[8] Eubel, *Hierarchia catholica medii aevi,* II, 6, n. 37; II, 6, n. 43; II, 8, n. 11; II, 9, n. 26; II, 11, n. 7.

[9] Raynaldus, Annales Eccl., ad a. 1454 (n. 1, 3, 4), t.X, 1-4; a. 1455 (n. 1) t.X, 13-14; ad 1456 (n. 17), t.X, 65-66.

[10] " . . . *nec miretur tua Celsitudo quod dicto Lud. instructionem eorum quae sibi commisimus in scriptis non dedimus; cognovimus enim ipsum ita providum et in agendis expertum, quod sine alia instructione existimamus ipsum ea quae sibi commisimus bene fideliter et diligenter tuae Serenitati relaturum,* — Richard, "Origines de la Nonciature de France," *RQH,* LXXVIII, (1905), 108, note 1.

his activities and interests himself in its progress; and while they render valuable service to the Curia, they are no less useful to the State. This applies in a special way to Spain. Spain was divided into three financial districts: 1) Castile; Leon; 2) Aragon; 3) Navarre. The influence of the collectors in the politics and in the unification of the Iberian countries in the second half of the fifteenth century may be called decisive. The succession of papal agents and the numerous faculties they possessed in religious and political matters would seem to indicate that their standing was of no less importance than that of the modern nuncios. The faculties granted to the collectors of Spain had, besides, a very special importance on account of the position of preeminence which that country was acquiring in the Christian world.[11] The nature of the collectorate of England, at least during the reign of Henry VII (1476-1496) when Giovanni Gigli was collector, was very similar to that of Spain.[12]

What was happening in point of fact was not yet recognized by law. The Curia retained its traditional practices, and such missions were always considered as extraordinary.

An attempt to introduce an innovation was made by Pope Sixtus IV (1471-1484). Going further than his predecessors he regarded the position of nuncio as a curial office, well defined and extending to all matters referring to the welfare of the Church in any nation, having attached to it suitable prerogatives and privileges together with the duty of representing the Pope before the laity, the hierarchy and the sovereign. In the brief appointing Gerard de Crussol nuncio to King Louis XI the qualifications of a plenipotentiary and permanent delegate are set down as follows:

> "Te apud regem (Ludovicum) nuncium procuratorem factorem et negotiorum gestorem facimus constituimus et deputamus tibique in omnibus et singulis causis et negotiis nos et prefatam Sedem (Apostolicam) concernentibus in quocumque loco comparendi ac omnia et singula faciendi,

[11] Richard, "Origines des Nonciatures permanentes," *RHE*, VII (1906), 321-327.

[12] Richard, *Op. cit.*, pp. 328-329.

procurandi et gerendi quae ad nostrum et prefatae Sedis honorem cedant, facultatem concedimus." [13]

This step, which was a distinct move towards the institution of nunciatures, was not followed up; even the same Pontiff returned to the practice of extraordinary legations. However, the legates in actual fact remained for a long time on their missions, and this contributed towards the development of the new system. In 1475 Sixtus IV proclaimed the jubilee, and Nicolo di San Donnino, Bishop of Modena, with the title of *"nuncius et orator, cum potestate legati a latere"* for France and the neighbouring territories, was entrusted with the following onerous missions: 1) to make peace between the Kings of France and England in preparation for a new crusade; 2) to promulgate the jubilee for the Holy Year; 3) to institute an inquiry for the repression of usury and the restitution of ill-gotten money, of which two-thirds were to be spent on the crusade and the remaining third used to erect a loan-office "Monte di Pieta"; and not long afterwards he had the duty of securing the appointment of Giuliano della Rovere, nephew of the Pope, to the legation of Avignon.[14]

Finally the legates have powers of a financial, diplomatic, disciplinary and spiritual order. Such is the case when the apostolic emissaries are sent *cum potestate legati a latere*: the powers ordinarily reserved to cardinals are extended by the Popes on such occasions to envoys of lower rank. Sixtus IV once more tried the experiment of a permanent nunciature in France, when, in 1482, he invoked the assistance of Louis XI against the aggression of Ferdinand of Naples. He invited the King of France to establish stable diplomatic relations in the following words of the brief nominating Raymond Peraud or Peraudi:

"Sit semper atque continuo in curia suae Regiae Maiestatis aliquis nuncius ex Gallis aut Italis ad beneplacitum Regiae Maiestatis, medio cuius possit utrique de mutua voluntate constare plenissime." [15]

[13] Combet, Louis XI et le Saint-Siège, p. 108, note 2; Richard, "Origines de la Nonciature de France," *RQH*, LXXVIII (1905) 114.

[14] Combet, *Op. cit.*, pp. 132-133, 245-250.

[15] Richard, "Origines de la Nonciature de France," *RQH* LXXVIII, (1905), 124; Combet, *Op. cit.*, p. 190.

This proposal was not put into effect. With regard to this nunciature of France, Richard [16] notes the presence of the following juridical elements: 1) the nuncios are appointed by brief and bring with them credential letters to the sovereign: 2) they receive instructions from Rome and maintain a correspondence with this centre; 3) they deal principally with ecclesiastical affairs but they also take part in diplomatic discussions of a political nature. As one can see, the fundamental element of permanent appointment, although mentioned in the brief, does not yet exist in actual fact. Still, while in previous centuries the legates had to deal with purely ecclesiastical affairs, it could now be said that the nuncios had a prolonged mission which, moreover, is of a twofold character: he has faculties of a spiritual order to deal with the hierarchy and faithful, and he performs diplomatic and civil functions as regards the sovereign.

The mission granted during the reign of Innocent VIII (1484-1492) to Nicolo Franco, Bishop of Treviso, nuncio *"cum potestate legati a latere in dominio Venetorum"* and at the same time collector for the provinces of the Venetian Republic, is worthy of note. The mission of the Bishop of Treviso had the character of what was then understood by the term "nunciature," and it was, to say the least, the final step from the collectorate to the nunciature properly so called.[17]

Innocent VIII did not greatly increase the scope of the nunciatures, but he made a definite contribution to the development of a diplomatic organization in the Roman Curia, namely, the Secretariate of State, and this he did by regulating the College of Apostolic Secretaries and creating of the "Segretario Domestico." [18] The duty of this last-mentioned personage seems to have been at first confined to the despatch of the personal correspondence of the Pope but soon nobody had greater importance than he in the activity for the Holy See. He is *au courant* with all ecclesiastical and civil affairs, counsellor of the Pope and general superintendent; he takes charge of the cor-

[16] *Op. cit., RQH,* LXXVIII, (1905), 125.

[17] Richard, "Origines des Nonciatures permanentes," *RHE* VII, (1906), 331-332.

[18] Bulla, "Non debet reprehensibile," (31 decembris 1487)—*Bullarium diplomatum et privilegiorum,* ed. Taurin., V, 330-338.

respondence, directs the action of the legates and the nuncios, and gradually controls all the internal and external activity of the Church.[19]

The period from Alexander VI to Clement VII, that is, from 1492 to 1534, is noted for the predominantly secular policy of the Popes. This had no small influence on the rapid growth of the nunciatures, which, through the regular and uninterrupted appointments of the holders, became permanent and ordinary.

During the pontificate of Alexander VI we find the first resident nuncios, sent *to remain,* (*per starvi*) as we are told by Marin Sanuto, Secretary and author of the *Diarii* of the Republic of Venice. The first resident nuncio is Angelo Leonini, sent to Venice May 25, 1500.[20] The scope of this mission is exclusively religious and political. It is completely separated from matters pertaining to the collectorate which, by this time, can hardly be said to exist.[21] The succession of the nuncios continues uninterruptedly from now on, except for the years 1505-1509, when diplomatic relations were broken off on account of the invasion of some cities of Romagna by the Republic. This series of apostolic nuncios presents all the features of a stable nunciature, the first of its kind, perfectly organized.[22]

In France the mission of Giovanni Ferreri, Bishop of Arles, commenced about 1500,[23] was followed by those of Carlo Domenico del Carretto, Marquis del Finale and Bishop-elect of Thebes (1503-

[19] Richard, "La Secretererie d'Etat Apostolique," *RHE,* XI, (1910), 69; Ancel, "La Secretererie pontificale sous Paul IV," *RQH,* LXXIX (1906), 410.

[20] "A di 25 Marzo. Vene poi lo episcopo da Thioli, nominato Angelo, orator dil papa . . . et presentó le letere di credenza, et il breve dil papa. *Sexto,* era venuto per star qui appresso questa Signoria per nontio dil papa . . . che il sia venuto per star qui, li disse saria ben visto."—Sanuto, *Diarii,* III, 343.

[21] Cf. Richard, "Origines des Nonciatures permanentes," *RHE,* VII (1906), 332.

[22] Biaudet, *Les Nonciatures Apostoliques permanentes jusqu'en* 1648, pp. 17-18; Cecchetti, *La Repubblica di Venezia e la corte di Roma nei rapporti della Religione,* I.

[23] Sanuto, Diarii, III, 295.

1505) [24] and of Pierre Le Filleul (1504-1507) to whom Julius II wrote: "Volumus ut continues et permaneas donec te duxerimus revocandum"—words which prove beyond doubt the permanent nature of the nunciature.[25]

In Germany after the missions of Leonello Chieregato, Bishop of Concordia, in (1496-1499) [26] and of Cardinal Peraudi (1500-1503 [27] during the pontificate of Alexander VI, there were lessening strained relations with Julius II, whose impetuous character could not easily tolerate the egoism of the Emperor Maximilian I.[28]

In Spain the financial and political nature of the nunciature of Ruffo dei Teodoli, Bishop of Bertinoro, was retained.[29]

In the year 1510 Pope Julius II sent missions to the different cantons of Switzerland with the object maintaining friendly relations and of enlisting soldiers for the papal army. At this time originated the tradition of having the Swiss Guard in the Vatican.[30]

When Leo X (1513-1521) ascended the papal throne it could be said that the nunciatures had been already firmly established. With the exception of Naples, Spain and Portugal, they had everywhere replaced the collectorates of the fourteenth century. To Leo X, however, is due the merit of definitely establishing the ordinary and permanent nunciatures by the regular succession of nuncios during his reign.[31]

As a result of the political events which transferred to Germany the crown of the Holy Roman Empire the relations of the Holy See

[24] Sanuto, *Op. cit.*, V, 638; Villari, *T. Dispacci di Antonio Giustinian,* II, 363-364; III, 81-99.

[25] Richard, "Origines de la Nonciature de France," *RQH* LXXVIII, (1905), 140.

[26] Sanuto, *Op. cit.*, II, 1253; cf. Pio Paschini, *Leonello Chieregato—Nuncio di Innocenzo VIII e Alessandro VI.*

[27] Eubel, *Hierarchia catholica medii aevi,* II, 23, n. 10.

[28] Richard, "Origines des Nonciatures permanentes," *RHE,* VII, (1906), 69; 336.

[29] Raynaldus, *Annales Eccl.,* ad a. 1508, n. 11, t.XI, 518-519.

[30] Guasti, *"I Manoscritti Torrigiani,"* *ASI,* XIX (1874), 56; 63; 65; XXVI (1877) 182; 200-202; Biandet, *Op. cit.*, p. 19.

[31] Richard, "Origines de la Nonciature de France," *RQH,* LXXX (1906), 112-113.

with central Europe could not be neglected, and in fact numerous missions were carried out there by papal representatives,[32] but a true nunciature did not appear until 1513, with the legation of Lorenzo Campeggio.[33]

The nunciature during the reign of Leo X which perhaps most closely approximates the modern conception is the French Nunciature of Lodovico di Canossa, Bishop of Tricarico, during the years 1514-1517. Leaving Rome on May 20, 1514, he had first of all the task of making peace between Louis XII of France and Henry VIII of England.[34] For some time he acted in conjunction with the Florentine ambassador, Francesco Pandolfini, but soon the Pope instructed him to assume the title of nuncio apostolic in order *to confer, to attend to and to deal with everything* (per conferire, intendere e trattare tutto),[35] that might be of advantage to the Holy See and the kingdom of France, and on him were conferred the powers of a *legatus a latere.*[36] Thus we find united in the person of Lodovico di Canossa diplomatic and ecclesiastical functions: there is the office of representing the Pope with the sovereign, with temporal and spiritual faculties for all affairs, together with authority over the hierarchy and faithful within the limits of a determined territory.

Papal diplomacy of this period has a predominantly political character directed towards the defence of the territory of the Papal States. It is, therefore, not surprising to find papal representatives, like the nuncios in France Carlo Domenico del Carretto and Le Filleul, who, though they are ecclesiastics, have no power in spiritual affairs. This seems to be chiefly due to the fact that ample power in ecclesiastical matters was given to the national legate. At this time, too, it happened that ordinary laymen were created apostolic nuncios. This was not

32 Cfr. Richard, "Origines des Nonciatures permanentes," *RHE,* VII (1906), 63-64.

33 Hergenroether, *Regesta Leonis X,* n. 4928; Guasti, *Op. cit.,—ASI,* XXVI (1877), 190; E. V. Cardinal, *Cardinal Lorenzo Campeggio,* p. 43. See the series of nuncios in Pius VI, *Responsio ad Metropolitanos,* cap. VIII, n. 133, in note.

34 Sanuto, *Diarii,* XVIII, 236-293.

35 Guasti, *Op. cit.,* — ASI, XIX (1874, 72.

36 Hergenroether, *Op. cit.,* n. 12033; cf. Richard, "Origines de la Nonciature de France," *RQH,* LXXX (1906), 123.

altogether an innovation: in 1447 Francesco Petrarca had been the ambassador of Clement VI with Mastino della Scala, Lord of Verona.[37] During the Renaissance period we find among the papal legates men of letters, writers, humanists, and the most illustrious figures in public life. It is hardly necessary to remark here that these emissaries, or *oratores,* dealt with ecclesiastical affairs in a rather wide sense inasmuch as the object of their missions was to foster devotion to the Church, to promote peace and the crusade; or their mission concerned questions in which sovereigns unlawfully interfered, as, for example, in the question of the benefices.[38] So far as we can gather, they were never entrusted with faculties regarding matters of conscience, such as, the granting of dispensations.

Among the principal lay papal nuncios of this period we may mention the following: Galeazzo Butrigaro, nuncio to the King of Spain, 1513-1517;[39] Giovanni Rucellai, nuncio to the King of France in 1520,[40] and Baldassare Castiglione, nuncio to the Emperor Charles V, 1524-1529.[41] While these laymen were the ordinary apostolic nuncios, *legati a latere* having the faculties usually conceded in spiritual matters since the middle ages they performed other special missions. Such were the missions of the Cardinals Egidio da Viterbo in Germany (1515-1516) [42] and in Spain (1518-1519), [43] Bernardo di Bibiena to the Emperor 1516),[44] and to the King of France (1518),[45]

[37] Cf. Cipolla, "Sui motivi del ritorno di Francesco Petrarca in Italia nel 1347," *Giornale Storico della Letteratura italiana,* XLVII (1906), 253-265.

[38] Hergenroether, *Regesta Leonis X,* n. 5621; 6654; 11566.

[39] Bembo, *Epistolae,* VII, 16; IX, 25; Sanuto, *Diarii,* XVII, 373; 544; Guasti, "I Manoscritti Torrigiani," *ASI,* XIX (1874), 59; XXI (1875), 197.

[40] Sanuto, *Op. cit.,* XXX, 221; Guasti, *Op. cit.* — *ASI,* XXV (1877), 387-403; XXVI (1877), 182; Richard, "Origines de la Nonciature de France," *RQH,* LXXX (1906), 163-165.

[41] Pieper, *Zur Entstehungsgeschichte der staendigen Nuntiaturen* pp. 67-69.

[42] Bembo, *Epistolae,* XI, 13; 14.

[43] Reynaldus, *Annales Eccl.,* ad a. 1518, n. 37, t.XII, 205-206; Guasti, *Op. cit.,* — *ASI,* XXIII (1876), 416.

[44] Guasti, *Op. cit.,* — ASI, XX (1874), 28.

[45] Bembo, *Epistolae,* XII, I.

Thomas de Vio (Cardinal Cajetan) in the Low Countries (1518-1519)[46] and Giovanni Salviati (1525-1526)[47] and Lorenzo Campeggio (1530-1532) to Charles V.[48]

During the pontificates of Leo X (1513-1521) and Clement VII (1523-1534), both of the House of the Medici of Florence, the question of lay nuncios becomes still more interesting. The papal and Florentine politics go hand in hand, and the apostolic nuncios have often to act in conjunction with the Florentine ambassadors. Besides, the Florentine ambassador is not infrequently raised to the office of apostolic nuncio. The Florentine ambassador to Venice, Pietro Dovizi di Bibiena, acts as apostolic nuncio during the years 1513-1514;[49] the Florentine ambassadors in France, Roberto Acciaiuoli and Francesco Pandolfini, for some years act semi-officially in the name of the Pope,[50] and finally Acciaiuoli is appointed by Clement VII nuncio along with Capino da Capo, with full power to deal with the war against the Turks, and for this purpose to establish relations with the King of England and the Duke of Milan and Venice.[51] Giovanni Corsi was in correspondence with the Roman Curia from 1514, and regularly performed the functions of nuncio to the emperor during the years 1523-1525.[52] By this procedure, which was by no means extraordinary at that time, it was intended to raise the apostolic nunciatures to the importance of civil legations. The Florentine ambassadors, famous for their finesse and ability in political affairs, had been the teachers of the Church diplomats.[53] The ecclesiastical dip-

46 The principal scope of this mission entrusted by Leo X to Cardinal Cajetan was to obtain the submission of Luther; cf. Hefele-Leclercq, *Histoires des Conciles,* VIII, 683-696.

47 Molini, *Documenti di Storia Italiana,* I, 191-200.

48 Cardinal, Cardinal Lorenzo Campeggio, pp. 140-162.

49 Bembo, *Epistolae,* I, 3; 4.

50 Guasti, *Op. cit.,* — *ASI,* XIX (1874), 58; 61; 64; 68-69.

51 Fraikin, *Nonciatures de France, Nonciatures de Clement VII;* I, 12-15; Richard, "Origines de la Nonciature de France," *RQH,* LXXXV (1909), 18-23.

52 Guasti, *Op. cit.* — *ASI,* XIX (1874), 61; Pieper, *Op. cit.,* p. 67, note 4.

53 Biaudet, *Les Nonciatures Apostoliques permanentes jusqu'en* 1648, p. 20.

lomatic organization was at the height of its efficiency; at the same time, we may observe with Richard [54] that at this period an ordinary nunciature was far from being regarded as an ecclesiastical administration attached to a definite place. The nuncios were sent to court rather than to a government, and they formed part of the entourage which accompanied the sovereign at the palace or elsewhere even in time of war. The direct relations with the sovereign and the frequent contact with court officials gave the nuncios an opportunity of serving the interests of the Church.

With the accession to the throne of Paul III (1534-1549) there commenced the religious reawakening known as the counter-reformation, and the papal representatives become somewhat less diplomatic, but much better versed in eccleesiastical discipline," and we shall never be able to fully appreciate their good services to the Church." [55]

The first result of this new policy was the exclusion of laymen from the ordinary nunciatures.[56] In the second was the increase in dignity and authority of the ecclesiastical nuncios, especially in the great nations, in preparation for the Council of Trent. The papal representatives were knit into a more compact body depending on the Secretariate of State, which was at that time headed by "the Cardinal nephew." [57] The nuncios and legates leave Rome with precise

[54] "Origines de la Nonciature de France," *RQH, LXXX* (1906), 124-125.

[55] Cf. Biaudet, *Op. cit.*, p. 21.

[56] e.g., the mission of Francesco Giucciardini to the Emperor lasted only a month (August 15 - September 15, 1536)—Pieper, *Op. cit.*, p. 112, note 1.

[57] "Non seulement le Cardinal neveu devait être, avec le tître de *Cardinal patron,* le chef de la politique extérieure, le ministre des affaires étrangères de l'Eglise, celui qui expédiait les ordres aux nonces, dans le choix desquels il avait une grande parte, qui règlait leur attitude, leur action, dictait leur language, les rappellait, les deplaçait, interpretait la pensée du pape, en dirigeait l'execution, la modifiat parfois plus ou moins selon son influence et le tempérament du maître; mais encore il devait avoir sous la main toutes les branches du gouvernement et de l'administration des Etats pontificaux, devenir maître de tout, argent, honneurs, affairs au dedans comme au dehors de Rome, en un mot le premier, si non le seul ministre du pouvoir pontifical." — Richard, "La Secretairerie pontificale sous Paul IV, "*RQH,* LXXIX (1906), 418-470.

instructions both with regard to the line of policy to be followed and the exercise of their spiritual powers. Usually they have instructions of a public nature for the general run of cases and then certain reserved faculties to be used only in extraordinary circumstances. While the permanent nuncios deal with most of the affairs, the temporary missions of the *legati a latere* are still continued. The spirtual faculties vary according to the different classes of papal representatives and the requirements of each mission.

With the aim of ending the political and hegemonic rivalries of Spain, France and Germany, in the attempt to arrest the advance of Lutheranism, and in preparation for the Council of Trent, Paul III multiplied his legations and enriched his emissaries with all the powers that papal supremacy could concede. His preoccupation was to elect by means of the nuncios, "persons of such education and character that their integrity and loyalty could be depended upon." [58]

With the Council of Trent the institution of the right of legation was directed and disciplined, if we may say so, on a juridical basis more effectively adapted to the needs of the Church. A fundamental innovation was introduced into the law of the Decretals when the hearing of ecclesiastical cases in the first instance was definitely committed to the Bishop's tribunal. Until this time metropolitans, vicars apostolic, *legati nati, legati a latere* and nuncios were permitted to receive and deal in the first instance with all the cases brought before them.[59] In fact we read in the brief of appointment of Stanislaus Hosius, sent as nuncio by Pius IV in 1559 "cum potestate legati a latere apud Imperatorem; matrimoniales et Beneficiales, ac alias Ecclesiasticas necnon spirituales et profanas causas ad forum ecclesiasticum quomodolibet pertinentes, tam *primae instantiae* quam appellationum quarumcumque a quibuscumque Iudicibus ordinariis . . . etiam summarie . . . sola veritate inspecta . . . audiendi cognoscendi et fine dèbito terminandi." [60]

However as a result of the new legislation [61] in all the briefs, the first example being that addressed to the nuncio Melchior Biglia,

[58] Cf. Pieper, *Op. cit.*, pp. 195; 196-199.

[95] C. I, X, *de officio legati,* I, 30.

[60] Pius VI, *Responsio ad Metropolitanos,* cap. VIII, n. 143 in note.

[61] Conc. Trident., Sess. XXIV, *de ref.,* c. 20.

sent in 1565 to replace Hosius, after enumerating the matters with which they could deal the following clause is added: "Sine praejudicio Ordinariorum quoad causas huiusmodi in prima instantia coram eis iuxta Concilii Tridentini decretum agnoscendas." [62] The Council of Trent, however, did not intend to take from the Holy See the right of acting as a supreme court,[63] nor the right of reserving certain cases nor the right of all the faithful of appealing to Rome, either directly or by means of the legates. The above-mentioned clause had an important exception in the case of the Nunciature of Spain where almost contemporaneously there was established the tribunal of the Apostolic Nuncio of Madrid.[64]

The Council of Trent urged that the reforms it had introduced should now be put into operation without delay. In the campaign thus inaugurated we find the last phase of the development of the apostolic nunciatures and of their complete organization. Pius IV (1559-1565) resumed diplomatic relations with the different European countries and even attempt a rapprochement with non-catholic countries.[65] The work of increasing and of organizing the nunciatures was completed by Gregory XIII (1572-1585). Under this Pontiff the nunciatures increased in number and were classified according to their importance into "greater" and "lesser" nunciatures. The "greater" nunciatures are those whose nuncios, immediately after the completion of their mission, are ordinarily created cardinals. To obtain the good-will of a personage influential in the Curia, and to increase their own prestige, the princes ask for a "greater" nunciature, but this opens the way to abuses on the part of certain nuncios, and to unjustified pretensions on the part of the princes.[66]

[62] Pius VI, *Op. cit.*, cap. VIII, n. 143.

[63] Conc. Trident., Sess. XXV, *de ref.*, c. 10; cf. Montini, *La "Responsio super Nunciaturis" di Papa Pio VI*, pp. 67-70.

[64] Picanyol, "De origine et evolutione historica Tribunalis Rotae Hispanicae," *Apollinaris*, V (1932), 222-229.

[65] Biaudet, *Les Nonciatures Apostoliques permanentes jusqu'en* 1648, p. 26, note 2.

[66] Pius IV, *"Etsi Romanum Pontificem"* (18 Maji 1565)—*Bullarium Romanum*, VII, 369-371; Biaudet, *Op. cit.*, pp. 47-55.

The number of the nunciatures rises to sixteen divided as follows: 6 Italian: Savoy, Genoa, Venice, Florence, Naples, Malta; 4 Latin: Spain,

With Gregory XIII there is a further determination of terminology regarding the classes of papal representatives. The *legati a latere* are cardinals sent as extraordinary ambassadors.[67] The nuncios are generally bishops and archbishops accredited only to the Emperor and to princes of the blood.[68] After these come the representatives of lower grade, or diplomatic agents in general.

One of the most deplorable abuses in ecclesiastical discipline at the time of the Council of Trent was the general laxity in the matter of the law of residence. This abuse was nothing new: in reference particularly to Papal legates, the fifth Lateran Council had already called attention to the obligation of residence and re-imposed it under pain of privation of revenues: "Quae quidem antiquitus ordinata et instituta fuerunt ut opportuna legatorum praesentia populis esset salutaris.[69] The Council of Trent insisted on the observance of this fundamental obligation of the pastoral office and the care of souls.[70]

Up to this time the Apostolic Nuncios were chosen from among the residential bishops. While on their missions which were often rather prolonged, they had to leave their sees in the hands of vicars, not without detriment to the spiritual welfare of their flocks. Besides, this was in open contradiction to the new laws and brought with it the danger of perpetuating the very abuses which these laws were intended to remedy. The difficulty, however, was to provide a means of support for the legates. The first Pope to give a salary to legates was Alexander VI,[71] but he did so only occasionally.

Portugal, France, Belgium; 5 German: Germany, England, Cologne, Bavaria, Switzerland: 1 Slav; Poland; but from the point of view of diplomatic character we may exclude from this list Bavaria, England, Genoa and Malta. Biaudet, *Op. cit.*, pp. 27-28; cf. Maere, "Origines de la Nonciature de Flandre," *RHE*, VII (1906), 569; 821.

67 Cf. Moroni, "Legato Apostolico," *Dizionario di erudizione eccl.*, XXXVII, 269.

68 Cauchie et Maere, *Instructions generales aux Nonces de Flandre*, XXIII; Biaudet, *Op. cit.*, p. 33 note 3; Maere, *Op. cit.*, *RHE, VII* (1906), 814-815.

69 Bulla *"Supernae dispositioni,"* (5 maji 1514—*Bullarium Romanum*, V, 604.

70 Conc. Trident., Sess. VI, *de ref.*, c. 1; Sess. XXIII, *de ref.*, c. 1.

71 Richard, "Origines de la Nonciature de France," *RQH*, LXXVIII (1905), 137-138.

But such assistance, was altogether exceptional, and was intended rather as a contribution towards travelling expenses. The nuncios lived on the revenues of their benefices and on the resources occasionally arising from the exercise of their faculties. Paul III assigned fixed allowances, but it was only under Gregory XIII that there was introduced a regular and uniform rate of salaries graded according to the classes of nunciatures.[72] Many years had to pass before Paul VI (1605-1621) chose nuncios from the inferior clergy, constituting them Archbishops with titular sees.[73]

The offices of the Nuncios Apostolic reached the height of its splendour at the time of the Peace of Westphalia (1648). During this period the Holy See used it to intervene, and often exercise a dominating influence in the political life of Europe. Thenceforward this intervention continued but the supremacy of the Holy See declined with the growing estrangement of certain nations from Rome.[74] The gradual dissemination of Gallican and Illuminist ideas led to a progressive weakening of the ties that once bound nations to the centre of Catholicism. *The "De Statu Ecclesiae et legitima potestate Romani Pontificis"* of Febronius (John Nicholas von Hontheim), a pernicious attack on papal supremacy, and the controversy which centred round the establishing of the Nunciature of Munich (1783), a controversy which was referred to the Congress of Ems (1786), compelled Pius VI to defend the right of papal legation with the *"Responsio ad Metropolitanos Maguntinum, Trevirensem, Coloniensem, et* Salisburgensem Super Nunciaturis" (1789). This "Responsio" consists of a brief followed by a large volume directed to the Ecclesiastical Electors of Germany, the Archbishop of Mainz, Trier and Cologne and the Archbishop of Salzburg. These had united in opposing the erection of a nunciature at Munich, for which the Palatine Elector of that principality had repeatedly petitioned the Pope. But the Munich Nunciature only provided the occasion; the real purpose of the controversy was to question the whole right of papal legation, on the pretext that it trenched on episcopal authority.

[72] Biaudet, *Op. cit.*, 70-79.

[73] Biaudet, *Op. cit.*, pp. 44-47.

[74] Karttunen, *Les Nonciatures apostoliques permanentes de* 1650 *a* 1800, p. X.

In the *Responsio* the rights of the Pope are exhaustively defended from the theological, juridical and historical points of view.[75]

At the time of the French Revolution the nunciatures were in a state of decline but a revival came with the Congress of Vienna (1815), where the custom of giving the apostolic nuncios precedence over all the civil diplomatic agents was confirmed.[76]

After this period the nunciatures continued to flourish. It is especially worthy of note that the diplomats of the Church continued to hold their position after the events of September 20, 1870. This fact of international importance affords a strong argument in favour of the right of the Holy See to be considered a member of the international community, but it is above all a proof of the entirely spiritual aims of the exercise of papal legation.

Article IX: Apostolic Internuncios

Throughout practically the whole of the sixteenth century the names *"nuntius," "internuntius,"* and *"interpres"* mean the same thing and denote a diplomatic agent without any reference to the rank of his mission.

"Internuntius" may be considered as a contraction of *"interim nuntius,"* or *"nuntius ad interim"* or perhaps even *"nuntius inter"*

[75] The contents of the whole work may be summarized as follows: c. 1—the persons and events which had given rise to the dispute; c. 2—the circumstances in which the Nunciature of Munich was erected; cc. 3-4—defence of the use of the faculties of the nuncio of Cologne, especially with regard to dispensations; cc. 516—controversy regarding the Pro-Synodal Tribunals and discussion of the arguments of the right claimed by the Elector of Cologne to take charge of the affairs which had already devolved upon the nunciature; c. 7—the prolongation of a tithe on ecclesiastical goods granted in favour of the Palatine Elector of Bavaria; c. 8—proof of the thesis: *"De Iure Apostolicae Sedis mittendi Nuncios tam Extraordinarios, quam Ordinarios* stabili jurisdictione pollentes . . ." this chapter, divided into seven sections, is most important for the history of the papal right of legation. For a commentary on the historico-juridical circumstances of the *Responsio,* cf. Montini, *La "Responsio super Nunciaturis" di Pio VI.*

[76] Reglement, art. IV, leaves unchanged the tradition of precedence for the representatives of the Pope; cf. Satow, *A Guide to Diplomatic Practice,* I, 244-245.

and, in this last case, it could be equivalent to the expression *"nuntius inter nos."* At all events, what interests us here is to determine how the word came to have a special meaning and to designate a kind of ecclesiastical diplomatic agent of secondary importance. Leo X frequently used the term. His representatives at Venice, Madrid and at the court of the Emperor were often designated by the title of internuncios.[1] A classification of the permanent diplomatic representatives seems to have been begun at the Council of Trent and to have been definitely established by Gregory XIII. It was natural to expect that the representatives sent to the court of the Emperor and to that of a petty prince would not be put on an equal footing; at the same time, it was not so much the place that counted as the important nature of the mission itself or the peculiar intricacy of a particular question demanding the services of a specially qualified person for its solution. The diplomatic service as we understand it to-day did not exist before 1560 and, if circumstances required or favoured it, a person could easily be transferred from one nunciature to another. The sending of a nuncio from a first class nunciature to one of lower grade did not in the least imply that he had fallen into disgrace.[2] The practice of the time was that papal representatives with the title of nuncio were sent to the Emperor and to princes of royal blood. A diplomatic agent of lower grade was sent to the other rulers. An example is furnished by the Nunciature of Belgium.[3] However, it does not appear that the rule was strictly observed in the positive sense, but one easily sees that if the Pope sent to the princes of the blood a representative who had not the title of nuncio, it would have been considered as an offence and a refusal to acknowledge the royal rank.[4]

Only in the seventeenth century did the term *"internuntius"* acquire the meaning of a second class diplomatic agent. It was the

[1] Bembo, *Epistolae,* I, 3, 13 and 30; II, 1, 9 and 32; VI, 17 and 24; VIII, 32; IX, 25; XV, 12.

[2] Biaudet, *Les Nonciatures Apostoliques permanentes jusqu'en* 1648, p. 47.

[3] Maere, "Origines de la Nonciature de Flandre," *RHE,* VII (1906), 810-216; Biaudet, *Op. cit.,* p. 33, note 3.

[4] Biaudet, *Op. cit.,* p. 322.

technical title of a representative of the House of Austria at the court of Constantinople, but this was a rather isolated case in civil diplomacy.[5] It does not appear to have been much in use even by the Holy See. The apostolic representatives of lower rank were more frequently known by the generic names of diplomatic agents and commissaries. Ordinarily the secondary positions were given to ecclesiastics who were not bishops but protonotaries apostolic and auditors of the Tribunals of the Curia.

Among the earliest apostolic Internunciatures were that erected in Brazil in 1829 (now a nunciature), and that erected in Holland in 1832, still existing.[6]

The use of the term "internuncio" by the Curia remained uncertain till shortly before the promulgation of the code. A clarification of this matter came from the Secretariate of State on May 8, 1916 when, on the proposal of Card. Peter Gasparri, Secretary of State, Pope Benedict XV decided that papal representatives who were not apostolic nuncios should henceforth be called apostolic internuncios instead of extraordinary delegates or envoys, the title of apostolic delegate being reserved to those representatives who had not diplomatic character.[7] The document was accompanied by an authentic interpretation which declared that the new terminology was adopted with the intention of indicating the categories of papal representatives in a manner corresponding better with ecclesiastical usage, and, at the same time, more honourable. The term "Envoy Extraordinary" belongs more appropriately to a lay representative. In virtue of the above document the title of *Apostolic Internuncio* besides being given to the Papal representative in the Argentine, Chile and Holland, was also given to the Papal representatives accredited to the Republics of Columbia, Costa Rica, Nicaragua, Honduras, Haiti, Peru and Bolivia, and Venezuela.[8] From the practice followed in these Re-

[5] Cf. Satow, *A Guide to Diplomatic Practice,* I, 243; Bolsover, "The meaning and history of the term 'Internuncio',*Bulletin of the Institute of Historical Research,* XII (1934-1935), 145-151.

[6] Giobbio, Lezioni di Diplomazia Ecclesiastica, I, 315-316.

[7] Segreteria Status (8 Maii 1916), Fontes, n. 6457.

[8] Cfr. *Il Monitore Eccl.* XXXVIII 1916), 254-255; cfr. Giobbio, *Op. cit.,* I, 316-322.

publics it would appear that the Internunciature is sometimes the first step in diplomatic relations between the Holy See and a government, a nunciature being erected when a greater spirit of understanding has developed.

Article X: Apostolic Delegates

In the specific sense of a papal envoy, the term *"Delegatus Apostolicus"* is comparatively recent.[1]

Towards the end of the eighteenth century the governors of the thirteen provinces into which the Papal States were divided were called apostolic delegates. After the Congress of Vienna in the general reorganization of the Papal States in the time of Pius VII (1800-1823), the different provinces were called apostolic delegations and were indicated by the name of the chief town and seat of the governor, for example, the Apostolic Delegation of Bologna, of Urbino, etc.[2] In 1827 Leo XII (1823-1829) introduced an innovation in this arrangement giving the name of legation to each of the four provinces of Bologna, Ferrara, Ravenna and Forli, whose governor was a Cardinal Legate. The provinces whose governor was not a cardinal continued to be known as delegations.[3]

The name of apostolic delegate attributed to these governors evidently connoted offices which were quite specific but were not different from the functions performed since the Middle Ages by the officials governing the papal territories. Judging from an expression of Innocent IV,[4] their duties were similar to those formerly carried out by the Roman consuls and proconsuls in the government of the provinces of the empire.

When the Sacred Congregation de Propaganda Fide was estab-

[1] For the meaning of the phrase, *"tamquam Apostolicae Sedis Delegati"* attributed to bishops by the Decretals and the Council of Trent, cf. Kearney, *The principles of Delegation,* pp. 38-40; Wernz, *Ius Decretalium,* II, 694-697.

[2] Cf. *Bullarii Rom. Continuatio,* ed. Prati, VII, 1300-1320.

[3] Cf. Moroni, "Delegazioni Apostoliche," *Dizionario di Erudizione eccl.,* XIX, 202-208.

[4] *C.* 2, de officio legati, I, 15, in VI°; cf. *C.* (I, 35); *D.* (I, 16); (1, 18).

lished (1622), the missionary activity of the Church was directed not only towards the conversion of the pagans but, with equal zeal, to the reunion of the Eastern Churches. Now, in the lands and among the peoples that are being converted to the Catholic religion, it is the recognised practice of the Holy See to erect the hierarchy by slow stages. We still find in Asia Minor, for example, some ecclesiastics who are Prefects or Vicars Apostolic for the newly converted of the Latin rite and are at the same time Apostolic Delegates for the Eastern Uniates. It seems that the Apostolic Delegations properly so called had their origin in this way. The most ancient of the Apostolic Delegations is that of Syria, established June 27, 1762 under Clement VIII, with its seat at Aleppo.[5]

In the year 1834 the Apostolic Delegation of Greece was erected by Gregory XVI (1831-1846). On that occasion the Pope recommended to the goodwill of Otho I, King of Greece, Louis Mary Blancis, Bishop of Sira, appointed apostolic delegate for the care of the Greek Catholics in the islands of the Aegean who were not subject to the jurisdiction of the other bishops of Greece.[6] The letter of commendation to the king regards this papal representative more as a nuncio than as an apostolic delegate, and the care he is to take of the faithful not subject to other jurisdictions is much the same as that of a present-day vicar apostolic. The Apostolic Delegations therefore, had not from the beginning a well-defined character; they were an adaptation to circumstances and the necessity the Pope was under of giving his support in situations of particular difficulty in the East.

All this seems to be confirmed by the practice of Leo XIII (1878-1903). This Pope re-enforced the laws of Benedict XIV,[7] regarding the relations between the Oriental Church and the Holy See, the preservation of the different rites, and the laws governing the changing from an oriental rite to the Latin rite and vice versa. To under-

[5] *Epist. ad Arnulphum Bossu* (27 junii 1762)—De Martinis, *Ius Pontificium de Propaganda Fide*, IV, 80.

[6] *Epist. ad Othonem regem* (25 augusti 1834)—*Bullarii Rom. Continuatio* (ed. Rev. Camerae Ap.), XIX, 583.

[7] Cf. Const. *"Demandatam"* (24 decembris 1743)—*Bullarium Benedicti XIV*, I, 328-334.

stand the great part played by the apostolic delegates in fostering a better spirit of understanding between the Holy See and the various branches of the Oriental Church it is sufficient to recall the prescriptions of Leo XIII directing that the patriarchs of the East should not only keep in frequent correspondence, but should also meet in local conferences at least twice a year to discuss everything of advantage to their churches.[8]

The apostolic delegations form a kind of papal representative body in those countries where the Catholic Church is not officially recognized by the civil authority. This mostly happens where the Catholics still constitute a minority of the population. The apostolic delegations, therefore, depended from the beginning on the Congregation de Propaganda Fide, for the double reason that they were situated in countries only partly converted to the true religion, and that their nature was not diplomatic. This form of papal representation developed more and more with the impetus given to the missions by Pius IX, Leo XIII and their successors.

The beginning of the Apostolic Delegation of the United States is connected with the arrival of Monsignor Gaetano Bedini in America in 1853-1854. Together with the commission to settle certain questions, he received from Pius IX instructions to enquire into the possibility of erecting an Apostolic Delegation. This enquiry was without result at the time. In 1889 Francesco Satolli, Archbishop of Lepanto, was sent as *Ablegatus Apostolicus* of Leo XIII on the occasion of the centenary of the constitution of the American hierarchy and the opening of the Catholic University of America in Washington, D.C. In 1893 Archbishop Satolli was entrusted with another American mission and during his stay the apostolic delegation was erected.[9]

On account of particular regulations in force before the Code a tribunal for certain cases was often erected at the seats of the Papal Representations, the auditor of the nunciature or apostolic

[8] Leo XIII, Const. *"Auspici rerum"* (19 martii 1896)—*Acta Leonis XIII*, XVI, 76-77.

[9] Leo XIII, Epist. *"Longinqua Oceani"* (6 januarii 1895)—*Fontes*, n. 628; Lallou, "The Apostolic Delegation at Washington," *ER*, XCV (1936), 576-592. Cerratti, "Legate," *The Catholic Encyclopedia*, IX, 120.

delegation being the judge. Mention is made of the tribunal of the Apostolic Delegate of the United States as late as 1914 in a document for the Orientals published by the Sacred Congregation de Propaganda Fide.[10]

Shortly after the erection of the Delegation of the United States followed that of Canada (1899-1900).[11]

With regard to their dependence on the Holy See the delegations follow the condition of the nations where they are constituted. As is well known all works directed towards the conversion of the heathen are in charge of the Congregation de Propaganda Fide but as soon as the faith develops a proper hierarchy is erected. The territory then passes from the *jus missionum* to the *jus commune* and the delegations formerly depending on Propaganda, *ipso facto* become subject to the *Sacred Congregation of the Concistory*.

Historical Résumé:

The Popes began to use the right of legation at the beginning of the fourth century. The most important factors in the public activity of the Church were then the Councils, both ecumenical and plenary. These were the guardians of the Faith and centres for the enactment of the first ecclesiastical laws. The Supreme Pontiffs could not intervene personally at the councils, and the tradition was soon established that he should not intervene except by means of his representatives. This practice was confirmed by Leo the Great. At the councils, the Papal representatives legalise the assemblies, formally approve of the measures taken, and refer them to the Pope with whom the final sanction rests.

However, the development of the Church in the different nations of the East and around the Mediterranean gave rise to the need of a more constant contact with Rome. The bishops of districts which are of greater importance either on account of the number of the faithful or because of their economic and political prestige, are granted special faculties and act as representatives of the Popes in

10 *Decretum pro Orientalibus* (17 augusti 1914), art. 15. *AAS* (1914), 461.

11 Leo XIII, Litt. Apost. *"Antiquissimi moris"* (3 augusti 1899)—*Acta Leonis XIII*, XIX, 128-130.

questions of ecclesiastical discipline and especially in the development and supervision of the hierarchy. Thus the apostolic vicars become the bonds of union with Rome; the Pope frequently corresponds with them, uses them as the means of conveying his orders, and is kept informed by them of the development of Christianity in the different countries.

In the fifth century we meet the first papal legates sent to civil governments. At the court of Constantinople the *apocrisiarii* are representatives of the Pope in matters both political and religious. It is worthy of note that the Apocrisiarii were permanent legates.

With the rise of new kingdoms in the West the Popes followed with keen interest the development of the religious and civil institutions of the different peoples, and there was gradually formed through *legati missi* and *legati a latere* a vast network of communication and of supervision. The widespread moral decadence of the ninth and tenth centuries was met by gradual but solid programmes of reform, which the Popes of the eleventh century made entirely their own and put into effect by means of their legates. Gregory VII constituted them into an organ of regular administration in the Church. Their importance continually increased, and in the thirteenth and fourteenth centuries we find a complete hierarchy of prelates who act with the authority of Rome, attend to the most varied tasks, and constitute the threads of that vast network of diplomatic activity which put the Pope at the centre of European life at the period of the crusades.

The great geographical discoveries of the fifteenth century made many changes in the life of the world. The idea of nationality dominated the minds of the people. We find the *apostolic nuncios* holding permanent posts with kings and princes, acting at first in the interests of the Papal States, and then in the Reformation period confining themselves more closely to the spiritual interests of the Church. On this account the office of apostolic nuncio retained its prestige at the different courts and reached its greatest splendour at the Peace of Westphalia. Then because of Illuminist ideas certain nations became estranged from the Pope and a wave of Ultramontanism attacked his prerogatives. After a while this difficulty disappeared, and gradually the ordinary course of papal representative bodies was resumed not only in the form directed towards maintaining religious and diplomatic relations, but the type associated with the ancient apostolic vicars was, in a certain sense, revived in the *apostolic delegates* who took the place of the Pope with the hierarchy and the faithful.

Through the difficult times of 1870 and during the period when the Church was being deprived of her temporal power the right of legation continued to be recognized, thus showing that the spiritual authority alone sustains it and constitutes the scope of its activity.

At the present time the apostolic nunciatures number 38; the apostolic delegations dependent on the Sacred Congregation of the Consistory 5; those dependent on the Oriental Congregation 8; and those dependent on the Sacred Congregation de Propaganda Fide 9.[12] The increase in number in recent years is undoubtedly to be attributed to the high aims of justice and peace constantly put before the world by the Holy See through its use of the right of legation.

12 Cfr. Annuario Pontificio (1945), pp. 722-731.

CHAPTER IV

THE PRINCIPLES OF THE RIGHT OF PAPAL LEGATION

Can. 265—Romano Pontifici ius est, a civili potestate independens, in quamlibet mundi partem Legatos cum vel sine ecclesiastica iurisdictione mittendi.

The above canon *directly* affirms the power of the Pope to send his representatives independently of the civil authority, and indirectly affirms the same right to be independent of the local ecclesiastical authority. By this canon therefore three classes of errors are rejected: 1) *a priori*, the Regalist Theory; 2) directly, the Gallican Theory; 3) indirectly, the Theory of Episcopal Febronianism.

Considered in its positive aspect, the canon asserts the right of papal legation; that is, the power of the Pope to send legates with or without ecclesiastical jurisdiction, namely, representatives who, in modern terminology, may be numbered among either permanent or temporary legates.

ARTICLE I: THE OPPONENTS OF THE RIGHT OF PAPAL LEGATION

I. *The Regalist Theory.* The first series of errors regarding papal legates arises from principles expounded by Marsilius of Padua in his "*Defensor Pacis.*" It is to be observed that the author speaks only indirectly of papal legates. First of all he would abolish the *plenitudo potestatis* of the Roman Pontiff in the Church, as being contrary to the will of Christ and the rights of the emperor; and consequently the legates, who are the instruments of this power, should also be abolished.[1]

II. *The Gallican Theory.* The Gallican Theory with regard to papal legates may be summarized as follows:

[1] Marsilius Patavinus, *Defensor Pacis,* dictio II, cap. 26; §§ 17-18, ed. Scholtz, pp. 511-514.

According to an axiom of the Liberties of the Gallican Church" the Pope could only send his legates at the request and with the consent of the civil authority. The legate had to promise verbally under oath and also in writing that he would confine his activity to the limits imposed by the French sovereign and would cease to use his faculties on being commanded to do so. By this promise it was intended to restrict the faculties of the legates to the application of the decrees and canons of the Ecumenical Councils and, in accordance with the liberties and privileges of the Gallican Church, of the State Universities and Academies. In order to avoid the risk of any infringement of the liberties of the Gallican Church to which the faculties were something contrary, it was required that the Pope should notify the civil authority of his intention of appointing a legate, and await its consent. On arriving at the frontier of the kingdom, the legate should send a messenger with a list of his Papal faculties for examination, so that it might be ascertained whether they contained anything contrary to the rights and liberties of the Gallican Church and the State. In practice, the list would be examined, not by the king himself, but by the Parliament of Paris. If found satisfactory, the faculties were to be noted in the acts of the government; if, on the contrary, anything opposed to the Gallican traditions and the rights of the State was detected, the people were to be notified that they were not bound to obey the legate until his faculties were modified. After this procedure, the legate could, with the consent of the civil authority, enter on the discharge of his duties.[2]

III. *Episcopal Febronianism:* One of the principal theses defended by Febronius[3] was vindication of the rights of the bishops against what he terms the abuse of papal supremacy. With this thesis is connected the theory of opposition to the establishment of permanent apostolic nunciatures inasmuch as they constitute a usurpation of the rights of the local hierarchy. This opposition was established as a system by Marc Antoine De Dominis, followed

[2] Pithou, *Liberties of the Gallican Church*, English translation of C. Vedder, pp. 4-5; De Marca-Baluze, *De Concordia Sacerdotii et Imperii*, lib. VI, cap. 58.

[3] *De Statu Ecclesiae et legitima potestate Romani Pontificis*, cap. II, § 4; cap. III, §§ 1-4.

by Edmund Richer and Eybel who declare that the power conferred by Christ on the Roman Pontiff is the same as that of the bishops, and so the apostolic nuncios should be regarded as ordinary diplomatic agents at the courts of sovereigns and as such should be deprived of all jurisdiction. Only in extraordinary circumstances would it be lawful for the Pope to send his legates to appeal for the observance of ecclesiastical discipline, but never could they exercise jurisdiction within the territories of the bishops.[4]

This doctrine was embraced and defended in open controversy by the Archbishop Electors of Cologne, Mainz and Trier together with the Archbishop of Salzburg when the nunciature was erected at Munich (1785). Apropos of this question of fact Archbishop Electors maintained the principle that the Pope could not send legates on his own initiative without usurping the rights of the bishops, and also that the bishops were the judges even of urgent cases, and so the Pope should always wait for their invitation.[5]

This brief exposition of the errors relative to the right of papal legation shows that the doctrines opposed to the Holy See are of two classes: those which refer to the internal ecclesiastical sphere, and those which refer to the relations between Church and State. The Regalist Theory alone, in opposition to the mind of the Church,[6] absolutely denies the rights of the Pope, and therefore the Code, presupposing these rights and stating them categorically, excludes this theory *a priori*. It therefore remains to analyse the right of legation firstly, with reference to the civil authority and secondly, with reference to the rights of the local hierarchy.

Article III: The Right of Papal Legation and the Civil Authority

The principle laid down by the Code is that the Pope is free and independent in sending his legates to every part of the world. Particular mention of this liberty and independence is made with reference to the State. The words of canon 265 constitute a general

[4] Cf. Pius VI, Responsio ad Metropolitanos, cap. VIII, n. 18-22.

[5] Cf. Pius VI, *Op. cit.*, cap. VIII, nn. 1-11.

[6] Denzinger-Bannwart, *Enchiridion*, nn. 495-500.

statement: no distinction is made between the different classes of papal legates, nor between the different duties entrusted to them, whether diplomatic or otherwise. A proper exposition of the theological principle stated in the above canon seems, however, to demand this distinction, and here the question is considered from the point of view of the different kinds of missions performed by the legates. The Pope, as Supreme Head of the Church, can send his legates on a purely religious mission, and then they are sent as his representatives to the hierarchy and faithful. Considered as a sovereign he can, according to the Ius Gentium, entrust to the same legates particular duties of a so-called diplomatic nature. In this latter case the legates are his representatives with the civil authority. But the religious mission sometimes assumes such solemn forms that it cannot be ignored by the State, and, furthermore, the diplomatic mission is nowadays ordinarily linked with a religious mission. While the civil authority, in some cases at least, cannot simply ignore one mission while acknowledging the other, the two different aspects of the work performed by the legates can be considered separately, each in its relations to the principles governing it, which are founded, in the first case, on the constitutional law of the Church, and in the second, on both the constitutional law of the Church and the Ius Gentium.

A. Papal Legates on Religious Mission

By a religious mission of the legates is meant any office not connected with the superior civil authority, or to put it in terms more positive and precise, one that deals rather with matters which directly refer to the internal administration of the Church. From this viewpoint the right of papal legation should be regarded as absolute and completely independent.

a) *The Church and State are two distinct societies.* The civil society constitutes the temporal, the ecclesiastical constitutes the spiritual order. The distinction and the independence of the two societies, due to their different ends, are responsible for the distinction and independence of the powers which govern them. When therefore, the Pope sends his representative on a religious mission, he does not exceed the limits of his powers, and no motive can justify a limitation of his rights on the part of the State. If ecclesiastical authority were to depend on the good-will of the civil authority, not only would the distinction between spiritual and temporal be destroyed, but the whole scale of values would be upset and the order of precedence inverted. Both societies remain distinct in their proper spheres: so the consent of the civil power is not required for the free use of the right of papal legation.

b) *The Holy See is a sovereign power.* To contest the right of a sovereign to be represented abroad is equivalent to a denial of his sovereignty, since the sovereign who, by definition, is independent, is thereby made subject to the will of another. It is furthermore worth while noting that here the expression "representation abroad" is not strictly speaking, juridically correct, as applied to the Church. In fact, no state is outside the Church: to see the truth of this it is sufficient to remember that wherever it is considered a foreign power it is inevitably persecuted and banned. The sphere of action of the legates is as wide as that of the Church itself. Since the Pope has power to rule the Church and the Church is a universal society, that is, one by its very nature destined to extend to the whole world, it follows that Papal legates are never in foreign territory. By means of them the Holy See carries out its mission on earth; and since the mission of the Church is not subject to any temporal power, the Holy See is independent in the exercise of the right of legation.

c) *Ius liberae communicationis.* Granted the distinction between the spiritual and temporal order, and the universal spiritual sovereignty of the Holy See, it follows that it is in possession of the *"ius liberae communicationis.*

The Pope has the right and the duty to extend the benefits of his spiritual mission to all the faithful and no human authority can lawfully prevent him from doing this. The *"ius liberae communicationis"* therefore means that he can correspond freely with the bishops and the faithful and that they can freely correspond with him. The right of free communication is exercised in two ways: by letter and personally. Both of these were at times contested on unjust grounds. It was said that the heads of states had the right and duty to control all the relations of their subjects with foreign powers, even to the extent of prohibiting all such relations, should the defense of the State require it. This theory was to be applied to the Pope as well as to other sovereigns and so his mandates could not be carried out before the *Royal Placet* was given. Furthermore, according to Van Espen,[7] even dogmatic bulls would have no value in the state before the examination and approval of the sovereign. The other way of using the *"ius liberae communicationis,"* if not entirely denied in theory, was in practice restricted by those who favoured the Gallican Theory, according to which the Pope could send his legates only with the consent of the civil power. They placed this restriction even when the legates were on purely religious business, as generally happened in the case of the *legati a latere*. They said that in order to defend the State the sovereign had the right to control or restrict the faculties of the legate.[8]

On the contrary, the Church maintains that the *"ius liberae communicationis"* is an attribute inherent in the nature of the Church itself as a juridically perfect society. Possessing all the means required for its end, it should be able to use them freely according to its needs, of which the Church alone is competent to judge. Against the partisans of the Royal Placet it is certain that the acts of the Pope have full value independently of any civil authority.[9]

Although the State has the right to watch and control its citizens in order to prevent conspiracies, nevertheless the Church which by reason of its purpose is superior to the State should not be molested on this account. In fact the Holy See reserves the *"ius liberae communicationis"* as an inalienable right both as regards the correspondence of the faithful with their immediate superiors, and as regards the correspondence of the faithful, the clergy and the hierarchy with the Pope. Explicit and solemn mention is made of this reservation in

[7] Van-Espen, *Ius Ecclesiasticum Universum,* IV, 132-140.

[8] Dupuy, *Commentaire sur le traite des libertes de l'Eglise Gallicane de P. Pithou,* I, 41-45.

[9] Cf. Matt. XVI, 19; XVIII, 18; Jn. XX, 21-23; Conc. Vaticanum. Sess. IV, cap. III—Denzinger-Bannwart, *Enchiridion,* n. 1829; Pius IX; Alloc. *"Luctuosis"* (12 March 1877) — Densinger-Bannwart. *Op. cit.,* n. 1847.

the concordats,[10] in which, on the one hand, the use of the Royal Placet is excluded and, on the other, the lawfulness of the *"ius liberae communicationis"* is recognized. Now, the right of papal legation is nothing more than an extension of the *"ius liberae communicationis"* so that the papal legates have the right to act freely without any interference from the State.

Before 1870, when the Papal States enjoyed some political power, and it was possible that the Pope would actually favour a particular belligerent, some reservation in the free exercise of the right of legation in time of war, might, perhaps, have been expected and granted, by way of exception,[11] but since the establishment of the Vatican City the Holy See has declared that in the event of political rivalries between nations it will remain strictly aloof, reserving to itself only a mission of peace to be exercised by the use of its spiritual and moral authority.[12] Therefore no exception is admitted, whether in times of peace or war, and so the right of free communication remains intact in every case. Since this point is connected with the position of the Holy See with regard to Italy more than to any other nation, in the Lateran Treaty special provision is made to ensure the right of free communication by the following words: "It is agreed that Italy pledges herself to allow always and in every case free correspondence between all States, even belligerents, and the Holy See, and viceversa, and to permit the free access of the bishops of the whole world to the Apostolic See." [13]

d) *Historical confirmation.* Having seen the historical development of the law of papal legation it is scarcely necessary to elaborate further the argument from tradition in favour of the liberty and independence of the Popes in sending their legates to all parts of the world.

The present-day legislation is already found ratified in the Decretals by the following words:

[10] Concordata cum Polonia, art. II; cum Lithuania, art. II; cum Italia, art. 2; cum Romania, Art. IV; VIII; cum Austria, art. 1 § 4; cum Germania, art. 4.

[11] Cf. Cavagnis, *Institutiones Iuris Publici Ecclesiastici* III, 271-272.

[12] Tractatus Lateranensis, art. 24.

[13] Tractatus Lateranensis, art. 12.

> "Super gentes et regna Romanus Pontifex a Domino constitutus, cum personaliter singulas regiones circuire non possit, nec circa gregem sibi creditum curam pastoralis sollicitudinis exercere: necesse habet interdum ex debito impositae servitutis, suos ad diversas mundi partes (prout necessitates emerserint) destinare legatos, qui vice ipsius supplendo errata corrigant, aspera in plana convertant, et commissis sibi populis salutis incrementa ministrent. Verumtamen aliqui huiusmodi officium et potestatem ipsius Romani Pontificis, quam non ab homine, sed a Deo recepit, sub suo arbitrio redigere molientes, legatos ipsos, nisi ab eis petiti fuerint, vel de beneplacito eorum transmissi, sibi terras subiectas (dicentes, hoc eis de consuetudine competere) ingredi non permittunt. Nos, huiusmodi consuetudinem non tam irrationabilem, quam nonnunquam animarum saluti contrariam detrahentemque Apostolicae potestati, auctoritate Apostolica penitus reprobantes, legatos ipsos ab omnibus, cuiuscumque praeeminentiae, conditionis aut status fuerint, debere admitti decrevimus, nec eos praetextu cuiusvis consuetudinis impediri posse a quoquam, Christiano nomine gloriante, quominus regna, provincias, et terras quaslibet, ad quae ipsos destinari contigerit, ingrediantur libere, ac commissae sibi legationis officium exerceant in eisdem." [14]

For the reasons mentioned in the Decretal, any custom contrary to the free exercise of the right of Papal legation must be considered as rejected by the Code, [15] and this irrespective of the religion of the sovereign, whether Catholic or non-Catholic.[16] For it is a right arising from the Divine mandate giving the Pope absolute authority in all religious questions.

The arguments set out above retain all their force for the case of papal diplomatic representatives such as nuncios and internuncios, as regards their spiritual faculties. Their mission in canon law is twofold and, while in their diplomatic capacity they must conform to the rules and customs prevailing in international law, in all that concerns the exercise of their spirtiual faculties which are directed

[14] C. un, *de consuetudine,* I, 1, in Extravag. com.

[15] Can. 27, § 1.

[16] Blat, *De personis,* p. 285.

solely towards the benefit of the Church, they are bound exclusively to the directions of the Pope and the prescriptions of canon law.

B. Papal Legates on Diplomatic Mission

I. THE BASIS OF THE DIPLOMATIC MISSION

The Holy See claims recognition as a juridical personality in the international community, basing this claim both on tradition and on the very nature of its mission in the world. A logical consequence of this status is the exercise of the right of diplomatic legation, in as much as this is essential for participation in international affairs.

It might be objected that politics are beyond the ends of the Church which are completely spiritual. However, international law extends beyond questions of a territorial nature or hegemonic questions between nations, or the equilibrium of the different powers for the preservation of peace or the development of economic and industrial relations. International law is concerned with all human activity and so questions of the intellectual order like cultural conferences, social questions, labour problems, and also a large number of religious questions, so far from being excluded, are positively desired.[17] Questions dealt with in the Ius Gentium extend even to matters of doctrine, and in this case the Church not only has the right to speak, but is alone competent to do so. In this way we determine the extent of the Church's power of teaching according to the clear statement of Pius X: "We understand indeed that it may sound strange to some people to say that we must interest ourselves in political things also. But, any just judge of things sees that the Pontiff can never separate the question of education from the magisterium of faith and morals. Furthermore, the Pope, since he is the supreme Head of a perfect society, the Church made up of men and constituted among men, must certainly desire to carry on relations with the rulers of nations and governors of peoples, if he wishes

[17] Cf. Hobza, "Questions de droit international concernant les religions," *Recueil des cours,* V (1924 IV), 368-423; Del Giudice, *Corso di diritto ecclesiastico,* I, 210.

to see to the security and liberty of Catholics in every land and in every part of the world."[18]

This fundamental principle has been developed by Pius XII: "If it is true that the Church does not wish to meddle in disputes concerning the timeliness, usefulness or earthly efficacy of the different temporal forms, which institutions or merely political activities may assume, it is not less true that the Church neither can nor will renounce being the light and the guide of consciences in all those questions of principles, in which men, their programmes, or their efforts, may run the risk of forgetting or denying the eternal fundamentals of Divine Law."[19] A means of attaining the aims here mentioned is the exercise of the right of active and passive legation. By legations the Holy See can take part in the social life of peoples and inculcate the respect due to the principles of faith and morals. In this way it furthers its own work, and not only maintains its traditional relations with States, but strengthens them with the solemn pledges of Concordats.[20] By means of these bi-lateral pacts the law of papal legation is formally inserted in Ius Gentium. Since, however, no international law strictly imposes the right of active and passive legation, it may be asked whether the Papal practice of sending diplomatic agents is founded simply on the concessions of certain States, or on international courtesy. Evidently the foundation of the right of papal legation is something deeper than custom. Since this right is based on the primacy of the Roman Pontiff it is clear that it is intimately bound up with the constitution of the Church. In the case of a Catholic country the Holy See justly demands this form of recognition, so that not to receive or worse still, to expel Papal

18 "Utique intelligimus nonnullis offensioni fore, quod dicimus curare nos etiam rem politicam oportere. Verum quisque aequus rerum iudex videt Pontificem a magisterio quod gerit, fidei morumque nequaquam posse politicorum genus disiungere. Praeterea caput quum sit rectorque summus perfectae societatis, quae est Ecclesia, ex hominibus coalescentis, inter homines constitutae, profecto velle debet cum principibus civitatum et gubernationibus rei publicae mutua sibi officia intercedere, si catholicorum in omni ora et parte terrarum velit et securitati et libertati esse consultum." Alloc. Concist. *"Primum vos"* (9 novembris 1903)—*Acta Pii X*, I, 57.

20 Cf. *supra*, pp. 33; 79181.

legates involves not only a rupture of friendly relations, but also a denial of the rights of the Church, a society that cannot be ignored. For this reason the Popes have always protested whenever governments have attempted to limit the exercise of the functions of even diplomatic legates, or on some pretext have expelled them from their territories. The nature of the permanent diplomatic legate is never separated from that of the representative sent to the hierarchy and the faithful, and so one cannot be violated without injuring the other.[21] In countries where a resident nuncio is traditional, the rupture of diplomatic relations is equivalent to depriving Catholics of the benefit of one of those ecclesiastical offices which renders easier and more secure the development of the Christian life. It very rarely happens that the Holy See sends, or rather can, without insurmountable obstacles, send a permanent representative for religious matters where a nuncio has formerly resided. An example of this happy reconquest after centuries of waiting occurred recently in the establishment of the Apostolic Delegation of England.[22]

II. *Ambassadors, Apostolic Nuncios and Internuncios.* Given the twofold representative character of the diplomatic agents of the Holy See, the fundamental question here arises what is the difference between the functions of an ambassador and those of an apostolic nuncio or internuncio. It is the business of the ambassador to maintain good relations between two nations, but he exercises no jurisdiction over the citizens of the country in which he lives. He always remains the representative of a foreign power. The apostolic nuncio, or internuncio, on the other hand, since he represents the Pope, can logically be said to enjoy faculties which are a participation of the supreme papal power. "They are true representatives of the Pope from whom they derive their authority to be exercised in the manner and form that he prescribes . . . they have a mission which is not purely diplomatic but authoritative with regard to the faithful and

[21] Leo XIII, Alloc. *"Summi Pontificatus"* (20 augusti 1880)—*Fontes,* n. 581.

[22] Pius XI, Litt. Ap. *"Paterna caritas"* (21 novembris 1938)—*AAS,* XXXI (1939), 100.

and to religious matters." [23] In other words, they exercise jurisdiction over the citizens of the state where they reside.

When the erection of permanent representative bodies was under consideration, the Holy See considered the advisability of sending two representatives: one with purely religious, the other with purely diplomatic duties. The experiment was tried in Sweden but it was not a success and so the idea was definitely abandoned.[24] In the seventeenth century M. Antoine De Dominis tried to put into effect his idea of nunciatures of a nature purely diplomatic, so that apostolic nuncios should be regarded as mere diplomatic agents without any jursidiction in ecclesiastical affairs.[25] During the last century the Spanish government put forward the same claim.

The distinction between ecclesiastical and political affairs is so clear that it is maintained by the Holy See not only with in regard to theory and practice in general, but also in regard to its representatives. There are in fact papal representatives without a diplomatic character resident in certain countries and this can be easily understood in ecclesiastical circles. It is fitting, however, that permanent legates should represent the person of the Pope in its entirety—as sovereign in both the spiritual and temporal order. The partisans of the system put forward by De Dominis intended, so to speak, to laicize the apostolic nunciatures with the aim of removing the supposed threats to the rights of the episcopate. But the existence of permanent papal representatives of a purely diplomatic nature character (when by this is understood a purely *political* character) constitutes a meaningless recognition for the Church, if not a contradiction in terms and an implicit negation of the spritual sovereignty of the Holy See. Even when the temporal power of the Holy See had some importance in political life, Pius VII replied to the Spanish government that "the temporal sovereignty of the Pope is purely secondary compared with his Supreme Apostolate." [26]

23 Letter of Card. Jacobini to the Nuncio of Madrid (15 April 1885)—*ASS,* XVII (1885), 561.

24 Cf. Biaudet, *Les Nonciatures Apostoliques permanentes jusqu' en* 1648, p. 10, note 2.

25 Cf. Pius VI, Responsio ad Metropolitanos, cap. VIII, n. 20.

26 Quoted by Werns, *Ius Decretalium,* II, n. 684, note 18.

The absurdity of having papal representatives of a purely political nature is even more evident since the constitution of the small Vatican City. The political question in which the nuncios can usefully intervene have no reference to temporal ambitions but are connected either with the teaching power of the Church (from whose ambit are not excluded the moral principles which regulate public life in the pursuit of the welfare of society), or with the defence of the rights of the Church. Just as the temporal power is accessory to the spiritual sovereignty and a guarantee of its independence, so the representation of the Vatican City is merely secondary in comparison with the representation of the Pope as Supreme Head of the Catholic Church.

On account of their duties the papal nuncios and internuncios occupy a singular position in international law, both with reference to the governments to which they are accredited and in comparison with all other diplomatic agents. The nuncios and internuncios have official relations with governments and in this respect are equivalent to ambassadors, but at the same time they essentially differ from these on account of the spiritual jurisdiction they exercise over citizens of the state in so far as these are Catholics and subject to the Church.[27]

II. *Agreement.* Even when the exchange of diplomatic agents is regulated or imposed by pacts, a sovereign can always in accordance with international law make reservations with regard to the person of the agent on account e.g. of his character or previous record. In order to avoid unpleasant complications, it is customary before proceeding to the exchange of diplomatic agents to conduct a confidential correspondence with the object of ascertaining whether a particular individual is "*persona grata*" to the sovereign or not.[28] This is a natural measure of prudence on the part of each sovereign and is all the more justified nowadays since diplomatic agents are not sent to deal with a particular matter only, but ordinarily reside for a period of time, more or less prolonged and their office is in itself permanent. This practice does not imply a negation of international rights; it may even be said to assist good relations in so

[27] Cf. Pinchetti-Sammarchi, *Guida Diplomatica Ecclesiastica,* I, 300-301.

[28] Cf. Satow, *A Guide to Diplomatic Practice,* I, 203-215.

far as it seeks to avoid suspicions and misunderstanding which are particularly harmful in this sphere.

Corollary: *The right of passive legation.* The canon which we have just explained asserts the power of the Pope to send his legates to represent him with the hierarchy, the faithful and the civil authority. In this consists the right of active legation. Corresponding to the exercise of active legation is the right of passive legation.

International law does not strictly impose the obligation of using the right of active and passive legation, but the most ancient customs demand the protection of legates, and especially do not allow any sovereign to prevent another from utilizing their services. Since authorities on legal matters are not in agreement as to whether diplomatic agents are entitled to the privileges of protection and immunity even outside the state to which they are accredited,[29] special provision is made in the Lateran Treaty for diplomatic representatives sent to the Holy See. They all live in Italian territory; and even when a certain government has no diplomatic relations with Italy, its diplomatic agents to the Holy See continue to enjoy all the privileges granted by international law. Even in time of war between Italy and a country having diplomatic relations with the Holy See, the diplomatic representatives to the Vatican may continue to reside in Italian territory. The articles of the Lateran Treaty state a general stipulation, and an exception, if any, should be expressly mentioned.[30] In strict international law all this is based on the neutrality of the Vatican City, but another and more fundamental reason can probably be added. For the same reason that the diplomatic representatives of the Holy See can, juridically speaking, be only in part compared with other diplomatic agents, the representatives sent by Governments to the Holy See have not a merely political character: the relations between the ecclesiastical and civil societies are concerned with a higher order, i.e., the spiritual which must be safeguarded in war time also.

[29] Cf. Satow, *A Guide to Diplomatic Practice,* I, 329-331; Pasquazi, *Ius Internationale Publicum,* p. 139-140.

[30] Cf. *Lateran Treaty,* arts. 12 and 19.

Article III: The Right of Papal Legation and Episcopal Authority

The right of papal legation is as free and independent with reference to episcopal authority as it is with regard to the civil authority. It has, however, been erroneously stated by some that the Pope by sending legates having the power of ecclesiastical jurisdiction usurps the rights of the bishops to whom is entrusted the entire government of their dioceses. It has also been asserted that only in exceptional circumstances could the Pope send his representatives, and even then not with stable power of jurisdiction, but only as inspectors and *amici curiae*. These ideas are evidently derived from a false conception of the primacy of the Roman Pontiff. It would be well, therefore, to recall briefly here the theological and juridical principles regarding the primacy in order to deduce the logical consequence of the legitimacy of the right of papal legation, which, in reality, neither usurps the rights of the bishops nor prejudices their jurisdiction.

A. Papal Primacy and the Right of Legation

As Vicar of Jesus Christ the Pope enjoys full and supreme authority not only regarding truths of faith and morals but in everything pertaining to the discipline and government of the Church. And there is not merely question of a primacy of honour or of a certain power of supervision, but of a true power of orders and jurisdiction, that is, the primacy of the power of ruling, teaching and governing the faithful according to the will of Christ and the special ends of the Church.

In the Church, which is a perfect religious society, there is a twofold power, that is, the *potestas ordinis,* and the *potestas iurisdictionis.* The *potestas ordinis* is directed towards the sanctification of souls by means of acts of worship; the *potestas iurisdictionis* is directed towards the government of the faithful by means of authoritative legislation. The *potestas ordinis* is conferred by means of an act of divine institution, and all who submit themselves to such an act equally participate in this power. The *potestas iurisdictionis* denotes the public power given to a lawful ecclesiastical superior either directly by God, or by the Church by means of canonical mission, and directed towards the government of the faithful in their pursuit of everlasting life. The *potestas iurisdictionis* coming directly from God is, according to the more common opinion, possessed only by the Roman Pontiff who acquires it by accepting his legitimate election.[1] Every other power of jurisdiction in the Church depends on the act of a lawful superior, and can vary in different persons and even in the same person according to the will of the superior.[2]

In Canon Law, power of jurisdiction means not only a restricted power according to the etymological sense of the word (*iurisdictio, ius dicere*—judicial power), but a public faculty in the comprehensive sense of legislative, judicial and executive power, aimed at the good government of the faithful, and so directed towards all the acts necessary for the attaining of eternal life.[3]

The twofold power bestowed on the Church by its Divine Founder is possessed in all its fulness by the Pope. The *potestas ordinis* of the Pope is of the highest grade, since by episcopal consecration he receives the fulness of the priesthood. His *potestas ordinis* is substantially the same as that of the other bishops, so that, considered from the point of view of validity, this power may be regarded as equal in Pope and Bishops. The lawful use of the *potestas ordinis,* however, depends on the *potestas iurisdictionis,* which is supreme and universal only in the Pope, so that he can regulate, qualify, and even limit the use of the *potestas ordinis* in the bishops.

The *potestas iurisdictionis* resulting from the primacy is:

a) *Supreme,* inasmuch as no authority superior to that of the Pope exists in the Church, nor is there any authority not subject to him. It follows that there is no appeal from his decisions and that all can appeal to him.

b) *Perfect,* so that nothing required for the plenitude of Ecclesiastical power is wanting.

c) *Universal,* so that it extends to all the faithful and the bishops,

[1] Can. 109; 219; *Conc. Trident.*, Sess. XXIV, *de ref.*, c. 1; Pius VI, Const. "*Super soliditate*" (28 nov. 1786)—*Fontes,* n. 473; Leo XIII, Enc. "*Satis Cognitum*" (29 jun. 1896)—*Fontes,* n. 630.

[2] Cf. Ottaviani, *Institutiones Iuris Publici Ecclesiastici,* I, 212-222.

[3] Wernz, Ius Decretalium, II, n. 3, note 19; Maroto, *Institutiones Iuris Canonici,* I, 660-661; Kearney, *The Principles of Delegation,* pp. 44-46.

even when convened in an Ecumenical Council, and to everything relating to questions of faith, morals and ecclesiastical discipline.

d) *Episcopal,* and not of mere supervision, but mainly directed towards teaching, ruling and governing the faithful; it is a legislative, judicial and coercive power.

e) *Ordinary.* It is not received by delegation, but is derived from the Pope's office as Supreme Head of the Church, and can be exercised over all the faithful, not only in extraordinary cases or when inferior ecclesiastical superiors fail in their duty, but in all times and places independently of special circumstances. It is, however, often fitting that such circumstances should be taken into consideration.

f) *Immediate,* so that the Pope can exercise his authority over all the faithful and over all the Churches not only through subordinate authorities e.g. the bishops, but directly, either personally or through his legates.

g) *Independent* of any human authority, civil or ecclesiastical, whether this be the authority of bishops, cardinals or even the Ecumenical Council.[4]

From all this it appears that the authority of the Pope is not subject to any human limitation; it is however limited by divine law. The primacy of the Roman Pontiff is directed towards the good of the universal Church, and to it may be applied the words of St. Paul regarding his own authority: that it was conferred on him for the faithful, *in aedificationem et non in destructionem;*[5] besides, the spirit of gentleness and moderation should reign in the Church.[6] Another limitation on the sovereignty o fthe Pope arises from the rights of the episcopate, which also has been placed by the Holy Ghost or rule the Church of God.[7] It is true that the bishops can act only with dependence on the Supreme Pastor, [8] but the Pope is bound not to limit their power more than the welfare of the Church requires. And it is also only fitting that the Supreme Legislator in the Church should not without a proportionate and just cause,

[4] Cf. Maroto, *Institutiones Iuris Canonici,* II, 158-160.

[5] II Cor. X, 8; XIII, 10.

[6] Matt. XXII, 8-11.

[7] Acts, IX, 28.

[8] Can. 329, § 1.

change the existing laws and sacred canons, or customs legitimately introduced and privileges previously granted; and the rules of a wise administration require the exercise of prudent consideration and sometimes on account of special circumstances even a temporary suspension of the exercise of his supreme power.[9]

The supreme power of the Pope therefore extends to all the faithful, that is, to all those who, united by the ties of a common faith, profess themselves followers of Jesus Christ and members of the society founded by Him, viz, the Holy Catholic Church. By the mere act of profession of faith, every member of this society submits himself to the supreme power of the Pope, so that it will never be true to say that any of the faithful, no matter to what class he may belong, can be called a member of the Church and still regard himself as exempt from the jurisdiction of its Supreme Head. Accordingly, the Roman Pontiff is not simply the direct and immediate Pastor of a part of the Church, such as the diocese of Rome, but the direct and immediate Pastor of the whole Church.[10] The power in question is comprehensive and is, as St. Bernard calls it, a singular privilege: *"Plenitudo siquidem potestatis super universas orbis ecclesias singulari praerogativa Apostolicae Sedi donata est."* [11]

The primacy puts the Pope in the position of Ruler of the universal Church. The authority of a Supreme Head is placed over the faithful and the bishops to preserve the unity of the faith against schisms and human inconstancy. The whole edifice of the Church rests on the rock of Peter, and the faithful share in the security and firmness of this foundation. The Pope, who, assisted by the divine Truth, is an infallible guide, proposes with authority what should be believed and what should be done in order to possess eternal life.[12]

By virtue of his universal jurisdiction the Pope is supreme judge in all matters connected with faith, morals and the disciplinary government of the Church, and in particular to him are reserved

9 Maroto, *Op. cit.*, II, 177-178.

10 Conc. Vaticanum, Sess. IV, cap. 3 — Denzinger-Bannwart, *Enchiridion*, nn. 1826-1831.

11 *Epist.* 131 — *MPL, CLXXXII*, 286.

12 Matt. XVI, 18; Lc. XXII, 32; Jn. XXI, 15-17.

the *causae majores* or the ecclesiastical affairs of major importance.[13] Of these matters some by their very nature pertain to the supreme ecclesiastical authority and are called *causae maiores per se vel essentialiter;* others per se would pertain to the hierarchy, but since the Pope can, and actually does, reserve them to himself, they become *causae maiores* by positive law and are called *causae maiores per accidens vel accidentaliter.*[14] As Chelodi observes,[15] a complete enumeration of the *causae maiores* is well nigh impossible since from the moment that the Pope reserves any such matter to himself it becomes *ipso facto* a *causa maior,* and on the other hand it can be said that a *causa maior* becomes *minor* when the Pope delegates it to an inferior authority. However, following the example of the code we may mention among the *causae essentialiter maiores*: 1) all those which require infallibility, like dogmatic definitions (can 1313, § 2), or those matters which are connected with a dogmatic fact, like the canonization of saints (can. 2137, § 3; 2140); 2) all those matters which, though they do not require infallibility, nevertheless demand the exercise of the supreme authority, since they refer to the government of the universal Church, or to the relations between particular churches and the supreme authority, or to the relations between these particular churches themselves (can. 1557, § 2, 2°); 3) the care of the missions throughout the world (can. 1350, § 2); 4) the convocation of Ecumenical Councils (can. 222); 5) the promulgation of laws for the whole Church (can. 227); 6) the erection of dioceses and ecclesiastical provinces, the delimitation of their territorial boundaries, their division, union and suppression (can. 215, § 1): 7) the election and translation of bishops (can. 329, § 2; 332, § 1; 350, § 1; 430, § 1), of apostolic administrators (can. 312), and of vicars and prefects apostolic (can. 293, § 1).

Among the *causae accidentaliter maiores* the following may be enumerated: 1) the beatification of servants of God (can. 1999, § 1); 2) the arrangement and publication of liturgical books (can. 1257); 3) the dispensation from matrimonial impediments iuris ecclesiastici (can. 1040); 4) the erection, suppression and provision of some minor

[13] Can. 220.

[14] Cavagnis, *Institutiones Iuris Publici Eccl.,* II, 21.

[15] Ius de Personis, p. 239.

benefices (can. 394, § 2; 1422; 1435); 5) judgment in the cases of certain dignitaries of Church or State (can. 1557); 6) absolution from certain censures (can. 2245): i.e. those incurred for a) profanation of the Sacred Species (can. 2320), b) ill-treatment of the person of the Pope (can. 2343, § 1), c) absolution or pretended absolution of an accomplice *in peccato turpi* (can. 2367, § 1), d) direct violation of the seal of confession (can. 2369, § 1) and e) violation of the canonical laws regarding the papal election (can. 2330), (all these being reserved *specialissimo modo*); and finally the absolution of censures incurred: a) for sins of apostasy, heresy and schism (can. 2314); b) for publication of the works of apostates, heretics and schismatics (can. 2318 § 1); c) for simulation of the celebration of Mass or of hearing confessions (can. 2322, § 1); d) for those who appeal from the judgment of the Pope to a Council (can. 2332), or appeal to the secular power to prevent the promulgation and execution of laws of the Holy See (can. 2333; 2334), e) for those who contravene the *privilegium* fori (can. 2341), or inflict grave personal violence on ecclesiastical dignitaries (can. 2343, §§ 2-3), f) for the usurpers of ecclesiastical goods (can. 2345) and g) for those who falsify papal documents (can. 2360).[16]

Others prefer to consider the affairs reserved to the Pope from the point of view of their subject-matter, and so divide them generally into *doctrinal* (e.g., can. 247, § 1, 1323, § 2; 1350, § 2; 1376; 1395, § 1; 1999), *legislative* (can. 3; 80), *administrative* (can. 215; 329; 492; 1145; 1244; 1499); *judicial* (can. 1557; 1962) and *penal* (can. 2245, §§ 2-3), *causae maiores*.[17]

Thus we find in the Roman Pontiff the prerogatives of High Priest, Supreme Doctor, Legislator, Judge, Governor and Administrator of the Universal Church.[18] This is tantamount to saying that the Pope can directly exercise power of orders and power of jurisdiction over the whole Church. If he can do this directly, he can also do it by means of persons to whom he entrusts part of his power;

[16] Cf. Cavagnis, *Op. cit.*, II, 19-22; Maroto, *Op. cit.*, II, 179-180; Wernz-Vidal, *Ius Canonicum*, II, 413-420.

[17] Vermeersch, *Epitome*, I, 222.

[18] Maroto, *Institutiones Iuris Canonici*, II, 180-183.

and so the right of legation is nothing more than a corollary resulting from the primacy.

That this right has been exercised from the earliest times we have already seen in the historical section of this work. We shall confine ourselves here, therefore, to a few explicit assertions of their claim at various times by the Pontiffs themselves.

Innocent I, on the 17 January 412, wrote to Rufus, Bishop of Thessalonica: "Divinitus haec procurrens gratia, ita longis intervallis disterminatis a me Ecclesiis discat consulendum . . . Arripe itque, dilectissime Frater, Nostra vice per supra-scriptas (in Illyrico) Ecclesias, salvo earum primatu, curam, et inter Primates primus." [19] Boniface I, on the 19 September 419, wrote to Rufus, Bishop of Thessalonica: "Non potest tibi esse non proximus qui pastor Dominicarum ovium est perpetuus constitutus, seu aliquam ubivis positam ecclesiam non curare, in quo universalis Ecclesiae positum legimus fundamentum . . . vice Sedis Apostolicae a nobis creditas (ecclesias) recognosces." [20]

Leo the Great (445-446) in a letter to Anastasius, Bishop of Thessalonica wrote: ". . . sicut predecessores mei predecessoribus tuis vices mei moderaminis delegavi, ut curam quam universis ecclesiis principaliter ex divina institutione debemus, imitator nostrae mansuetudinis adiuvares et longinquis a nobis provinciis praesentiam quodammodo nostrae visitationis impenderes, siquidem continenti opportunoque prospectu promptum tibi esset agnoscere, quid in quibusque rebus vel tuo studio componeres vel nostro iudicio reservares." [21]

St. Gregory the Great informed the *"Rector patrimonii Siciliae"* (at the end of the sixth century): "Ubi nos praesentes esse non possumus nostra per eum cui praecipimus repraesentetur auctoritas." [22]

Gregory VII writing to the Bishop of Corsica (A.D. 1077) said: "Reverentiam his (i.e. legatis) exhiberi oportet quos Sancta et Apostolicae Sedes in partes suae sollicitudinis assumendos quibusque vicem Romani Pontificis committendam esse praevidet." [23]

[19] Innocentius I, *Epist.* 13—*MPL,* XX, 515.
[20] Bonifacius I, *Epist.* 5—*MPL,* XX, 761.
[21] Leo Magnus, *Epist.* 14—*MPL,* LIV, 668.
[22] Gregorius Magnus, *Epistolae,* I, 1—*MPL,* LXXVII, 442.
[23] Caspar, *Register Gregorii VII, Epistolae selectae,* V, 2.

Gregory VII writing to Manasses, Archbishop of Rheims, after proving from Church history that the Popes have power to send legates, adds: "Miramus nimium prudentiam vestram eo usque perductam ut precamini benevolentiam nostram iura Sedis Apostolicae debere imminuere, idque nobis in solius vestri negotiis non debere licere quod in negotiis omnium predecessores nostri sine omni contradictione et licitum et legitimum tenuerunt." [24]

Alexander II in a letter to the Archbishops of Gaul (A.D. 1063) wrote: "Ex auctoritate Sedis Apostolicae cui nos indignos clementia divina praefecit, totius universalis Ecclesiae regendus ac disponendis nobis status incumbit. Quoniam igitur pluribus ecclesiarum negotiis occupati ad vos ipsi venire non possumus, talem vobis virum destinare curavimus . . . Huic itaque vicem nostram pleno iure commisimus, ut quidquid in illis partibus Deo auxiliante statuerit ita ratum teneatur ac firmum, ac si speciali nostri examinis fuerit sententia promulgatum." [25]

Pius VI in his *"Responsio"* to the Archbishops of Mainz, Cologne, Trier and Salzburg (A.D. 1789) wrote: "Agitur de graviori atque insigniori iure Primatus in Petro eiusque Successoribus a Christo instituti; quo praeditus Romanus Pontifex, dum Agnorum et Ovium Sibi concreditarum curam gerit universam, suo fungitur Apostolico munere per Ecclesiasticos Viros, sibi stabiles, sive ad tempus, veluti magis expedire censuerit, delegatos in iis dissitis locis, ubi Ipse interesse non potest, praecipiens Eisdem, ut ibi Suas vices obeant, eamque iurisdictionem exerceant, quam Ipse per Se, si adesset, exerceret.

Ius est Romano Pontifici habendi aliquos in dissitis praesertim locis, qui Sui absentis Personam repraesentent, qui iurisdictionem Suam, atque auctoritatem stabili Delegatione collatam exerceant; qui denique Suas vices obeant, idque ex intima vi ac natura Primatus, ex iuribus dotibusque cum Primatu ipso coniunctis, ex constanti Ecclesiae disciplina a primis usque saeculis deducta." [26]

Leo XIII in an Encyclical Letter to the Hierarchy of the United States of America (January 6, 1895) writes: "Romani Pontifices ob hanc causam quod rei christianae administrandae divinitus tenent

[24] Caspar, *Register Gregorii VII, Epistolae selectae,* VI, 2.

[25] Alexander II, *Epist. ad Archiep. Galliae*—Mansi, XIX, 958.

[26] Pius VI, *Responsio ad Metropolitanos,* cap. VIII, n. 1 et n. 24.

principatum suos peregre legatos ad gentes populosque christianos mittere vel ab ultima antiquitate consueverunt. Id autem non extrinsecus quaesitum, sed nativo iure suo." [27]

The right of papal legation is therefore legitimate because of the source from which it arises and the relations which must necessarily exist between the supreme authority of the Sovereign Pontiff and the authority of the Bishops, his subordinates.

Besides, since the primacy confers on the Pope a power which is exercised directly over the universal Church, it follows that it can be exercised not only in exceptional circumstances, but as an ordinary means of warding off errors and abuses and of safeguarding the faith and the growth of the Christian life. If the Pope could intervene only to correct and punish, his duties as teacher, which require direct and positive action, would not be effectually fulfilled.

B. The jurisdiction of Ordinaries and the jurisdiction of Apostolic Legates

Can. 269, § 1. Legati Ordinariis locorum liberum suae iurisdictionis exercitium relinquant.

Together with the supreme and universal power of jurisdiction which belongs to the Pope there exists in the Church *"ex iure divino"* the power of jurisdiction of the Bishops, to whom is entrusted the office of teaching, ruling, and governing certain sections of the faithful. The power of jurisdiction of residential Bishops, according to the commonly accepted doctrine,[28] comes from the Pope and cannot be exercised independently of him (can. 329, § 1).

While the power of jurisdiction of the Pope is certain and unchangeable with regard to its subjects (all the faithful), to its territory (all the world), as well as to the matters that are its object, and consequently it can be said to be incapable of increase or decrease in the Church, the power of episcopal jurisdiction on the other hand is limited first with regard to territory which varies in extent

[27] Leo XIII, Ency. *"Longinqua oceani"* (6 januarii 1895)—*Fontes,* n. 628.

[28] Cf. Cavagnis, *Institutiones Iuris Publici Ecclesiastici,* II, 35-40; Wernz-Vidal, *Ius Canonicum,* II, 613-618.

and is subject to division, union and suppression (can. 215, § 1), then, with regard to the subjects living there, some of whom can enjoy the privilege of exemption like certain religious (can. 615), and finally, with regard to the acts and matters that are its object: for example, ordinaries cannot constitute matrimonial impediments "*iuris ecclesiastici*" (can. 1040), and can not dispense from the universal laws of the Church except in certain circumstances (cf. can. 15; 81; 459, § 3, 3°; 978; 990, § 1; 1028; 1043; 1045; 1245; 1313; 1320; 1402; 2237).

The power of episcopal jurisdiction is conferred by the Pope by means of that act of ecclesiastical power called "*missio canonica.*" The idea of "*missio canonica*" does not seem to differ from that of "*provisio canonica*" with the Code defines as follows: "Nomine *canonicae provisionis* venit concessio officii ecclesiastici a competente auctoritate ecclesiastica ad normam sacrorum canonum facta."[29] This provision by the competent ecclesiastical authority is necessary in order that a bishop may be said to be lawfully in charge of the government of a diocese, and pertains to the Pope alone (can. 332, § 1).

The nature and scope of the power of episcopal jurisdiction are thus defined by the Code:

"Episcopi residentiales sunt ordinarii et immediati pastores in dioecesibus sibi commissis" (can. 334, § 1).

"Ius ipsis et officium est gubernandi dioecesim tum in spiritualibus tum in temporalibus cum potestate legislativa iudiciaria, coactiva ad normam sacrorum canonum exercenda" (can. 335; § 1).

The power of residential bishops is ordinary, that is, annexed *ipso iure* to their office,[30] and immediate, so that it can be exercised directly over every member of their flock. Their power does not ordinarily extend beyond the limits of their diocese. This power of jurisdiction is put into operation in the functions proper to every power of government, i.e., in legislative, judicial and executive acts.

By his power of jurisdiction the ordinary is authorized to urge the observance of ecclesiastical laws and, in particular, to maintain

[29] Can. 147 § 2; cf. Wernz, *Ius Decretalium,* II, n. 284.

[30] Can. 197, § 1.

the canonical prescriptions regarding the administration of the sacraments, divine worship, preaching of the word of God, christian education of youth and the administration of legacies in favour of pious causes, "in such wise that, by preventing abuses, the purity of faith and morals of clergy and people is preserved and increased." [31] If they are to be really effective for their purpose it is necessary that these acts of jurisdiction be exercised freely and independently of all interference from the civil authority. Lay intervention by the princes is therefore justly condemned and punished.[32]

Since the power of episcopal jurisdiction is subject to that of the Pope, there exist in each diocese two ordinary and immediate jurisdictions. But this does not imply any incompatibility, for these powers are not independent of each other but hierarchically subordinated,[33] the inferior being perfectly free to move in its proper sphere provided that the superior power does not, for special and just reasons, intervene.

Now it is certain that the Pope in virtue of his primacy can exercise authority over the Ordinaries and can for just reasons increase or limit their jurisdicton. For the same just reasons he could delegate, even permanently, this authority to those who take his place in countries which on account of their distance from Rome he cannot keep under his direct control. According, however, to the existing law of the Code, legates are obliged to leave the exercise of the power of episcopal jurisdiction completely free. The legislator is quite definite on this point: "Legati Ordinariis locorum liberum suae iurisdictionis exercitium relinquant" (can. 269, § 1). The expression is general and includes all legates, whether *legati a latere* or legates on permanent mission in particular countries, whether the mission is diplomatic or purely religious. It is, of course, true, as stated in canon 266, that nowadays the powers of the *legatus a latere* are expressly determined each time in the apostolic mandate, and this mandate could contain a derogation from the ordinary law. But it is a case of the exception confirming the rule. Canon 269, § 1

[31] Can. 336.

[32] Cf. can. 2334; Pius IX, *Syllabus errorum,* propos. 51—Denzinger-Bannwart, *Enchiridion,* n. 1451.

[33] Cf. Cavagnis, *Op. cit.,* II, 34.

establishes a *praesumptio iuris,* and so episcopal jurisdiction should remain unaltered until the contrary is proved in each case. This interpretation is confirmed by explicit statements of the Popes. The following statement of Leo XIII is typical:

> "Quare Legati Apostolici, *qualicumque demum potestate augeatur,* cum haec persona, atque hae partes sint, Pontificis a quo mittitur, mandata facere et voluntatem interpretari, *tantum abest ut ordinariae potestati episcoporum quicquam parit detrimenti, ut potius firmamentum ac robur sit allaturus.* Eius quippe auctoritas non parum est habitura ponderis ad conservandam in multitudine obedientiam; in clero disciplinam debitamque Episcopis verecundiam; in Episcopis caritatem mutuam cum intima animorum coniunctione. Quae quidem tam salutaris tamquam expetenda coniunctio, cum in hoc potissimum sita sit et sentire concorditer et agere, plane efficiet, ut *quisque vestrum in administratione rei dioecesanae suae* diligenter versari pergat: nemo alterum in regundo impediat." [34]

Permanent papal legates certainly exercise some jurisdiction in the territory assigned them. Their jurisdiction is a participation in the *potestas regiminis* of the Pope. Here again there is a subordination of power: the ordinary is not impeded in the exercise of his jurisdiction, and the rights of the legate are clearly set forth in his special faculties in regard to the exercise of order and jurisdiction. It is natural to expect that the papal legate should be granted some jurisdiction in matter reserved to the Pope; but this is altogether in order and does not injure the rights of the episcopate. Episcopal authority, therefore, suffers neither directly nor indirectly from the presence of papal legates.

In the law of legation as stated in canon 265 it is said that the Pope can send legates with or without jurisdiction. According to can. 201, § 1, power of jurisdiction can be exercised directly only over subjects, so it can easily be understood how the permanent papal legates have a certain power of jurisdiction "ex officio." Since they have a permanent office and a definite territory, we can, at least by

[34] Ency. *"Longinque oceani"* (6 ian. 1895)—*Fontes,* n. 628.

analogy, speak of their subjects. At any rate they can receive such power by delegation since the Pope possesses the very fulness of all power in the Church. So the exercise of the power of jurisdiction can be granted even to papal representatives whose office is not permanent. In this last case, however, express mention of this concession should be made in the letters of appointment or it should be inferred from the nature of their mission.

CHAPTER V

THE NATURE OF THE POWER OF PAPAL LEGATES

Apart from any considerations based on names by which the representatives of the Pope are designated, it should be admitted that, in accordance with the principles put forward by the Code, at least some of these representatives are vested with the double power of ordinary vicarial and delegated jurisdiction.[1]

ARTICLE I: THE POWER OF ORDINARY VICARIAL JURISDICTION

The power of ordinary jurisdiction is that recognized by law as being joined to a certain ecclesiastical office. The power of delegated jurisdiction is that which is entrusted to a *person* by the superior who, legitimately possessing it can legitimately communicate it.[2]

The elements required by the Code for *potestas ordinaria* are two: a) an ecclesiastical office; b) an attribution of power to this office made by law. The power of legates of the Pope satisfy these two requirements.

First of all the duties of a papal legate constitute an ecclesiastical office in the strict sense of the term.[3] The institution in question is very ancient, permanently established in the Church, and always united to a certain use of the power of orders on the power of ecclesiastical jurisdiction. Now, with regard to permanence of an ecclesiastical office this permanence can be considered: 1) *subjectively,* in the person who holds the office, i.e. when a certain individual having a legal title is in peaceful possession of that office, of which he cannot be deprived except in the way specified by law; 2) *objectively,*

1 "*Legati Pontificii* personam et auctoritatem Romani Pontificis gerunt in aliquo regno, ditione, etc., *cum potestate etiam ordinaria;* nonnulli profecto ex his Legatis Papae dicuntur *Delegati Apostolici,* sed nomini non est insistendum, quoniam et ipsis competit auctoritas ordinaria."—Maroto, *Institutiones Iuris Canonici,* I, 838, note 1.

2 Can. 197, § 1.

3 Cf. can. 145, § 1.

in the office itself which, once constituted, becomes a permanent juridical entity and which, whenever vacated, immediately calls for a successor. Jurists maintain that ***objective*** permanence is sufficient for an ecclesiastical office in the strict sense of the term, to which, therefore, ordinary power can be joined.[4] The application of this principle to legates calls for a distinction between extraordinary and permanent legates. In the case of extraordinary legates, stability is obviously wanting, and therefore the question of ordinary jurisdiction does not arise. This even holds for *legati a latere*: their faculties are specially determined in their letters of appointment and it does not appear that any power is annexed *ipso iure* to their office: hence their power is delegated.[5]

On the other hand, the permanence of the office of nuncios and internuncios admits of no doubt. The Apostolic Letters declare the stability of the relations established with governments by means of the nuciatures;[6] and canon 267, § 1, 1°, expressly states that nuncios Apost. *"Spectat ad Romanum Pontificem,"* for the establishing of the and internuncios are permanent representatives (*legatione stabili funguntur*).[7]

Apostolic delegations also have the permanent nature required for what are strictly called ecclesiastical offices. They do not properly constitute a definitive form of representation, since the Holy See has in view eventual recognition by the State, but it is none the less true that the office of apostolic delegate taken in the sense of canon 267, § 2, is permanently established. Apostolic delegates are representatives normally sent to the hierarchy and faithful. Their regular succession

[4] Maroto, *Op. cit.*, I, 675; Vermeersch, *Epitome*, I, n. 227; Kearney, *The Principles of Delegation*, pp. 53-54.

[5] Can. 266.

[6] " . . . in perpetuo erigimus et constituimus eique (Nunciaturae) omnia et singula deferimus iura, privilegia, honores, praerogativas, indulta, quae praestatiorum huiusmodi Legationum propria sunt."—Litt. Italian Nunciature (24 June 1929)—*AAS*, XXI (1929), 762; Litt. Apost. *"De Romanorum Pontificum,"* for the establishing of the Irish Nunciature (27 November 1929)—*AAS*, XXII (1930), 131; Litt. Apost. *"Cum in Republica Estoniensi,"* for the establishing of the Esthonian Nunciature (11September 1933)—*AAS, XXVIII* (1936). 102.

[7] Cf. Pius VI, *Responsio ad Metropolitanos*, cap. VIII, n. 32-33.

shows that the office is not linked with one particular person; it exists as a juridical entity and forms a part of the general machinery of administration used by the Pope for the efficient performance of his duties as universal Pastor.

The second element required for *potestas ordinaria* is that to a certain office a participation of ecclesiastical power of orders or of jurisdiction should be joined *ipso iure*. Canon 267, § 1, 3° and § 2, speaks of *potestates ordinariae* when it prescribes that permanent apostolic legates should on the one hand *foster good relations between the Holy See and the government to which they are accredited*, and on the other hand *watch over the state of the dioceses in the territory assigned them and make reports thereon to the Pope*. Though the content of these prescriptions may seem rather indefinite, nevertheless the code calls them *potestates ordinariae*. Besides, the distinction between ordinary and delegated powers referred to by this canon leads one to infer that both are to be found in papal legates. These powers can well be conceived as a general rule and as being joined to the office of a permanent apostolic legate irrespective of the actual holder. Apart from these general duties the code expressly attaches to the office of permanent apostolic legates the power of settling disputes regarding the competence of judges not subject to a superior local tribunal.[8] Canon law also assigns to legates, together with ordinaries and rectors of Catholic universities, the special duty of taking cognizance of the publication of books dangerous to faith and morals and of indicating them to the Holy See.[9] That these powers are joined to the office by law is confirmed by the fact that the duties of the permanent representatives continue with the death of the Pope.[10] Now, by reason of the presence of the two necessary elements, viz., a permanent office and powers attributed to it by law, the permanent apostolic legates must be said to have power of ordinary jurisdiction. There are, however, two classes of power of ordinary jurisdiction: one is exercised in one's own name, the other in the name of another.[11] We can speak of ordinary power exercised in

[8] Can. 1612, § 2.

[9] Can. 1397, § 1.

[10] Cf. can. 268, § 1.

[11] Can. 197, § 2.

the name of another person without denoting delegated power. The reason is that power of ordinary *vicarial* jurisdiction is joined to *an office,* while the power of delegated jurisdiction is entrusted to *a person.* Permanent papal representatives discharge their duties within the limits of territory over which other ecclesiastical superiors have ordinary jurisdiction, and the authority of residential bishops is subordinated only to that of the Pope. If, therefore, the legates supervise and control dioceses, this cannot be done except by participating in the supreme *potestas regiminis* which the Pope exercises over the whole Church. Therefore the power of legates should be called ordinary vicarial jurisdiction. Here again the name of these legates (nuncios, internuncios and apostolic delegates) makes no essential difference: they are all in this matter true vicars of the Pope.[12]

Article II: The power of delegated jurisdiction

As opposed to the power of ordinary jurisdiction which is *ipso iure* joined to an ecclesiastical office, the Code in canon 197 § 1, defines delegated power as that entrusted to a person. The basis of the distinction is to be found in this that the ordinary is attached to an office and is a power previously determined by the law of the Church; the delegated is given to a person and is determined each time by the ecclesiastical superior who delegates.

The power of delegated jurisdiction expressly referred to in Canon 267, § 1, 3 and § 2, is granted to legates in order to facilitate the exercise of their ordinary power, and is fully in accord with the nature of their work. They represent the Pope and to a certain extent take his place when his presence is impossible.

The delegated powers come from the Holy See,[1] that is, either directly from the Pope, or indirectly, through the Congregations, Tribunals and Offices used by the Pope to deal with affairs affecting the universal Church. These powers must be interpreted, first of all in the light of the competency of the particular *Dicasteri* from which they emanate and, secondly, in the light of the special rules of the Congregation on which the Nunciatures or Apostolic Delegations particularly depend. They can be either *general,* i.e., contained

[12] Cf. Maroto, *Institutiones Iuris Canonici,* I, 835.

[1] Can. 7.

and embodied in general *Formulae* for all the Papal representatives depending on special circumstances of person, time and place. The variations are explained by *aequitas canonica,* and may be more or less frequent or extensive according to distance from Rome, development of the Church in a certain country or diversity of rite.[2] Finally, faculties are sometimes delegated *"de industria personae."* This may be done either in view of the mission he is performing, or in view of his particular merits, or as a personal favour. The delegated powers can therefore be granted *"ratione officii"* or *de industria personae."* [3] This twofold aspect must be carefully considered especially in relation to subdelegation. Powers delegated by the Holy See can be subdelegated unless 1) this is expressly forbidden by the person delegating, or 2) they are granted *"de industria personae."* [4] To determine when subdelegation can be employed, or when account should be taken of the two exceptions is a question of practical interpretation which can generally be decided without difficulty from the tenor of the rescripts.

[2] Cf. e.g., *Index Facultatum*—Appendix I; Bouscaren, *The Canon Law Digest, I,* 175-187; Vermeersch, "Facultatum quae, post Codicem, Legatis Apostolicis concedi consueverunt breve commentarium." *Periodica,* XII (1924), (69) - (98); (129) - (159); Petrani, "De S. C. pro Ecclesia Orientali eiusque facultatibus, "*Apollinaris,* X (1937), 28-46.

[3] Maroto, *Op. cit.,* I, 844; Kearney, *The Principles of Delegation,* p. 59.

[4] Can. 199, § 2.

CHAPTER VI

APPOINTMENT. CLASSIFICATION AND DUTIES OF PAPAL LEGATES

1. *Appointment*—The very nature of the office of legates requires that their appointment be reserved to the Pope. They are in fact his representatives and, though the positions of some of them are permanent, they hold these positions *"ad nutum."*

The appointment of a civil diplomatic agent also is reserved to the head of the state.[1]

2. *Classification* — Papal legates are distinguished according to the nature of their mission.

a) The *Legati a latere* are entrusted with duties, generally ecclesiastical, to be performed on extraordinary occasions.

b) The *Nuncios* and *Internuncios* have both diplomatic and ecclesiastical duties. Their representative character, therefore, has a double aspect—with governments, and with the hierarchy and faithful.

c) The *Apostolic Delegates* have ecclesiastical duties only, and represent the Pope only with the hierarchy and the faithful.

The Nuncios, Internuncios and Apostolic Delegates have permanent positions; in their absence, or during the temporary vacancy of the Nunciature, their place is taken by second class agents, like

d) *Extraordinary Envoys, Charges d'Affaires.*

The Pope very seldom sends a permanent diplomatic representative lower than a nuncio or internuncio.

e) The *Legati nati*[2] have only this title of honour which is connected with their episcopal see on account of the fact that Papal representation had been attached to it in the past.

[1] Satow, *A Guide to Diplomatic Practice,* I, 191.

Article I: The Legatus a latere

Can. 266. Dicitur *Legatus a latere* Cardinalis qui a Summo Pontifice tamquam *alter ego* cum hoc titulo mittitur, et tantum potest, quantum ei a Summo Pontifice demandatum est.

The title of legatus *a latere* is *per se* reserved to cardinals. They represent the Pope on particular occasions and for ecclesiastical events of special importance and solemnity. Nowadays it is customary for international and national Eucharistic Congresses, centenary celebrations and solemnities, and similar functions to be honoured by the presence of a *legatus a latere*.[3]

However, cardinals are not always sent to these celebrations, as on the occasions, e.g. of the National Eucharistic Congresses of Madras, India and of Iquique, Chile, to which the apostolic delegate and the apostolic nuncio of the respective countries were sent with the title of legate.[4] It is not always easy to determine whether on all these occasions the title of *legatus a latere*, or simply that of legate has been conferred. In every case the *legatus a latere* is appointed to such an office for a special purpose and his powers are determined on each occasion in the apostolic letters of nomination. Here there is a distinct difference between the present legislation and that in force before the Code. Formerly one had to have recourse

[2] Can. 270; Blat, *De personis*, p. 289.

[3] Cf. e.g. Pius XI, *Epist. ad Card. D. Dougherty*, for the International Eucharistic Congress of Manila (1 January 1937)—*AAS*, XXIX (1937), 54; *Epist. ad Card. A. Hlond*, for the International Congress in honour of Christ the King at Posnan (May 16, 1837) — *ibid.* p. 338; *Epist. ad Card. E. Pacelli*, for the Consecration of the Basilica in honour of St. Teresa of the Infant Jesus in Lisieux (June 29, 1937)—*ibid.* p. 432; *Epist. ad Card. J. Verdier*, for the Marian Congress of Aiguebelle (September 7, 1937)—*AAS*, XXX (1938), 18; *Epist. ad Card. A. Dolci*, for the Italian National Eucharistic Congress of Tripoli (October 24; 1937)—*ibid.* p. 60; *Epist. ad Card. R. Villeneuve*, for the National Eucharistic Congress of Canada (May 31, 1938)—*ibid.* p. 264: *Epist. ad Card. E. Suhard*, for the ceremony of the restoration of Rheims Cathedral (June 29, 1938—*ibid.* p. 316.

[4] Pips XI, *Epist. ad P. Kierkels* (November 22, 1937)—*AAS*, XXX (1938), 94; *Epist. ad H. Felici* (November 30, 1937—*ibid.* p. 96.

to various heads of the Decretals to determine what was granted and what was forbidden to the legati *a latere*.[5] Now, on the other hand, all their power apart from liturgical privileges is contained in the letters of nomination. Generally these legates are deputed *"ad caeremoniam"* and so have no ecclesiastical jurisdiction. Accordingly, the duties of *legati a latere* generally remain within the ambit of the ecclesiastical of order but, on account of the dignity of their person and the solemnity attached to their position as representatives, they cannot be ignored by the civil authority. So it is usual that civil honors are given to the *legati a latere* both in the countries where the Catholic Church is formally recognized and in countries where such official recognition has not yet been granted.

Article II: Juridical aspects of the functions of Apostolic Nuncios and Internuncios in their mission to the State

Nuncios and Internuncios occupy an official position with respect to the civil authority, and represent the Pope with governments according to the rules of international law concerning diplomatic representatives. Besides the duties directly connected with the Church in the territory assigned to them, they have other duties in regard to the state to which they are accredited. Canon law specifies their position in the following terms:

> Can. 267, § 1. Legati qui mittuntur cum titulo Nuntii aut Internuntii:
>
> 1° Fovent secundum normas a Sancta Sede receptas relationes inter Sedem Apostolicam et civilia Gubernia apud quae legatione stabili funguntur.

In this paragraph the permanent nature of the papal representatives is stressed. The permanence of diplomatic offices is now common, and has been accepted in international law since the Italian Renaissance. A long residence affords the representative of the Pope the best opportunities of securing a first-hand knowledge of place and people, of fostering a friendly understanding and promoting better co-operation between Church and State, and of securing facility and dispatch in dealing with affairs. The object of the mis-

[5] Cf. Wernz, *Ius Decretalium,* II, n. 690.

sion of nuncios and internuncios is the development of good relations between Church and State. In everything pertaining to this mission the Holy See observes the accepted international diplomatic procedure. The recognition given to the Church in this respect meets the Papal claim to recognition as a member of the international community. It serves, besides, the respective interests of the civil and ecclesiastical authorities, and also of the people, who, under different aspects to be sure, are subjects of the two authorities.

The Catholic Church justly claims not only toleration but the recognition of what is an independent and a noble social institution. Though she possesses all the means required to attain her ends, she does not proclaim complete separation, which, besides, would be "*absurd,*[1] *false* and *dangerous,*"[2] but approaches the State and asks for recognition on equal juridical terms, as Leo XIII teaches:[3] "si nullus adversetur, si nulla res impedimento sit, (Ecclesia) se sponte effert atque effundit, longe tamen uberiores editura fructus, si, praeter libertatem, gratia legum fruatur patrocinioque publicae potestatis." The nuncios and internuncios have the obligation of fostering good relations between Church and State, so that by mutual understanding peace be maintained. By means of the nuncios, and of the ambassadors accredited to the Holy See, diplomatic notes are exchanged in order to determine their fields of action, to communicate their wishes and to settle differences more easily. Without these relations good understanding between the two supreme authorities, the ecclesiastical and the civil, would be very difficult on account of distance, difference of manners and customs and the general inconstancy of all things human.

As to the manner of promoting good relations between the two powers, the nuncios and internuncios should in accordance with canon 267, § 1, 1°, observe the instructions issued by the Holy See. These may refer in general to the defence of the rights of the Church, or they may be dictated by particular circumstances that

1 Leo XIII, Ency. "*Libertas*" (20 iundii 188)—*Fontes,* n. 600.

2 Pius X, Ency. "*Vehementer Nos*" (11 feb. 1906)—*Fontes,* n. 671.

3 Epist. "*Longinqua oceani*" (6 ian. 1895)—*Fontes,* n. 628; Pius IX, "*Syllabus*" (8 dec. 1864), prop. 55 — Denzinger-Bannwart, *Enchiridion,* n. 1755; Ottaviani, *Institutiones Iuris Publici Ecclesiastici,* II, 81-99.

is to say, in connection with the development of events in a certain State. When relations between Church and State have been agreed upon and previously established in concordats, it is the special duty of the nuncios and internuncios to see that all the clauses of the concordats are observed: all the more so because they are generally responsible for these agreements and become the natural *trait-d'union* between the two powers.

Article III: Juridical aspects of Apostolic Delegates in ecclesiastical law

Can. 267, § 2. Qui vero mittuntur cum titulo *Delegati Apostolici* unam habent ordinariam potestatem de qua in § 1, n. 2, praeter alias facultates delegates ipsis a Sancta Sede commissas.

I. *Apostolic Delegates in general.* Apostolic delegates are sent to a definite country to represent the Pope with the faithful and with the local hierarchy. Apostolic delegates are also permanent representatives: for they deal with all the ecclesiastical affairs in the territories to which they are assigned. They have no official position with the civil authority, but attend only to matters of ecclesiastical jurisdiction. This means that in the countries where they live the Church is not officially recognized as a member of the international community, and this explains how apostolic delegations are generally constituted in countries recently converted to the faith, even though these countries may have a regularly established hierarchy and be in a condition much superior to that of a missionary country. Since this institution is altogether internal to the Church, no previous consent of the State is necessary, but at the same time in establishing a Delegation the Church proceeds with caution in order to avoid the possible opposition of the State.

II. *Apostolic Delegates in missionary countries.* When the apostolic delegate is sent to a regularly established hierarchy, his position in canon law is perfectly clear. He is in fact sent to supervise the ecclesiastical administration of a territory entirely entrusted to the jurisdiction of ordinaries who govern it in their own name. The juridical position of apostolic delegates with regard to prefects and vicars apostolic in missionary countries seems to be somewhat different.

Since the care of the missions is entirely reserved to the Holy See,[1] prefects and vicars apostolic do not receive the prefectures and vicariates as their own dioceses but administer them in the name of the Pope. Their power also is an ordinary *vicarial* power of the Pope. Should it then be said that there are two kinds of papal representatives in missionary countries? To be sure, juridical status of prefects and vicars apostolic and that of apostolic delegates are very much alike, especially since both representatives act immediately in the name of the Holy See and both are bound, not by a strict obligation of justice to the faithful but by the obedience which they have promised to the Pope. This explains why before the Code the juridical status of both was discussed under the titles: *de officio vicarii* and *de officio et potestate iudicis delegati.*[2] In modern law, however, their positions are rightly considered separately. Both represent the Pope, but in different ways. Apart from the difference in their office and dignity there is a very important technical difference. The prefects and vicars apostolic are really ordinaries of the place;[3] the apostolic delegates enjoy powers which are also ordinary but they are not properly speaking in charge of the administration of the place which they supervise. In practice, it follows that the apostolic delegates represent the Pope in the duties of supervision and control with the prefects and vicars apostolic as with bishops. In other words, the juridical status of apostolic delegates, as defined in canon 267, § 2, is the same both in places where there is a regularly established hierarchy and in missionary lands.

III. *The Apostolic Delegates in relation to the Oriental Church.* From a strictly juridical point of view there is no difference between the apostolic delegations established in the Latin Church and those in the Eastern Church. The same remark may be made regarding the nunciatures and internunciatures: they represent the Pope, irrespective of the rite of the countries to which they are accredited, since the Pope is the pastor of the universal Church. The question is here considered from the point of view of the apostolic delegates

[1] Can. 1350, § 2.

[2] C. 1-6, X, *de officio vicarii,* I, 28; c. 1-43, X, *de officio et potestate iudicis delegati,* I, 29; cf. Wernz, *Ius Decretalium,* II, n. 692-710.

[3] Can. 198, § 1; 294.

only, since at the present time actually only a few Apostolic Delegations and no Nunciature or Internunciature depend on the Oriental Congregation.[4] And just as the Apostolic Delegates represent the Sovereign Pontiff in the Eastern or Western Church, so do they represent him in respect of the different Rites into which the Eastern Church is sub-divided. In all cases they exercise the same ordinary power of supervision. Naturally the supervision here will be in relation to the local disciplinary laws which not infrequently differ considerably from those of the Latin Church.[5] Naturally the office of vigilance attends to the state of the dioceses in relation to their own law which often differs from the canon law of the Latin Church. In particular the apostolic delegates must see that the Apostolic Constitutions and Decrees referring to the purity of the different rites and missionary work among the Orientals are put into effect.[6] It may be noted that the legates of the Pope used to have the power to grant a dispensation to the faithful who wished to pass from the Oriental Church to the Latin rite Church. But in the case of priests, it is always necessary to have recourse to the Sacred Congregation.[7] However, on November 23rd, 1940 this faculty was revoked, and all matters pertaining to the transfer from one rite to another, both in the case of clerics and faithful, are directly reserved to the judgment of the Sacred Congregation for the Oriental Church.[8] We have here an example that delegated faculties are subject to recall or modification.

To conclude our remarks on the juridical status of apostolic delegates we need only add here that the special feature of their office is permanence, and they must therefore be carefully distinguished from the ecclesiastics delegated for some particular mission on each separate occasion. The Apostolic Delegates to whom a certain

[4] Cf. *Annuario Pontificio* (1945), pp. 729-730.

[5] Cf. *Notificatio Secreteriae Status—AAS,* XXIII (1931), 62.

[6] Petrani, "De S. C. pro Ecclesia Orientali eiusque facultatibus,"—*Apollinaris,* X 1937), pp. 34-35.

[7] *Decretum S. C. pro Ecclesia Orientali* (6 dec. 1928)—*AAS,* XX (1928), 416.

[8] *Decretum S. C. pro Ecclesias Orientali* (23 nov., 1940) — *AAS,* XXXIII (1941), 28.

territory is assigned hold an ecclesiastical office, with which are connected duties and special faculties determined by canon law which are always permanent. It is an office established canonically in countries far from the centre of Catholicism, as a means normally used by the Pope to bring to the faithful, with whom he is not in immediate contact, the benefits of his apostolic mission.

Article IV: Canonical Supervision

The ordinary power common to all permanent papal representatives, whether their duties are diplomatic or simply religious, is summed up briefly in the words of canon 267, § 1, 2°, "In territorio sibi assignato advigilare debent in Ecclesiarum statum et Romanum Pontificem de eodem certiorem reddere." This paragraph therefore, states the duty entrusted to the Papal representatives of supervising the administration of the dioceses in the territory of their mission.

The extension of this *"potestas vigilandi"* cannot be determined directly, but some idea of it may be formed by referring to parallel passages of the Code where mention is made of similar duties entrusted to certain ecclesiastical authorities in respect to their inferiors.

Vicars forane have the right and the duty of supervising the conduct of the ecclesiastics of their district with a view to the observance of the laws regarding residence, religious instruction, care of the sick and the fulfilling of the instructions given by the bishop during canonical visitation.[1]

Similarly, a religious who is a parish priest is subject to the supervision of his religious superior, especially in regard to the administration of the revenue and distribution of funds collected for the good of the parish.[2]

Again, the ordinary of the place has the duty of supervising financial investments, the administration and the safeguarding of the property of female religious institutes and dowries of the religious.[3]

[1] Can. 447.

[2] Can. 630, § 4.

[3] Can. 533, § 1, 1°; 535; 550, § 2.

He is also bound to control the proper administration of ecclesiastical goods,[4] and the fulfilment of the provisions of last wills.[5]

And finally, it is the duty of the metropolitan to see that ecclesiastical discipline is observed in the suffragan dioceses and to report to the Pope any abuses which may have arisen.[6]

In all these cases the power of supervision is not confined to the passive attitude of observation and report but involves the duty of warning, counselling, and directing all who are subject to his authority, while these, on their side, are bound to pay due deference to this duty and responsibility of his.

The power of supervision of the apostolic legates extends to everything connected with the development of the Church in the countries committed to their care. In the examples quoted above one notes a certain hierarchy of supervision and also a detailed description of the matters to which the power of those in question extends. It may be said that by the office of supervision of papal representatives this hierarchy is completed, in regard to territorial, and, above all, to juridical extension. It is an office of general supervision to which are subject, to a certain extent, ecclesiastical persons and matters in the territories assigned them. Here again the hierarchy of powers is observed, but it does not follow that the legate cannot, for just reasons, intervene even directly.

Since this office should be exercised without putting obstacles in the way of episcopal jurisdiction, it is easier to mention examples of acts which are forbidden to the legate than to determine what is exempted from his supervision. The legate cannot, for example, assume the administration of a diocese, even *sede vacante;* he cannot appoint parish priests or curates; he cannot change the orders given by residential bishops to their flocks. But he has the right to know the economic state of the dioceses and to demand at least a summary account of the administration of the ordinaries. Together with this right of control the legate has also the right of warning, counselling and directing whatever may be for the greater good of the dioceses in the actual circumstances; he can enforce the observance

4 Can. 1478.
5 Can. 1515, § 2.
6 Can. 274, 4°.

of ecclesiastical discipline and intervene in time to prevent abuses; he has the right to coordinate the activity of the bishops and to encourage their cooperation for the attainment of end that are of common interest to them all.[7]

Since Nuncios, Internuncios and Apostolic Delegates have to give the Pope an account of the general condition of the dioceses, they certainly have the right to the cooperation necessary to learn the true state of affairs, and in special circumstances they can even intervene personally. If it appears to them that changes should be made in the method of administration, they cannot take direct action with the faithful, but can merely make suggestions to the ordinaries. Whenever such an act of control has been exercised, it should be reported to the Pope. The exercise of acts of jurisdiction over the faithful does not strictly speaking enter into the ordinary power of the legates, and may be said to depend on the use of the delegated faculties. These are granted liberally in order to make the office of representing the Pope really effective.

[7] Cf. Benedictus XV, Epist. ad Delegatum Apostolicum Indiarum, (15 oct. 1921)—*AAS,* XIV (1922), 7-10; Vromant, "Délégués Apostoliques et Ordinaires des Missions," *Nouvelle Revue Théologique,* LIX (1932), 63-64.

CHAPTER VII

THE DURATION AND CESSATION OF THE OFFICE OF PAPAL LEGATION

Can. 268, § 1. Legatorum munus cum omnibus facultatibus eisdem commissis non expirat vacante Sede Apostolica nisi aliud in litteris pontificiis fuerit statutum.

§ 2. Cessat autem expleto mandato, revocatione eisdem intimata, renuntiatione a Romano Pontifice accepta.

Article I: Duration of the delegated power

In the Decretals provision was already made to ensure the permanence of the office of the legates even while the Holy See was vacant: on this point the law of the Code is in complete conformity with that previously in force.[1] The Gloss attributed to Joannes Andrea had already given the reason for this legal provision: i.e. the legates, to whom a definite province is entrusted, have duties which are ordinary and which exist *per se* independently of the person granting the office. According to canon 208 ordinary power is not extinguished by the death of the person who concedes it. We have already seen that the power of permanent legates is ordinary: the reason there given show why the office of Nuncios, Internuncios and Apostolic Delegates should be permanent even while the Holy See is vacant. Canon 268, § 1, however, does not distinguish between the kinds of legates, and merely states that their office and faculties do not expire with the death of the Pope. Canon 207, § 1, lays down that delegated power is not lost *"resoluto iure delegantis,"* except in two cases expressly determined by the law itself. (The power of the person who delegates can be lost, according to Schmalzgrueber,[2] in two ways, namely by natural death, or by legal death, meaning by the latter any way in which, according to law, juridical

[1] C. 2, *de officio legati,* I, 15 in VI°.

[2] *Ius Ecclesiasticum Universum,* Lib. I, tit. XXIX, n. 48.

capacity is extinguished, e.g., by resignation duly accepted.) The two exceptions are:[3] a) when this is either expressly or implicitly laid down in the very conferring of the delegation; and b) when the delegation consists in the power of granting a favour to persons mentioned in the rescript and no step has yet been taken to execute the mandate, or as the canon puts it, *quando res adhuc integra sit.*[4]

In regard to the present case, therefore, the delegated power of papal representatives is not extinguished at the death of the Pope unless this is stated expressly in the Apostolic Letters. Such an exception is generally expressed by the clauses: *ad beneplacitum nostrum, donec vixero, quandiu mihi placuerit,* or something similar.[5] If, on the other hand, the phrase: *ad beneplacitum Sedis Apostolicae,* were inserted, the power of the legates would not expire on the death of the Pope. For, the Holy See is perpetual: *"non moritur."*[6] The death of the occupant does not affect its own juridical personality. In the absence however of such clauses the general principle holds and the power of a legate is not extinguished even in the hypothesis that he had not yet commenced his mission at the time of the death of the Pope.

The positive ways in which the power of legates ceases are determined in canon 268 § 2. This is nothing more than a combined application of canon 183, § 1, and canon 207, § 1, for the reason, perhaps, that the power of papal legates is partly ordinary and partly delegated. Canon 183, § 1, gives a list of the different ways in which the holder of an ecclesiastical office can be removed from it, and canon 207, § 1 eumerates the ways in which delegated power in general can cease.

[3] Can. 61; 183, § 2: 207, § 1.

[4] Cf. Cicognani, Canon Law, pp. 774-777; Kearney, *The Principles of Delegation,* p. 115.

[5] Maroto, *Institutiones Iuris Canonici,* I, 347; Michiels, *Normae Generales Iuris Canonici,* II, 299-303.

[6] C. 5, *de rescriptis,* I, 3 in VI°; Wernz, *Ius Decretalium,* II, n. 691 (II); Cicognani, *Op. cit.,* pp. 808-810.

Article II: Cessation of the Office of Papal Legation

Canon 268, § 1, reduces the causes which terminate the office and faculties of legates to three. These are: 1) the completion of the mission entrusted to them; 2) recall from office; 3) resignation accepted by the Pope.

§ 1 ***Legatorum munus cum omnibus facultatibus eisdem commissis cessat expleto mandato.*** In the first place, the mission of legates ceases on the fulfilment of the tasks entrusted to them. In this way the power granted for legations of a temporary character is naturally extinguished. The expression: *"temporary or extraordinary legation"* is here contrasted with the expression: *"permanent or ordinary legation"* in the sense we have already accepted when discussing the exercises of the right of legation. The time element is only secondary, since by a temporary legation is meant that which has for its object only one affair, in contradistinction to a permanent legation whose object is affairs in general.

Since permanent legates have an office determined by the Code, to which a certain power of ordinary jurisdiction is joined, it can never be said that their mandate is ended, and so their mission can never expire in this way. But the extraordinary legations of the *legati a latere* and inferior legates cease with the fulfilment of their mission. In the expression *"expleto mandato"* is included the cessation of power delegated for a certain number of cases, since the word *mandatum* can probably be employed to denote a number of acts. On account of the character of the specific mandate of a legation it can happen that its purpose coincides with a time limit. This usually happens, for example, in the case of legations to Eucharistic Congresses and similar events. Here in fact the office of the legate ceases *"elapso tempore,"* or, when the ceremony is finished. However it still remains true that the time limit cannot be always accurately determined. It can, however, be said with certainty that the legation is completed when the legate gives a report of it to the Pope.

Let us suppose that the object of the legation is to deal with a particular matter. Such a legation should end only when the affair has been brought to a successful conclusion.[1] If, however, the issue

[1] Cf. Kearney, *Op. cit.*, pp. 112-114.

is not successful, the legation can only be completed in one of the other ways mentioned here.

§ 2) *Legatorum munus cum omnibus facultatibus eisdem commissis cessat revocatione eisdem intimata.* The revocation is an act contrary to delegation. Since the office of the legates is *"ad nutum,"* it begins with the act of formal appointment and ceases with the revocation properly intimated. Here it is necessary to note that, while the office commences with a positive act of the will of the person who accepts it, the juridical effect of revocation comes only from the will of the superior. In other words, in order that the revocation have juridical effect it is sufficient that it be officially communicated to the person in question. This communication should therefore come through an act of the competent authority, or as canon 207, § 1, determines: "potestas delegata extinguitur revocatione delegantis delegato directe intimata." Hence forward acts performed in virtue of the delegated power are invalid.

By revocation every legation, whether extraordinary or permanent, ceases.

Translatio, which combines the revocation of one office and the acceptance of another by means of two logically and juridically distinct acts, is practically the same as revocation. The office of *legatus natus* ceases *ipso iure* by transfer from one episcopal see, to which this title is joined, to another which has no such title. However, the *legati nati* are not included in the terms of canon 268, § 2, since their position does not really constitute an office but is merely an honorary title, as stated in canon 270.

§ 3) *Legatorum munus cum omnibus facultatibus eisdem commissis cessat renuntiatione a Romano Pontifice acceptata.* An ecclesiastical office can be declined, at the time when the superior offers it or, for a just cause, when resigned, if it has already been accepted. Resignation (*renuntiatio*) is regulated by the general principles laid down in canons 184-190. In order that the resignation of the office of legate take effect the following acts are required: 1) that it be made freely; 2) that it be duly communicated to the Pope; 3) that it be accepted by the Pope.

The acceptance by the Pope is required for the reason that, since an ecclesiastic cannot assume to himself the office of legate without being appointed by the Pope, neither can he be relieved of it without his consent. But if the resignation is accepted, the office of legate expires when its holder has been notified.

By means of resignation duly accepted every form of legation ceases.

§ 4. *Other ways in which Papal legation may cease.* The Code contents itself with enumerating three general ways in which the office of legate ceases but it is clear that it can also expire in other ways, for example, by the fact that the Pope recalls for his own consideration and decision the affair previously entrusted to the legate, and especially by the natural death of the legate, or by his "legal death" as a result of crimes which demand that he be deprived of every office in the Church.[2]

On the other hand the office does not expire through the absence of the legate from his territory. In this case, the exercise of contentious jurisdiction is suspended, that of voluntary jurisdiction remains intact.[3]

[2] Cf. e.g. can. 188, 4°; 5°; 2314.

[3] Can. 201, §§ 2, 3; Wernz, *Ius Decretalium,* II, n. 681 (IV).

CHAPTER VIII

THE RIGHTS AND PRIVILEGES OF PAPAL LEGATES

Can. 269, § 2. Licet forte (Legati) charactere episcopali careant, precedunt tamen omnibus Ordinariis qui non sint cardinalitia dignitate insigniti.

§ 3. Si charactere episcopali sint aucti, possunt sine Ordinariorum licentia in omnibus eorum ecclesiis, excepta cathedrali, populo benedicere et officia divina etiam in pontificalibus, adhibito quoque throno et baldachino, peragere.

ARTICLE I: RIGHTS AND PRIVILEGES IN ECCLESIASTICAL LAW

The *legatus a latere* takes precedence not only over all other legates but, outside the city of Rome, over all the cardinals.[1]

In canon 269, § 2 and § 3, we find no ruling as to the grade of Order the Papal legates should have. However, a custom has been introduced in this matter from which a departure, at least in the case of permanent representatives, is very rare: Nuncios, Internuncios and Apostolic Delegates are made Titular Archbishops (*Archiepiscopi in partibus, nempe infidelium*). All papal legates, even those who are not bishops, take precedence over ordinaries unless these are cardinals. Canon 269, § 2, determines the precedence of ordinaries who are cardinals over legates, unless these are *legati a latere;* and the precedence of cardinals in general over Nuncios, Internuncios and Apostolic Delegates, and precedence *a fortiori* over legates of lower rank is laid down in canons 239, § 1, 21°, and in canon 347, where the following order is established 1° Cardinals, 2° Papal Legates, 3° Metropolitans, 4° residential Bishops in their own dioceses, 5° Archbishops and Bishops in order of seniority.

Apart from precedence legates who are bishops enjoy certain liturgical privileges as to prelaticial insignia and the exercise of the

[1] Can. 239, § 1, 21°.

power of orders. Without the permission of the ordinary of the place they can celebrate *divina officia* vested *in pontificalibus* and with the use of a throne with *baldachino* in all the churches of the diocese except the cathedral (for which such permission is required). Since privileges are in question, and the only exception made is the cathedral, it seems that the expression of canon 269, § 3: "*in omnibus ecclesiis,*" taken in conjunction with canon 239, § 1, 9°, should be understood, not in the restricted sense of canon 1161, but as a generic term to indicate all sacred places of the diocese. According to canon 2256, 1°, by *divina officia* is meant in general all acts of worship in which the power of orders is exercised. The legates who are bishops can also bless the people according to the rules prescribed by the *Caerimoniale Episcoporum.*[2]

Article II: Rights and Privileges in International Law

The general rules of international law accord to diplomatic agents the right of personal and local immunity. The international position of the diplomatic legates of the Pope naturally depends on the recognition given to the Holy See. In this way is explained the fact that during the controversy regarding the juridical personality of the Holy See a number of authors held that the position given to the legates of the Pope was more of a special concession granted by each state than a right inherent in the very nature of the sovereignty of the Holy See.[1] The use of the right of diplomatic legation arises naturally from the position occupied by the Holy See in the community of nations, and is now recognized by the majority of countries.[2] The diplomatic legates of the Holy See have, therefore, the right to all the prerogatives accorded to diplomatic agents in general by international law. Furthermore, by virtue of custom sanctioned at the Congress of Vienna by an act of June 9, 1815 the Papal diplomats take precedence over all diplomatic agents of the same grade, and are the Doyens of the Diplomatic Corps of the

[2] Lib. I, cap. IV, § 4; cap. XXV.

[1] Cf. supra, pp. 15-16.

[2] Cf. Pasquazi, *Ius Internationale Publicum,* pp. 154-155.

state to which they are accredited.[3] The act of the Congress of Vienna was authoritatively interpreted in this sense by a regulation made in London in the year 1856, the text of which is as follows: "If it is intended, that by the invariable custom of any court, the representative of the Pope had at the time of the Congress been allowed to take precedence of all other diplomatic agents of the same class, without reference to the date of his arrival, that custom should not be affected by the new regulation."[4]

Since July 6, 1940, the personnel of all Papal Representations are Vatican citizens, according to the following statement of Pope Pius XII made officially known by the Secretariate of State:

"The Holy Father, Pius XII, happily reigning, on July 6, 1940 has graciously deigned to order that the personnel of the Papal Representations (Nunciatures, Internunciatures and Apostolic Delegations) *durante munere* be accorded Vatican citizenship."[5]

[3] Cf. Reglement, art. IV, — Satow, *A Guide to Diplomatic Practice,* I, 244-245; Lateran Treaty, art. 12.

[4] Quoted by Satow, *Op. cit.,* I, 245, note 1.

[5] *AAS,* XXXII (1940) 383.

CONCLUSIONS

1. The Pope has always made use of the right of legation whenever circumstances and his duties as Supreme Pastor of the Church required him to do so.

2. The right of legation manifests itself under various forms, but until the fifteenth century the different classes of legates had duties which were predominantly religious, the exceptions to this being the representatives called *Apocrisiarii* who resided at the court of Constantinople. The use of the right of legation within the Church is an argument in favour of the Primacy and a proof of the influence in ecclesiastical tradition and legislation exercised by the Pope since the early centuries of the Church.

3. From the middle of the fifth century till the beginning of the eighth the Pope is the natural *trait-d'union* of relations between the East and West. During this period we have the first clear manifestation of the international activity of the Holy See. The relations between the Pope and Emperor are conducted by an ecclesiastic whose office is both diplomatic and religious.

4. The position of representatives sent to the Councils was by its very nature temporary, but the exercise of the right of papal legation appears more frequently in the permanent representative position held by the bishops whose sees are situated in the more important and highly-developed centres of civil and ecclesiastical culture. After the ninth century the *legati missi* gradually increased in number and importance in view of the programmes of reform begun in the eleventh century and the unification of the Christian world against the Turks during the period of the Crusades.

5. The evolution of the right of papal legation along the lines with which we are familiar in modern times came about by means of a financial organization—the *Collectoriae* established in nearly all the countries of Europe for defence against the Turks and the reconquest of the Holy Land.

6. From the second half of the fifteenth century the forms of

papal legation became adapted to the representations of a permanent character introduced among civil governments. In the period 1492-1535 the legations were predominantly political, but through the action of the Council of Trent, and particularly through the work of Gregory XIII, the completely religious character of the legates of the Pope was re-established.

7. The first permanent Apostolic Nunciature was that established with the Republic of Venice in the year 1500. There is no proof that before the seventeenth century Internuncios were regarded as second class diplomatic agents, and, even if this were so, it would seem that their grade was derived from that of a similar civil diplomatic agent of the Emperor of Austria who resided at the court of Constantinople. It seems that the first Apostolic Delegations were erected in the near East during the eighteenth century in the form of temporary papal representatives sent to the Catholics of the Latin rite and those of the different Oriental rites. The first apostolic delegation was that of Syria established in the year 1762.

The terminology classifying Apostolic Delegates, Chargés d'Affaires and Internuncios was not definitely established before the decree of the Secretariate of State of 1916.

8. The question of the international personality of the Holy See became a live issue. After 1870 the principal reason alleged by those who denied this personality was based on the prevalent doctrine of the period according to which juridical capacity in the Law of Nations was granted only to States. The Holy See is, however, a juridical person in the international community since it enjoys the quality of sovereignty, which is the necessary and sufficient title for juridical persons in international law.

9. A proof of the international juridical personality of the Holy See was the use of the right of legation during the whole period of spoliation, and this, moreover, in the forms in use before 1870.

10. The exercise of the right of legation is a manifestation of participation in international life, and for this reason alone it is due to the Holy See. Nevertheless the right of papal legation is based on theological and juridical principles which transcend international law: its foundation is the primacy of the Pope.

11. Against the claims of the Gallicans we maintain that the

exercise of the right of papal legation is independent of the good-will of the civil authority. It constitutes no danger for the State, since its sole aim is the defence of the rights of the Church, rights which should be respected in international law.

12. Similarly, against the Febronian theories we maintain that the exercise of the right of papal legation is also independent of the authority of the bishops. It is not a usurpation of the rights of the episcopate, since it results from the primacy of jurisdiction exercised by the Pope over the universal Church and since it expressly respects episcopal jurisdiction.

13. The power of permanent legates is twofold: partly ordinary and partly delegated. The ordinary power is connected with the duty of supervising the dioceses; the delegated faculties vary according to circumstances of time, persons and place, and are conferred to facilitate the exercise of ordinary power.

14. At the present time the permanent representatives of the Pope are as a rule Titular Archbishops and the diplomatic representatives of the Holy See take precedence over all diplomatic agents in international law.

BIBLIOGRAPHY

1. Sources

Acta Apostolicae Sedis, Commentarium Officiale, Romae, 1909—

Acta Leonis XIII, 23 vol., Romae: Ex Typographia Vaticana, 1881-1905.

Acta Pii X, 3 vol., Romae: Ex Typographia Vaticana, 1905-1908.

Acta Sanctae Sedis, 41 vol., Romae, 1865-1908.

Acte finale de la première conference de la Paix (1899): Publications de l'Institute international de la Paix, n. 12, Monaco, 1910.

Annuario Pontificio, Roma, 1912—

Bembo, Card. Petrus, *Epistolarum Leonis X Pont. Max. nomine Scriptarum libri sexdecim,* Venetiis: Apud Gualterum Scottum, 1552.

Bullarii Romani, Continuatio Summorum Pontificum, 19 vol., Romae: Ex Typographia Rev. Camerae Apostolicae, 1835-1857.

Bullarii Romani Continuatio Summorum Pontificum, 13 vol., Prati; Typographia Aldina, 1845-1854.

Bullarium Diplomatum et Privilegiorum Sanctorum Romanorum Pontificum Taurienensis Editio, 25 vol., Augustae Taurinorum; 1857-1872.

Bullarium SSmi Domini Nostris Benedicti Papae XIV, 4 vol. Prati: Typographia Aldina, 1845.

Bouquet, Martin, *Recueil des Historiens des Gaules et de la France,* Edit. Brial, ed. 2 publiee sous la direction de M. Leopold Delisle, 19 vol., Paris, 1869-1880.

Caeremoniale Episcoporum, editio Quinta Taurinensis, Taurini: Ex officina Libraria Marietti, 1935.

Codex Iuris Canonici Pii X Pontificis Maximi iussu digestus, Benedicti XV Papae auctoritate promulgatus, Romae: Typis Polyglottis Vaticanis, 1917.

Codex Theodosianus, ed. Th. Mommsen et Paulus M. Meyer, 2 vol., Berolini, 1905.

Codicis Iuris Canonici Fontes cura Emi. Petri Card. Gasparri editi, 8 vol., Romae: Typis Polyglottis Vaticanis, 1923-1938 (vol. VII-VIII, cura Emi. Iustiniani Card. Seredi editi.

Concilii Tridentini Canones et Decreta, Romae: Ex Typographia Polyglotta S. C. de Propaganda Fide, 1882.

Corpus Iuris Canonici, Editio Lipsiensis II (Richter-Friedberg), 2 vol., Lipsiae: Tauchnitz, 1928.

Corpus Iuris Civilis, 3 vol., Berolini, 1922. Digesta, quae recognovit Th. Mommsen et retractavit P. Krueger; Codex *Iustinianus,* quem recognovit et retractavit P. Krueger; *Novellae,* quas recognovit R. Schoell, et absolvit G. Kroll.

De Martinis, Raphael, *Ius Pontificum de Propaganda Fide,* 7 vol., Romae, 1888-1897.

Denzinger, H., Bannwart, C., *Enchiridion Symbolorum et Definitionum,* Editio Decima Quarta et Quinta, quam paravit J. Umberg, Friburgi Brisgoviae: Herder et Co., 1922.

Eubel, C., *Hierarchia Catholica medii aevi* (1198-1600), 3 vol., Munster, 1898-1910.

Gerarchia Cattolica, La, Roma: Tipografia Vaticana, 1872-1911.

Guasti, Cesare, "I Monoscritti Torrigiani," *ASI,* XIX (1874)—XXVI (1877).

Hardouin, Jean, *Acta Conciliorum et Epistolae Decretales ac Constitutiones Summorum Pontificum,* 12 vol., Parisiis, 1715.

Hergenroether, Card. Joseph, *Regesta Leonis* X, Friburgi Brisgoviae: Herder et Co., 1884.

Jaffe, Philippus, *Regesta Pontificum Romanorum ab condita* Ecclesia ad a. 1198, editionem secundam curaverunt S. Loewenfeld, F., Kaltenbrunner, P. Ewald, Lipsiae, 1881.

Jemolo, A. C., *La Questione Romana* (Documenti), Istituto per gli Studi di Politica Internazionale, Milano, 1938.

Kirch, Conradus, *Enchiridion Fontium Historiae Ecclesiasticae Antiquae,* Friburgi Brisgoviae: Herder et Co., 1910.

Lettres des Papae du XIVe siècle, Les, publiées par les Ecoles Françaises d'Athènes et de Rome:

Tome I: Coulon, A., *Lettres secrêtes et curiales du Pape Jean XXII* (1316-1334), Paris; Albert FoFntemoing, 1900-1906.

Tome I bis: Mollat, P., *Jean XXII. Lettres communes,* 14 vol., Paris: Albert Fontemoing, 1904-1933.

Tome II: Vidal, J. M., *Benoit XII. Lettres closes et patentes* (1334-1342), 2 vol., Paris: Albert Fontemoing, 1903-1920.

Liber Censuum, Le, ed. par P. Fabre et L. Duchesne, Paris: Albert Fontemoing, 1889-1905.

Liber Diurnus Romanorum Pontificum, ed. Sickel, Vindobonae, 1889.

Liber Pontificalis, Le, par L. Duchesne, 2 vol., Paris: Albert Fontemoing, 1886-1892.

Lo Grasso Ioannes, *Ecclesia et Status: De Mutuis Officiis et Iuribus Fontes Selecti,* Romae: apud Aedes Universitatis Gregorianae, 1939.

Mansi, Joannes, *Sacrorum Conciliorum Nova et Amplissima Collectio,* 58 vol., Paris-Leipzig-Arnheim. 1901-1927.

Mercati, Angelo, *Raccolta di Concordati, su materie ecclesiastiche tra la Santa Sede e le Autorita Civili,* Roma: Tipografia Vaticana, 1919.

Migne, Jacques Paul, *Patrologiae Cursus Completus, Series Graeca,* 161 coll., Paris 1856-1866.

Migne, *Patrologiae Cursus Completus, Series Latina,* 221 vol., Paris, 1844-1864.

Molini, Giuseppe, *Documenti di Storia Italiana,* 2 vol., Firenze, 1836-1837.

Monumenta Germaniae Historica, Defensor Pacis Marsilii Patavini, ed. Richard Scholz, Hannover, 1932.

———, *Diplomata (Merovingorum)* 1 vol. edidit C. Pertz, Hannoverae, 1872.

———, *Epistolae VII; Johannis VIII Papae Registrum* edidit Ericus Caspar, Berolini, 1912.

———, *Epistolae saeculi XIII,* 3 vol., per G. H. Pertz, ed. Carolus Rodenberg, Hannover, 1883-1894.

———, *Registrum Gregorii VII Libri IX: Epistolae selectae,* cura Erici Caspar, Berolini, 1920.

———, *Scriptores,* Georgius Heinricus Pertz edidit, 30 vol., Hannover, 1826.

Muratori, Ludovicus Antonius, *Antiquitates Italicae Medii Aevi,* 6 vol., Mediolani: Ex Typographia Societatis Palatinae, 1738-1742.

Muratori, *Rerum Italicarum Scriptores,* 25 vol., Mediolani, 1723-1751.

Perugini, Angelus, *Concordata Vigentia,* notis historicis et iuridicis declarata, Romae: Pontificium Insttutum Utriusque Iuris, 1934.

Pius PP. VI, *Responsio ad Metropolitanos Maguntinum, Trevirensem, Coloniensem et Salisburgensem super Nunciaturis Apostolicis,* Romae, 1789.

Pontificale Romanum, Romae: Typis Rev. Camerae Apostolicae, 1848.

Potthast, *Regesta Pontificum Romanorum inde ab A. post Christum natum MCXCVIII ad A. MCCCIV,* 2 vol., Berolini, 1874-1875.

Registres des Papes du XIIIe siècle, Les, publiés par les Ecoles Françaises d'Athènes et de Rome:

Tome I: Berger, E., *Les Registres d'Innocent IV* (1243-1254), 3 vol., Paris, 1884-1897.

Tome IV: Digard, G., Faucon, M., et Thomas, A., *Les Registres de Boniface VIII* (1294-1303), 4 vol., Paris, 1884-1909.

Tome V: Langlois, M. E., *Les Registres de Nicolas IV* (1288-1292), 2 vol., Paris, 1886-1893.

Tome VII: Prou, M., *Les Registres d'Honorius IV* (1285-1287), Paris, 1888.

Tome IX: Auvray, L., *Les Registres de Grégoire IX* (1227-1241), 3 vol., Paris, 1896-1910.

Tome XII: Guiraud, M. J., *Les Registres de Grégoire X* (1271-1277), Paris 1892-1896.

Tome XIII; Guiraud, M. J., et Dorez, L., *Les Registres d'Urbain IV* (1261-1264), 3 vol., Paris 1892-1906; *Le Registre Cameral d'Urbain IV,* Paris, 1904.

Sanuto, Marino, *I Diarii* (1494-1533), pubblicati per cura di R. Fulin, F. Stefani, N. Barozzi, G. Berchet, M. Allegri auspice la R. Deputazione Veneta di Storia Patria, 58 vol., Venezia: F. Visentini, 1879-1903.

Thiel, Andreas, *Epistolae Romanorum Pontificum genuinae,* I, in aedibus Eduardi Peter, Brunsbergae, 1868.

Villari, P., *I Dispacci di Antonio Giustinian,* 3 vol., Firenze, 1876.

2. AUTHORS

Amelot de la Houssaye, *Histoire du Government de Venise,* 2 vol., Lyon, 1740.

Annales Ecclesiastici, Baronii Caesaris, denuo excusi et ad nostra usque tempora perducti ab A. Theiner, 37 vol., Barri-Ducis, 1864-1883.

Annales Ecclesiastici, auctore C. Raynaldo, ab a. 1198 ubi desinit Card. Baronius, 15 vol., Lucae: Typis Leonardi Venturini, 1753.

Anzilotti, Dionisio, *Corso di Diritto Internazionale,* 3 ed. Roma; Athenaeum, 1928.

Bastgen, H., *Die Roemische Frage. Dokumente und Stimmen,* 3 vol., Freiberg im Breisgau: Herder, 1917-1919.

Biaudet, H., *Les Nonciatures Apostoliques permanentes jusqu'en* 1648, Annales Academiae Scientiarum Finnicae: Helsinki, 1910.

Blat, Albertus, O.P., *Commentarium Textus Codicis Iuris Canonici,* 6 vol., Romae: Libreria del Collegio "Angelico," 1921-1927.

Bouscaren, T. Lincoln, *The Canon Law Digest,* 2 vol., The Bruce Publishing Company: Milwaukee, 1934-1943.

Bracci, M., *Italia, S. Sede e Citta del Vaticano,* Padova: Cedam, 1931.

Brazzola, Marcel, *La Cité du Vatican est-elle un Etat?* Paris: Librairie du Recueil Sirey, 1932.

Calvo, C., *Le droit international, théorique et pratique,* 5 ed., 6 vol., Paris: Arthur Rousseau, 1896.

Cammeo, F., *Ordinamento giuridico dello Stato della Città del Vaticano,* Firenze Bemporad, 1932.

Cathrein, V., *Philosophia Moralis in usum scholarum,* 7 ed., Friburgi Brisgoviae, 1911.

Cauchie, A., et Maere, R., *Instructions generales aux Nonces de Flandre,* Bruxelles, 1904.

Cavaglieri, Arrigo, *Corso di Diritto Internazionale,* 2 ed. Napoli, 1932.

Cavagnis, F., *Institutiones Iuris Publici Ecclesiastici,* 4 ed. 3 vol., Romae: Desclée, Lefebvre et Cie. 1906.

Cecchetti, B., *La Repubblica di Venezia e la Corte di Roma nei rapporti della Religione, 2 vol., Venezia;* Stabilimento Tipografico P. Naratovich, 1874.

Chelodi, Ioannes, *Ius de Personis,* Tridenti: Liberia Ed. Tridentum, 1922.

Chénon, E., *Histoire des rapports de l'Eglise et de l'Etat du Ier au XXe siecle, Paris*: Libraire du Recueil Sirey, 1913.

Chklaver, G., *Le Doit International dans ses rapports avec la Philosophie du Droit,* Paris, 1929.

Chiesa e Stato: Studi Storici e giuridici per il Decimale della Conciliazione tra la Santa Sede e l'Italia, Universita Cattolica del S. Cuore, Scienze Giuridiche, serie seconda, vol. LXV-LXVI, Milano, Societa Editrice "Vita e Pensiero" 1939.

Cicognani, A. G., *Canon Law,* 2 ed., Philadelphia; Dolphin Press, 1935.

Combet, Joseph, *Louis XI et le Saint-Siege,* Paris: Librairie Hachette, 1903.

Del Giudice, V., *Corso di Diritto Ecclesiastico Italiano,* a cura di M. Petroncelli, 2 vol., Milano; A. Guiffre, 1933.

De Louter, J., *Le droit international public positif,* 2 vol., Oxford, 1920.

De Marca-Baluze, *De Concordia Sacerdotii et Imperii,* 2 vol., Neapoli: Apud Vincentium Ursinum, 1771.

Despagnet, F., *Cours de Droit International Public,* 4 ed., Paris: Librairie de la Societe Recueil Sirey, 1910.

Diena, Giulio, *Principi di Diritto Internazionale,* 2 vol., Napoli: L. Pierro, 1908-1910.

Donati, Donato, *La Citta del Vaticano nella teoria generale dello Stato,* Padova: Cedam, 1930.

Duchesne, L., *Fastes épiscopaux de l'ancienne Gaule,* 2 vol., Paris: Thorin et Fils, 1894.

L'Eglise au Vime siècle, Paris: E. De Boccard, 1925.

Dupuy, *Commentaire sur le Traité des libertés de l'Eglise Gallicane de P. Pithou,* 2 vol., Paris, 1715.

Durandus, Gulielmus, *Speculum Iuris,* Venetiis: Apud Iuntas, 1577.

Engelmann, O., *Die paepstlichen Legaten in Deutschland bis zur Mitte des II. Jahrhunderts,* Marburg, 1913.

Eppstein, J., *The Catholic Tradition of the law of Nations,* Washington, Carnegie Endowment for International Peace, 1935.

Fabre, Paul, *Etude sur le Liber Censuum de l'Eglise Romaine,* Paris: Thorin et Fils, 1892.

Falco, Mario, *The Legal Position of the Holy See before and after the Lateran Agreements,* Oxford University Press, London: Humphrey Milford, 1935.

Fauchille, P., *Traité de Droit International* (8 ed., del Manuel di Bonfils,) Paris, 1921-1926.

Febronius, Justinus, (John von Hontheim), *De Statu Ecclesiae et Legitima Potestate Romani Pontificis,* Bullioni: Apud G. Eurardi, 1764.

Fedozzi, Prospero, *Trattato di Diritto Internazionale*: vol. I. *Introduzione e Parte Generale,* Padova: Cedam, 1933.

Felici, Guglielmo, *La Reverenda Camera Apostolica,* Roma, Tipografia Poliglotta Vaticana, 1940.

Ferraris, Lucius, *Prompta Bibliotheca Canonica Iuridica Moralis Theologica Necnon Ascetica Polemica Rubricistica Historica,* 9 vol., editio novissima, Romae: Ex Typographia Polyglotta, 1885.

Fiore, Pasquale, *Il Diritto Internazionale Codificato,* 5 ed., Torino, 1915.
———, *Trattato di Diritto Internazionale Pubblico,* 3 ed., 3 vol., Torino, 1887.
Fliche, A., *Étude sur la polémique religieuse a l'époque de Gregoire VII,* Paris: Soliete Française d'Imprimerie et de Librairie, 1916.
———, *La Chrétienté médiévale,* Paris: E. De Boccard, 1929.
———, *La Reforme grégorienne,* 2 vol., Louvain, 1924-1925.
Fraikin, J., *Nonciatures de France, Nonciatures de Clément VII,* Tome I, Paris: Alphonse Picard et Fils, 1906.
Gentili, Albericus, *De Legationibus Libri Tres;* Carnegie Endowment for International Peace; The Classics of International Law: Number 12, Washington, D. C., 1924.
Giannini, A., *I Concordati Postbellici,* 2 vol., Milano: Vita e Pensiero, 1929-1936.
Gigli, G., *Brevi Genni di Storia del Diritto Romano,* Livorno: R. Giusti, 1921.
Giobbio, A., *Lezioni di Diplomazia Ecclesiastica,* 3 vol., Roma: Pustet, 1899-1907.
Güenechea, Joseph, N., *Principia Iuris Politici,* 2 vol., Roma, Apud Aedes Universitatis Gregorianae, 1938-1939.
Hefele-Leclercq, *Historire des Conciles,* 10 vol., Paris: Letouzey et Ane, 1907-1931.
Hill, David J., *A History of Diplomacy in the International Development of Europe,* 2 vol., London: Longmans, Green and Co., 1905.
Hinschius, Paul, *System des atholischen Kirchenrechts,* vol. I, Berlin, 1869.
Hostiensis (Henricus de Segusio), *Summa Aurea,* Lugduni, 1568.
Iannacone, C., *La personalità giuridica internazionale della Chiesa,* Roma, 1930
Jarrige, R., *La condition internationale due Saint-Siège avant et aprés les accords du Latran,* Paris, Rousseau, 1930.
Imbart-Latour, J., *La papauté en droit international,* Paris, 1893.
Karttunen, Liisi, *Les Nonciatures Apostoliques permanentes de* 1650-*à* 1800, Annales Academiae Scientiarum Finnicae, series B.T.V, numeri 2-3, Helsinki, 1912 (Geneve: Imprimerie E. Chaulmontet, 1912).
Kearney, Raymond A., *The Principles of Delegation,* The Catholic University of America, Canon Law Studies, n. 55, Washington: The Catholic University of America, 1929.
Lapôtre, A., *L'Europe et le Saint-Siège à l'époque carolingienne, Ie partie: Le Pape Jean VIII,* Paris, A. Picard, 1895.
Le Fur, L., *Etat federal et Confederation d'Etats,* Paris, 1896.
———, *Le Saint-Siège et le Droit des Gens,* Paris: Recueil Sirey, 1930.
———, *Précis de Droit International Public,* Paris: Librairie Dalloz, 1937.
Luchaire, A., *Innocent III, vol. VI: Le Concile du Latran,* Paris, 1908.

Lunt, William E., *Papal Revenues in the Middle Ages,* 2 vol., New York: Columbia University Press, 1934.

Maroto, Philippus, *Institutiones Iuris Canonici,* 2 vol., Madrid: Editorial del Corazon de Maria, 1919.

Micossi, Giuseppe, *Le Piena Personalità Giuridica Internazionale della Chiesa Cattolica secondo la Dottrina dei Civilisti,* Roma, Pontificio Ateneo Lateranense, 1939.

Montini, Giovanni Battista: *La "Responsio Super Nunciaturis" di Papa Pio VI,* Roma: Editrice Studium, 1936-1937.

———, *Note Scolastiche per la Storia della Diplomazia Ecclesiastica,* Roma: Editrice Studium, 1933-1934.

Moore's, *Digest of International Law,* New York: The McMillan Co., 1930.

Moore, T. E., *Peter's City, An Account of the Origin, Development and Solution of the Roman Question,* New York, The McMillan Co., 1930.

Müller, J., *Die volkerrechtliche Stellung des Papstes und die* Friedenskonferewsen, Einsiedeln, 1916.

Nys, E., *Les origines du Droit international,* Bruxelles: Alfred Castaigne, 1894.

Oppenheim, L., *International Law: A Treatise,* 5 edit. by H. Lauterpacht, 2 vol., London, Longmans, Green and Co., 1937.

Ottaviani, Alafridus, *Institutiones Iuris Publici Ecclesiastici,* 2 vol., Romae: Apud Aedes Facultatus Iuridicae ad S. Apollinaris, 1925.

Papiensis, Bernardus, *Summa Decretalium,* edidit Em. A. Laspeyres, Ratisbonae, 1861.

Pasquazi, Iosephus, *Ius Internationale Publicum, vol. I: De Iure Pacis,* Romae: Apud Custodiam Librariam Pont. Instituti Utriusque Iuris, 1935.

Pieper, *Zur Entstehungsgeschichte der Staendigen Nuntiaturen,* Freiburg, 1894.

Pinchetti-Sanmarchi, *Guida Diplomatica Ecclesiastica, vol. I,* 2 ed.. Roma: Desclée, 1908.

Piola, A., *La Questione Romana nella storia e nel diritto. Da Cavour al Trattato del Laterano,* Padova: Cedam, 1931.

Pithou, P., *Liberties of the Gallican Church,* English version by C. Vedder, Upland, 1911.

Plati, H., *De Cardinalis dignitate et officio, Romae,* 1836.

Poletti, Vincenzo, *La natura giuridica dei Concordati Postbellici nella Dottrina Canonica a nel Diritto Pubblico Internazionale,* Roma: Scuola Tipografica Missionaria Domenicana, 1938.

Rivet L., *La question romaine et le traité du Latran,* Paris, Librairie du Recueil Sirey, 1931.

Rivier, A., *Principes du Droit des Gens,* 2 vol., Paris, 1896.

Romano, S., *Corso di Diritto Internazionale,* 3 ed., Padova: Cedam, 1933.

Ruess, Karl, *Die rechtliche Stellung der paepstlichen Legaten* bis Bonifaz VIII, Paderbon: Ferdinand Schoeningh, 1912.

Samaran et Mollat, *La fiscalité pontifical en France au XIVe siècle,* Paris: A. Fontemoing, 1905.

Satow, Ernest, *A Guide to Diplomatic Practice,* 2 ed., 2 vol., New York, Longmans, Green and Co., 1922.

Schmalzgrueber, F., *Ius Ecclesiasticum Universum,* 12 vol., Romae, 1843-1945.

Schroeder, H. J., *Disciplinary Decrees of the General Councils,* St. Louis: B. Herder Book Co., 1937.

Solieri, F., *Institutiones Iuris Ecclesiastici,* 2 ed., Romae: F. Pustet, 1921.

Stefenelli, *Die Wahrheit über die römische Frage,* Munchen, 1928.

Strupp, K., *Elements du droit international public universel européen et américain,* 3 vol., Paris, 1930.

Thomassinus, Ludovicus, *Vetus et Nova Ecclesiae Disciplina,* 3 vol., Parisiis, 1688.

Van-Espen, Z. B., *Ius Ecclesiasticum Universum,* 4 vol., Venetiis, 1753.

Vasiliev, A. A., *History of the Byzantine Empire,* 2 vol., translated from the Russian by Mrs. S. Ragozin, Madison University, 1928.

Vergnes, A., *La condition internationale de la Papauté,* Paris, 1905.

Vermeersch, A., Creusen, J., *Epitome Iuris Canonici,* 4 ed., 3 vol., Mechliniae-Romae: H. Dessain, 1929.

Wagnon, H., *Concordats et Droit International,* Universitas Catholica Lovaniensis: Dissertationes ad gradum magistri, series II, Tomus 29, Gembloux: J. Duculot, Editeur, 1935.

Wernz, F. X., *Ius Decretalium,* 3 ed., 6 vol., Prato: Libreria Giachetti, 1911-1915.

Wernz-Vidal, *Ius Canonicum,* 2 ed., 9 vol., Romae: Universitas Gregoriana, 1923-1938.

Williamson, B., *The Treaty of the Lateran,* London, Burns Oates and Washbourne, 1929.

Winslow, Francis J., *Vicars and Prefects Apostolic,* The Catholic Universitf of America, Canon Laws Studies, n. 24. Washington: The Catholic University of America, 1924.

3. Monographs

Battifol, P., *Saint Grégoire le Grand,* Paris: Lecoffre, 1928.

Biron, R., *Saint Pierre Damiani,* Paris: Lecoffre ,1908.

Cardinal, Edward V., *Cardinal Lorenzo Campeggio,* Boston: Chapman and Grimes, 1935.

Fliche, A., *Saint Grégoire VII,* Paris: Lecoffre, 1928.

McNeill, Eoin, *St. Patrick, Apostle of Ireland, New York*: Sheed and Ward, 1934.

Morris, William B., *Life of St. Patrick, Apostle of Ireland,* 6 ed., London: Burns and Oates, 1908.

Paschini, Pio, *Leonello Chieregato. Nunzio di Innocenzo VIII e Alessandro VI,* Roma: "Lateranum," 1935.

Pollard, Albert F., *Wolsey,* London: Longmaris, Green and Co., 1929.

Riguet, Abbé, *Saint Patrick,* English translation by C. W. W., London: Duckworth and Co., 1912.

Sentis, F., *Die Monarchia Sicula,* Frieburg: Herder, 1869.

4. Periodicals

Acta Congressus Iuridici Internationalis, 5 vol., Romae: Apud Custodiam Librariam Pont. Instituti Utriushue Iuris, 1935-1937.

American Historical Review, New York, 1896—

Apollinaris, Romae, 1928—

Archivio Storico Italiano, 3 serie, 26 vol., Firenze, 1863-1877.

Byzantinische Zeitschrift, Leipzig, 1892—

Bulletin of the Institute of Historical Research, London, 1923—

Civiltà Cattolica, La, I-II vol. Napoli 1850; III volume Roma, 1850—

Diritto Ecclesiastico, Il, 3 serie, Roma: Athenaeum, 1921—

Ecclesiastical Review, The (originally) *The American Ecclesiastical Review*), Philadelphia, 1889—

Giornale Storico della Letteratura Italiana, Torino, 1859—

Irish Ecclesiastical Record, The

Journal of Egyptian Archeology, London, 1914—

Jus Pontificium, Romae, 1921—

Monitore Ecclesiastico, Il, Roma, 1888—

Nouvelle Revue Théologique, Louvain, 1869—

Proceedings of the American Society of International Law, Washington, D. C., 1907—

Recueil des Cours de l'Académie de droit international de la Haye, Paris, 1923-1932.

Revue de droit international et de legislation comparée, Bruxelles, 1869—

Revue d'Histoire Ecclesiastique, Louvain, 1900—

Revue des Questions Historiques, Paris, 1866—

Revue générale de droit international public, Paris, 1894—

Revue Historique, Paris, 1876—

Rivista di Diritto Internazionale, 3 serie, Roma: Athenaeum, 1921—

Rivista Internazionale di Scienze Sociali e Discipline Ausiliarie, Roma, 1893-1926. Milano, 1927—

Vie Intellectuelle, La, Paris, 1928—

5. Articles

Ancel, René, "La Secrétererie pontifical sous Paul IV," *RQH,* LXXIX (1906), 408-470.

Balladore Pallieri, Giorgio, "La sovranità temporale della Santa Sede e i Trattati del Laterno" *Chiesa e Stato—Studi Storici e Giuridici per il Decennale della Conciliazione tra la Santa Sede e l'Italia,* II, 3-11.

———, "Il Rapporto fra Chiesa Cattolica e Città del Vaticano," *RISS* XXXVIII (1930), 195-221.

Baynes, N. H., "Alexandria and Constantinople, A Study in Ecclesiastical Diplomacy," *Journal of Egyptian Archeology,* XII (1926), 149-158.

Bolsover, G. H., "The meaning and history of the term 'InterNuncio'," *Bulletin of the Institute of Historical Research,* XII (1934-1935), 145-151.

Bourgain, L., "Contribution du clergé a l'impôt sous la monarchie Française, *RQH,* XLVIII (1890), 62-132.

Brown Scott, James, "The Treaty between Italy and the Vatican," *Proceedings of the American Society of International Law,* 23d Meeting (1929), pp. 13-23.

Brusa, E., "La jurisdiction du Vatican," *RDILC,* XV (1883), 114-145.

Checchini, A., "La natura giuridica della Città del Vaticano e del 'Trattato" Lateranense," *RDI,* IX (1930), 196-211.

Cipolla, C., "Sui motivi del ritorno di Francesco Petrarca in Italia nel 1347," *Giornale Storico della Letteratura Italiana,* XLVII (1906), 253-265.

Daux, "La protection apostolic au moyen age," *RQH, LXXII* (1902), 5-60.

D'Avack, Pietro A., "Qualifica giuridica della Santa Sede nella stipulazione del Trattato Lateranense," *RDI,* XIV (1935), 83-124; 217-237.

Degert, "Louis XI et ses Ambassadeurs" *RH,* CLIV (1927), 1-19.

de Vabres, H. Donnedieu, "La souvrainete du Pape et la separation de l'Eglise et de l'Etat," *RGDIP,* XXI (1914), 339-379.

Duchesne, L., "L'Illyrium Ecclesiastique," *Byzantinische Zeitschrift,* I (1892), 531-550.

Flaischlen, G., "La situation juridique du Pape comme Chef Suprême de la religion catholique," *RDILC,* XXXVI (1904), 89-95.

Gidel, G., "La condition internationale de la Papauté," *RGDIP,* XVIII (1911), 589-620.

Gwyn, Aubrey, S.J., "Papal Legates in Ireland during the Twelfth Century," *IER,* LXIII (1944), 361-370.

Hobza, A., "Questions du droit international concernant les religions," Recueil des Cours, V (1924-IV), 368-421.

Lallou, W., "The Apostolic Delegation at Washington," *ER,* XCV (1936), 576-592.

Lunt, William E., "The First Levy of Papal Annates," *AHR,* XVIII (1912), 62-64.

Jannaccone, C., "La personalità giuridica della Chiesa," *DE,* XLI (1930), 381-443.

Jemolo, A. C., "Carattere dello Stato della Città del Vaticano," *RDI,* VIII (1929), 188-196.

Kneller, C. H., "Das Papsttum auf dem ersten Konzil Zu Nicaea, *Stimmen ans Maria Laach,* LXXVII (1909), 503-522.

Maere, R. "Origines de la Nonciature de Flandre," *RHE,* VII (1906), 565-584; 805-829.

Morelli, G., "Il Trattato fra l'Italia e la Santa Sede," *RDI,* VIII (1929), 197-236.

Mostaza, M., "Sanctae Sedis personalitas internationalis in Decretalibus et iure gentium," *ACII,* III (1936), 77-93.

Nys, Ernest, "Les commencements de la diplomatie et le droit d'ambassade jusqu'à Grotius," *RDILC,* XV (1883), 577-586; XVI (1884), 55-70; 167-189.

Ottolenghi, G., "Sulla condizione giuridica della Città del Vaticano," *RDI,* IX (1930), 180-195.

Pennisi, "La personalità internazionale della Chiesa Cattolica e il rapporto giuridico tra la Chiesa Cattolica e la Città del Vaticano," *Acta Congressus Iuridici Internationalis,* V (1937), 1-16.

Petrani, A., "De S. C. pro Ecclesia Orientali eiusque facultatibus," *Apollinaris,* X (1937), 28-46.

Petroncelli, Mario, "La Santa Sede e lo Stato della Città del Vaticano," *RISS,* III (1932), 169-193.

Picanyol, L., "De origine et evolutione historica Tribunalis Rotae Hispanicae," *Apollinaris,* V (1932), 218-237; 326-364.

Pillet, A., "Note au Sirey," *Recueil général des lois et des arrêts,* a. 1895, IIe partie, pp. 57-61.

Piola, A., "Per una bibliografia ragionata dei Patti del Laterano," *DE,* XLV (1934), 479-484.

Renard, G., "L'Eglise et la souveraineté," *La Vie Intellectuelle,* XIV (1932), 8-30.

Richard, P., "La Secrétererie d'Etat Apostolique," *RHE,* XI (1910), 56-72; 505-529; 728-754.

———, "Origines de la Nonciature de France," *RQH.* LXXVIII (1905), 103-147; LXXX (1906), 112-180; LXXXV (1909, 5-40.

———, "Origines des Nonciatures permanentes," *RHE,* VII (1906), 52-70; 317-338.

Rousseau, C., "L'État de la Cité du Vatican," *RGDIP,* XXXVII (1930), 145-153.

Siotto Pintor, M., "Les sujets du droit international autres que les Etats," *Recueil des Cours,* XLI (1932-III), 248-360.

Vermeersch, A., "Facultatum quae, post Codicem, Legatis Apostolicis concedi consuerunt breve Commentarium," *Periodica,* XII (1924), (69)-(98); (129)-(159).

Vromant, G., "Délégués Apostoliques et Ordinaires des Missions," *NRT,* LIX (1932), 57-65.

———, "De habitudine Delegatos Apostolicos inter et Ordinarios Messionum," *Jus Pontificium,* XII (1932), 30.

6. Dictionaries

Dictionnaire d'Archéologie Chrétienne et de Liturgie, public par F. Cabrol et H. Leclercq, Paris: Librairie Letouzey et Ane, 1924—

Dizionario di erudizione ecclesiastica del Comm. G. Moroni, 103 vol., Venezia: Tipografia Emiliana, 1840-1861.

Enciclopedia Italiana, Istituto dell'Enciclopedia Italiana fondata da Giovanni Treccani, Roma, 1929—

The Catholic Encyclopedia, in Fifteen Volumes, London: Caxton Publishing Company—New York: Robert Appleton Company, 1907-1912.

7. Articles

Carusi, E., "Nunzio Apostolico," *Enciclopedia Italiana,* XXV, 47-48.

Cerretti, B., "Legate," *The Catholic Encyclopedia,* IX, 118-120.

Fanning, William H. W., "Vicar Apostolic," *The Catholic Encyclopedia,* XV, 401.

Moroni, G., "Delegazioni Apostoliche," *Dizionario di erudizione ecclesiastica,* XIX, 202-208.

———, "Legato Apostolico," *Dizionario di erudizione ecclesiastica,* XXXVII, 226-288.

Pargoire, J., "Apocrisiare," *Dictionnaire d'Archéologie Chrétienne et de Liturgie,* I, 2537-2555.

Picotti, G. B., "Giovanni VIII," *Enciclopedia Italiana,* XVII, 252-253.

Soranzo, G., "Gregorio VII," *Enciclopedia Italiana,* XVII, 933-935.

ABREVIATIONS

AAS—Acta Apostolicae Sedis.
ACII—Acta Congressus Iuridici Internationalis.
ASI—Archivio Storico Italiano.
ASS—Acta Sanctae Sedis.
C—Codex Iustinianus.
C.Th.—Codex Theodosianus.
D—Digesta.
DE—Diritto Ecclesiastico, Il.
ER—Ecclesiastical Review, The.
Fontes—Codicis Iuris Canonici Fontes.
Hardouin—*Hardouin, Jean, Acta Conciliorum et Epistolae Decretales ac Constitutiones Summorum Pontificum.*
IER—The Irish Ecclesiastical Record.
Jaffé—Jeffé, Philippus, *Regesta Pontificum Romanorum ab condita Ecclesia ad* a. 1198.
Mansi—Mansi, Joannes, *Sacrorum Conciliorum Nova et Amplissima Collectio.*
MGH—Monumenta Germaniae Historica.
MPG—Migne, Jacques Paul, *Patrologiae Cursus Completus — Series Graeca.*
MPL—Migne, Jacques Paul, *Patrologiae Cursus Completus — Series Latina.*
N—Novella.
NRT—Nouvelle Revue Theologique.
Periodica—Periodica de Re Canonica et Morali Utili praesertim Religiosis et Missionariis.
Potthast—Potthast, A., *Regesta Pontificum Romanorum inde ab a. post Christum natum MCXCVIII ad a. MCCCIV.*
RDI—Rivista di Diritto Internazionale.
RDILC—Revue de Droit Internationale et de Legislation comparée.
Recueil des Cours—Recueil des Cours de l'Académie de Droit International de La Haye.
RGDIP—Revue général de Droit International Public.
RH—Revue Historique.
RHE—Revue d'Histoire Ecclesiastique.
RSIS—Rivista Internationale di Scienze Sociali e Discipline Ausiliarie.
RQH—Revue des Questions Historiques.

ALPHABETICAL INDEX

BIOGRAPHICAL NOTE

Gino Paro was born in Ponte di Piave, Province of Treviso, Italy, June 17, 1910. He attended the Seminary courses in Treviso, where he was ordained on July 5, 1936. In following autumn he entered the School of Canon Law at the Catholic University of America, Washington, D. C., from which he received the Baccalaureate degree in Canon Law in June, 1937 and Licentiate Degree in June, 1938.

CANON LAW STUDIES*

1. Freriks, Rev. Celestine A., C.PP.S., J.C.D., Religious Congregations in Their External Relations, 121 pp., 1916.
2. Gallagher, Rev. Daniel M., O.P., J.C.D., Canonical Elections, 117 pp., 1917.
3. Borkowski, Rev. Aurelius L., O.F.M., J.C.D., De Confraternitatibus Ecclesiasticis, 136 pp., 1918.
4. Castillo, Rev. Cayo, J.C.D., Disertacion Historico-Canonica sobre la Potestad del Cabildo en Sede Vacante o Impedida del Vicario Capitular, 99 pp., 1919 (1918).
5. Kubelbeck, Rev. William J., S.T.B., J.C.D., The Sacred Penitentiaria and Its Relation to Faculties of Ordinaries and Priests, 129 pp., 1918.
6. Petrovits, Rev. Joseph, J.C., S.T.D., J.C.D., The New Church Law on Matrimony, X-461 pp., 1919.
7. Hickey, Rev. John J., S.T.B., J.C.D., Irregularities and Simple Impediments in the New Code of Canon Law, 100 pp., 1920.
8. Klekota, Rev. Peter J., S.T.B., J.C.D., Diocesan Consultors, 179 pp., 1920.
9. Wanenmacher, Rev. Francis, J.C.D., The Evidence in Ecclesiastical Procedure Affecting the Marriage Bond, 1920 (Printed 1935).
10. Golden, Rev. Henry Francis, J.C.D., Parochial Benefices in the New Code, IV-119 pp., 1921 (Printed 1925).
11. Koudelka, Rev. Charles J., J.C.D., Pastors, Their Rights and Duties According to the New Code of Canon Law, 211 pp., 1921.
12. Melo, Rev. Antonius, O.F.M., J.C.D., De Exemptione Regularium, X-188 pp., 1921.
13. Schaff, Rev. Valentine Theodore, O.F.M., S.T.B., J.C.D., The Cloister, X-180 pp., 1921.
14. Burke, Rev. Thomas Joseph, S.T.D., J.C.D., Competence in Ecclesiastical Tribunals, IV-117 pp., 1922.
15. Leech, Rev. George Leo, J.C.D., A Comparative Study of the Constitution "Apostolicae Sedis" and the "Codex Juris Canonici," 179 pp., 1922.
16. Motry, Rev. Hubert Louis, S.T.D., J.C.D., Diocesan Faculties According to the Code of Canon Law, II-167 pp., 1922.

* Below no. 100 only the following numbers are still available: Nos. 25, 57, and 75. Beginning with nos. 100 only the following numbers are unavailable: Nos. 100-111, 113 and 115-117.

17. MURPHY, REV. GEORGE LAWRENCE, J.C.D., Delinquencies and Penalties in the Administration and the Reception of the Sacraments, IV-121 pp., 1923.
18. O'REILLY, REV. JOHN ANTHONY, S.T.B., J.C.D., Ecclesiastical Sepulture in the New Code of Canon Law, II-129 pp., 1923.
19. MICHALICKA, REV. WENCESLAS CYRILL, O.S.B., J.C.D., Judicial Procedure in Dsimissal of Clerical Exempt Religious, 107 pp., 1923.
20. DARGIN, REV. EDWARD VINCENT, S.T.B., J.C.D., Reserved Cases According to the Code of Canon Law, IV-103 pp., 1924.
21. GODFREY, REV. JOHN A., S.T.B., J.C.D., The Right of Patronage According to the Code of Canon Law, 153 pp., 1924.
22. HAGEDORN, REV. FRANCIS EDWARD, J.C.D., General Legislation on Indulgences, II-154 pp., 1924.
23. KING, REV. JAMES IGNATIUS, J.C.D., The Administration of the Sacraments to Dying Non-Catholics, V-141 pp., 1924.
24. WINSLOW, REV. FRANCIS JOSEPH, O.F.M., J.C.D., Vicars and Prefects Apostolic, IV-149 pp., 1924.
25. CORREA, REV. JOSE SERVELION, S.T.L., J.C.D., La Potestad Legislativa de la Iglesia Catolica, IV-127 pp., 1925.
26. DUGAN, REV. HENRY FRANCIS, A.M., J.C.D., The Judiciary Department of the Diocesan Curia, 87 pp., 1925.
27. KELLER, REV. CHARLES FREDERICK, S.T.B., J.C.D., Mass Stipends, 167 pp., 1925.
28. PASCHANG, REV. JOHN LINUS, J.C.D., The Sacramentals According to the Code of Canon Law, 129 pp., 1925.
29. PIONTEK, REV. CYRILLUS, O.F.M., S.T.B., J.C.D., De Indulto Exclaustrationis necnon Saecularizationis, XIII-289 pp., 1925.
30. KEARNEY, REV. RICHARD JOSEPH, S.T.B., J.C.D., Sponsors at Baptism According to the Code of Canon Law, IV-127 pp., 1925.
31. BARTLETT, REV. CHESTER JOSEPH, A.M., LL.B., J.C.D., The Tenure of Parochial Property in the United States of America, V-108 pp., 1926.
32. KILKER, REV. ADRIAN JEROME, J.C.D., Extreme Unction, V-425 pp., 1926.
33. MCCORMICK, REV. ROBERT EMMETT, J.C.D., Confessors of Religious, VIII-266 pp., 1926.
34. MILLER, REV. NEWTON THOMAS, J.C.D., Founded Masses According to the Code of Canon Law, VII-93 pp., 1926.
35. ROELKER, REV. EDWARD G., S.T.D., J.C.D., Principles of Privilege According to the Code of Canon Law, XI-166 pp., 1926.
36. BAKALARCZYK, REV. RICHARDUS, M.I.C., J.U.D., De Novitiatu, VIII-208 pp., 1927.
37. PIZZUTI, REV. LAWRENCE, O.F.M., J.U.L., De Parochis Religiosis, 1927. (Not Printed.)
38. BLILEY, REV. NICHOLAS MARTIN, O.S.B., J.C.D., Altars According to the Code of Canon Law, XIX-132 pp., 1927.

39. BROWN, MR. BRENDAN FRANCIS, A.B., LL.M., J.U.D., The Canonical Juristic Personality with Special Reference to its Status in the United States of America, V-212 pp., 1927.
40. CAVANAUGH, REV. WILLIAM THOMAS, C.P., J.U.D., The Reservation of the Blessed Sacrament, VIII-101 pp., 1927.
41. DOHENY, REV. WILLIAM J., C.S.C., A.B., J.U.D., Church Property: Modes of Acquisition, X-118 pp., 1927.
42. FELDHAUS, REV. ALOYSIUS H., C.PP.S., J.C.D., Oratories, IX-141 pp., 1927.
43. KELLY, REV. JAMES PATRICK, A.B., J.C.D., The Jurisdiction of the Simple Confessor, X-208 pp., 1927.
44. NEUBERGER, REV. NICHOLAS J., J.C.D., Canon 6 or the Relation of the Codex Juris Canonici to the Preceding Legislation, V-95 pp., 1927.
45. O'KEEFE, REV. GERALD MICHAEL, J.C.D., Matrimonial Dispensations, Powers of Bishops, Priests, and Confessors, VIII-232 pp., 1927.
46. QUIGLEY, REV. JOSEPH A. M., A.B., J.C.D., Condemned Societies, 139 pp., 1927.
47. ZAPLOTNIK, REV. JOHANNES LEO, J.C.D., De Vicariis Foraneis, X-142 pp., 1927.
48. DUSKIE, REV. JOHN ALOYSIUS, A.B., J.C.D., The Canonical Status of the Orientals in the United States, VIII-196 pp., 1928.
49. HYLAND, REV. FRANCIS EDWARD, J.C.D., Excommunication, Its Nature, Historical Development and Effects, VIII-181 pp., 1928.
50. REINMANN, REV. GERALD JOSEPH, O.M.C., J.C.D., The Third Order Secular of Saint Francis, 201 pp., 1928.
51. SCHENK, REV. FRANCIS J., J.C.D., The Matrimonial Impediments of Mixed Religion and Disparty of Cuilt, XVI-318 pp., 1929.
52. COADY, REV. JOHN JOSEPH, S.T.D., J.U.D., A.M., The Appointment of Pastors, VIII-150 pp., 1929.
53. KAY, REV. THOMAS HENRY, J.C.D., Competence in Matrimonial Procedure, VIII-164 pp., 1929.
54. TURNER, REV. SIDNEY JOSEPH, C.P., J.U.D., The Vow of Poverty, XLIX-217 pp., 1929.
55. KEARNEY, REV. RAYMOND A., A.B., S.T.D., J.C.D., The Principles of Delegation, VII-149 pp., 1929.
56. CONRAN, REV. EDWARD JAMES, A.B., J.C.D., The Interdict, V-163 pp., 1930.
57. O'NEILL, REV. WILLIAM H., J.C.D., Papal Rescripts of Favor, VII-218 pp., 1930.
58. BASTNAGEL, REV. CLEMENT VINCENT, J.U.D., The Appointment of Parochial Adjutants and Assistants, XV-257 pp., 1930.
59. FERRY, REV. WILLIAM A., A.B., J.C.D., Stole Fees, V-136 pp, 1930.
60. COSTELLO, REV. JOHN MICHAEL, A.B., J.C.D., Domicile and Quasi-Domicile, VII-201 pp., 1930.

61. Kremer, Rev. Michael Nicholas, A.B., S.T.B., J.C.D., Church Support in the United States, VI-136 pp., 1930.
62. Angulo, Rev. Luis, C.M., J.C.D., Legislation de la Iglesia sobre la intencion en la application de la Santa Misa, VII-104 pp., 1931.
63. Frey, Rev. Wolfgang Norbert, O.S.B., A.B., J.C.D., The Act of Religious Profession, VIII-174 pp., 1931.
64. Roberts, Rev. James Brendan, A.B., J.C.D., The Banns of Marriage, XIV-140 pp., 1931.
65. Ryder, Rev. Raymond Aloysius, A.B., J.C.D., Simony, IX-151 pp., 1931.
66. Campagna, Rev. Angelo, Ph.D., J.U.D., Il Vicario Generale del Vescovo, VII-205 pp., 1931.
67. Cox, Rev. Joseph Godfrey, A.B., J.C.D., The Administration of Seminaries, VI-124 pp., 1931.
68. Gregory, Rev. Donald J., J.U.D., The Pauline Privilege, XV-165 pp., 1931.
69. Donohue, Rev. John F., J.C.D., The Impediment of Crime, VII-110 pp., 1931.
70. Dooley, Rev. Eugene A., O.M.I., J.C.D., Church Law on Sacred Relics, IX-143 pp., 1931.
71. Orth, Rev. Clement Raymond, O.M.C., J.C.D., The Approbation of Religious Institutes, 171 pp., 1931.
72. Pernicone, Rev. Joseph M., A.B., J.C.D., The Ecclesiastical Prohibition of Books, XII-267 pp., 1932.
73. Clinton, Rev. Connell, A.B., J.C.D., The Paschal Precept, IX-108 pp., 1932.
74. Donnelly, Rev. Francis B., A.M., S.T.L., J.C.D., The Diocesan Synod, VIII-125 pp., 1932.
75. Torrente, Rev. Camilo, C.M.F., J.C.D., Las Procesiones Sagradas, V-145 pp., 1932.
76. Murphy, Rev. Edwin J., C.PP.S., J.C.D., Suspension Ex Informata Conscientia, XI-122 pp., 1932.
77. MacKenzie, Rev. Eric F., A.M., S.T.L., J.C.D., The Delict of Heresy in its Commission, Penalization, Absolution, VII-124 pp., 1932.
78. Lyons, Rev. Avitus E., S.T.B., J.C.D., The Collegiate Tribunal of First Instance, XI-147 pp., 1932.
79. Connolly, Rev. Thomas A., J.C.D., Appeals, XI-195 pp., 1932.
80. Sangmeister, Rev. Joseph V., A.B., J.C.D., Force and Fear as Precluding Matrimonial Consent, V-211 pp., 1932.
81. Jaeger, Rev. Leo A., A.B., J.C.D., The Administration of Vacant and Quasi-Vacant Episcopal Sees in the United States, IX-299 pp., 1932.
82. Rimlinger, Rev. Herbert T., J.C.D., Error Invalidating Matrimonial Consent, VII-79 pp., 1932.
83. Barrett, Rev. John D. M., S.S., J.C.D., A Comparative Study of the Third Plenary Council of Baltimore and the Code, IX-221 pp., 1932.

84. CARBERRY, REV. JOHN J., PH.D., S.T.D., J.C.D., The Juridical Form of Marriage, X-177 pp., 1934.
85. DOLAN, REV. JOHN L., A.B., J.C.D., The Defensor Vinculi, XII-157 pp., 1934.
86. HANNAN, REV. JEROME D., A.M., S.T.D., LL.B., J.C.D., The Canon Law of Wills, IX-517 pp., 1934.
87. LEMIEUX, REV. DELISE A., A.M., J.C.D., The Sentence in Ecclesiastical Procedure, IX-131 pp., 1934.
88. O'ROURKE, REV. JAMES J., AB.. J.C.D., Parish Registers, VII-109 pp., 1934.
89. TIMLIN, REV. BARTHOLOMEW, O.F.M., A.M., J.C.D., Conditional Matrimonial Consent, X-381 pp., 1934.
90. WAHL, REV. FRANCIS X., A.B., J.C.D., The Matrimonial Impediments of Consanguinity and Affinity, VI-125 pp., 1934.
91. WHITE, REV. ROBERT J., A.B., LL.B., S.T.B., J.C.D., Canonical Ante-Nuptial Promises and the Civil Law, VI-152 pp., 1934.
92. HERRERA, REV. ANTONIO PARRA, O.C.D., J.C.D., Legislation Ecclesiastica sobra el Ayuno y la Abstinencia, XI-191 pp., 1935.
93. KENNEDY, REV. EDWIN J., J.C.D., The Special Matrimonial Process in Cases of Evident Nullity, X-165 pp., 1935.
94. MANNING, REV. JOHN J., A.B., J.C.D., Presumption of Law in Matrimonial Procedure, XI-111 pp., 1935.
95. MOEJER, REV. JOHN M., J.C.D., The Proper Bishop for Ordination and Dismissorial Letters, VII-135 pp., 1935.
96. O'MARA, REV. WILLIAM A., A.B., J.C.D., Canonical Causes for Matrimonial Dispensations, IX-155 pp., 1935.
97. REILLY, REV. PETER, J.C.D., Residence of Pastors, IX-81 pp., 1935.
98. SMITH, REV. MARINER T., O.P., S.T.Lr., J.C.D., The Penal Law for Religious, VIII-169 pp., 1935.
99. WHALEN, REV. DONALD W., A.M., J.C.D., The Value of Testimonial Evidence in Matrimonial Procedure, XIII-297 pp., 1935.
100. CLEARY, REV. JOSEPH F., J.C.D., Canonical Limitations on the Alienation of Church Property, VIII-141 pp., 1936.
101. GLYNN, REV. JOHN C., J.C.D., The Promoter of Justice, XX-337 pp., 1936.
102. BRENNAN, REV. JAMES H., S.S., M.A., S.T.B., J.C.D., The Simple Convalidation of Marriage, VI-135 pp., 1937.
103. BRUNINI, REV. JOSEPH BERNARD, J.C.D., The Clerical Obligations of Canons 139 and 142, X-121 pp., 1937.
104. CONNOR, REV. MAURICE, A.B., J.C.D., The Administrative Removal of Pastors, VIII-159 pp., 1937.
105. GUILFOYLE, REV. MERLIN JOSEPH, J.C.D., Custom, XI-144 pp., 1937.
106. HUGHES, REV. JAMES AUSTIN, A.B., A.M., J.C.D., Witnesses in Criminal Trials of Clerics, IX-140 pp., 1937.

107. JANSEN, REV. RAYMOND J., A.B., S.T.L., J.C.D., Canonical Provisions for Catechetical Instruction, VII-153 pp., 1937.
108. KEALY, REV. JOHN JAMES, A.B., J.C.D., The Introductory Libellus in Church Court Procedure, XI-121 pp., 1937.
109. MCMANUS, REV. JAMES EDWARD, C.SS.R., J.C.D., The Administration of Temporal Goods in Religious Insttiutes, XVI-196 pp., 1937.
110. MORIARITY, REV. EUGENE JAMES, J.C.D., Oaths in Ecclesiastical Courts, X-115 pp., 1937.
111. RAINIER, REV. ELIGIUS GEORGE, C.SS.R., J.C.D., Suspension of Clerics, XVII-249 pp., 1937.
112. REILLY, REV. THOMAS F., C.SS.R., J.C.D., Visitation of Religious, VI-195 pp., 1938.
113. MORIARITY, REV. FRANCIS E., C.SS.R., J.C.D., The Extraordinary Absolution from Censures, XV-334 pp., 1938.
114. CONNOLLY, REV. NICHOLAS P., J.C.D., The Canonical Erection of Parishes, X-132 pp., 1938.
115. DONOVAN, REV. JAMES JOSEPH, J.C.D., The Pastor's Obligation in Pre-nuptial Investigation, XII-322 pp., 1938.
116. HARRIGAN, REV. ROBERT J., M.A., S.T.B., J.C.D., The Radical Sanation of Invalid Marriages, VIII-208 pp., 1938.
117. BOFFA, REV. CONRAD HUMBERT, J.C.D., Canonical Provisions for Catholic Schools, VII-211 pp., 1939.
118. PARSONS, REV. ANSCAR JOHN, O.M.Cap., J.C.D., Canonical Elections, XII-236 pp., 1939.
119. REILLY, REV. EDWARD MICHAEL, A.B., J.C.D., The General Norms of Dispensation, XII-156 pp., 1939.
120. RYAN, REV. GERALD ALOYSIUS, A.B., J.C.D., Principles of Episcopal Jurisdiction, XII-172 pp., 1939.
121. BURTON, REV. FRANCIS JAMES, C.S.C., A.B., J.C.D., A Commentary on Canon 1125, X-222 pp., 1940.
122. MIASKIEWICZ, REV. FRANCIS SIGISMUND, J.C.D., Supplied Jurisdiction According to Canon 209, XII-340 pp., 1940.
123. RICE, REV. PATRICK WILLIAM, A.B., J.C.D., Proof of Death in Prenuptial Investigation, VIII-156 pp., 1940.
124. ANGLIN, REV. THOMAS FRANCIS, M.S., J.C.D., The Eucharistic Fast, VIII-183 pp., 1941.
125. COLEMAN, REV. JOHN JEROME, J.C.D., The Minister of Confirmation, VI-153 pp., 1941.
126. DOWNS, REV. JOHN EMMANUEL, A.B., J.C.D., The Concept of Clerical Immunity, XI-163 pp., 1941.
127. ESSWEIN, REV. ANTHONY ALBERT, J.C.D., Extrajudicial Penal Powers of Ecclesaistical Superiors, X-144 pp., 1941.
128. FARRELL, REV. BENJAMIN FRANCIS, M.A., S.T.L., J.C.D., The Rights and Duties of the Local Ordinary Regarding Congregations of Women Religious of Pontifical Approval, V-195 pp., 1941.

129. Feeney, Rev. Thomas John, A.B., S.T.L., J.C.D., Restitutio in Integrum, VI-169 pp., 1941.
130. Findlay, Rev. Stephen William, O.S.B., A.B., J.C.D., Canonical Norms Governing the Deposition and Degradation of Clerics, XVII-279 pp., 1941.
131. Goodwine, Rev. John, A.B., S.T.L., J.C.D., The Right of the Church to Acquire Property, VIII-119 pp., 1941.
132. Heston, Rev. Edward Louis, C.S.C., Ph.D., S.T.D., J.C.D., The Alienation of Church Property in the United States, XII-222 pp., 1941.
133. Hogan, Rev. James John, A.B., S.T.L., J.C.D., Judicial Advocates and Procurators, XIII-200 pp., 1941.
134. Kealy, Rev. Thomas M., A.B., Litt.B., J.C.D., Dowry of Women Religious, IX-152 pp., 1941.
135. Keene, Rev. Michael James, O.S.B., J.C.D., Religious Ordinaries and Canon 198, V-164 pp., 1942.
136. Kerin, Rev. Charles A., S.S., M.A., S.T.B., J.C.D., The Privation of Christian Burial, XVI-279 pp., 1941.
137. Louis, Rev. William Francis, M.A., J.C.D., Diocesan Archives, X-101 pp., 1941.
138. McDevitt, Rev. Gilbert Joseph, A.B., J.C.D., Legitimacy and Legitimation, X-247 pp., 1941.
139. McDonough, Rev. Thomas Joseph, A.B., J.C.D., Apostolic Administrators, X-217 pp., 1941.
140. Meier, Rev. Card Anthony, A.B., J.C.D., Penal Administrative Procedure Against Negligent Pastors, X-240 pp., 1941.
141. Schmidt, Rev. John Rogg, A.B., J.C.D., The Principles of Authentic Interpretation in Canon 17 of the Code of Canon Law, XII-331 pp., 1941.
142. Slafkosky, Rev. Andrew Leonard, A.B., J.C.D., The Canonical Episcopal Visitation of the Diocese, X-197 pp., 1941.
143. Swoboda, Rev. Innocent Robert, O.F.M., J.C.D., Ignorance in Relation to the Imputability of Delicts, IX-271 pp., 1941.
144. Dube, Rev. Arthur Joseph, A.B., J.C.D., The General Principles for the Reckoning of Time in Canon Law, VIII-299 pp., 1941.
145. McBride, Rev. James T., A.B., J.C.D., Incardination and Excardination of Seculars, XX-585 pp., 1941.
146. Król, Rev. John T., J.C.D., The Defendant in Ecclesiastical Trials, XII-207 pp., 1942.
147. Comyns, Rev. Joseph J., C.SS.R., A.B., J.C.D., Papal and Episcopal Administration of Church Property, XIV-155 pp., 1942.
148. Barry, Rev. Garrett Francis, O.M.I., J.C.D., Violation of the Cloister, XII-260 pp., 1942.
149. Bolduc, Rev. Gatien, C.S.V., A.B., S.T.L., J.C.D., Les Études dans les Religions Cléricales, VIII-155 pp., 1942.

150. BOYLE, REV. DAVID JOHN, M.A., J.C.D., The Juridic Effects of Moral Certitude on Pre-Nuptial Guarantees, XII-188 pp., 1942.
151. CANAVAN, REV. WALTER JOSEPH, M.A., LITT.D., J.C.D., The Profession of Faith, XII-143 pp., 1942.
152. DESROCHERS, REV. BRUNO, A.B., PH.L., S.T.B., J.C.D., Le Premier Concile Plénier de Québec et le Code de Droit Canonique, XIV-186 pp., 1942.
153. DILLON, REV. ROBERT EDWARD, A.B., J.C.D., Common Law Marriage, X-148 pp., 1942.
154. DODWELL, REV. EDWARD JOHN, PH.D., S.T.B., J.C.D., The Time and Place for the Celebration of Marriage,X-156 pp., 1942.
155. DONNELLAN, REV. THOMAS ANDREW, A.B., J.C.D., The Obligation of the Missa pro Populo, VII-131 pp., 1942.
156. ELTZ, REV. LOUIS ANTHONY, A.B., J.C.D., Cooperation in Crime, XII-208 pp., 1942.
157. GASS, REV. SYLVESTER FRANCIS, M.A., J.C.D., Ecclesiastical Pensions, XI-206 pp., 1942.
158. GUINIVEN, REV. JOHN JOSEPH, C.SS.R., J.C.D., The Precept of Hearing Mass, XIV-188 pp., 1942.
159. GULCZYNSKI, REV. JOHN THEOPHILUS, J.C.D., The Desecration and Violation of Churches, X-126 pp., 1942.
160. HAMMILL, REV. JOHN LEO, M.A., J.C.D., The Obligations of the Traveler According to Canon 14, VIII-204 pp., 1942.
161. HAYDT, REV. JOHN JOSEPH, A.B., J.C.D., Reserved Benefices, XI-148 pp., 1942.
162. HUSER, REV. ROGER JOHN, O.F.M., A.B., J.C.D., The Crime of Abortion in Canon Law, XII-187 pp., 1942.
163. KEARNEY, REV. FRANCIS PATRICK, A.B., S.T.L., J.C.D., The Principles of Canon 1127, X-162 pp., 1942.
164. LINAHEN, REV. LEO JAMES, S.T.L., J.C.D., De Absolutione Complicis In Peccato Turpi, 114 pp., 1942.
165. MCCLOSKEY, REV. JOSEPH ALOYSIUS, A.B., J.C.D., The Subject of Ecclesiastical Law According to Canon 12, XVII-246 pp., 1942.
166. O'NEILL, REV. FRANCIS JOSEPH, C.SS.R., J.C.D., The Dismis:(. of Religious in Temporary Vows, XIII-220 pp., 1942.
167. PRINCE, REV. JOHN EDWARD, A.B., S.T.B., J.C.D., The Diocesan Chancellor, X-136 pp., 1942.
168. RIESNER, REV. ALBERT JOSEPH, C.SS.R., J.C.D., Apostates and Fugitives from Religious Institutes, IX-168 pp., 1942.
169. STENGER, REV. JOSEPH BERNHARD, J.C.D., The Mortgaging of Church Property, 186 pp., 1942.
170. WALDRON, REV. JOSEPH FRANCIS, A.B., J.C.D., The Minister of Baptism, XII-197 pp., 1942.
171. WILLETT, REV. ROBERT ALBERT, J.C.D., The Probative Value of Documents in Ecclesiastical Trials, X-124 pp., 1942.

172. WOEBER, REV. EDWARD MARTIN, M.A., J.C.D., The Interpellations, XII-161 pp., 1942.
173. BENKO, REV. MATTHEW ALOYSIUS, O.S.B., M.A., J.C.D., The Abbot *Nullius,* XVI-148 pp., 1943.
174. CHRIST, REV. JOSEPH JAMES, M.A., S.T.L., J.C.D., Dispensation from Vindicative Penalties, XIII-285 pp., 1943.
175. CLANCY, REV. PATRICK M. J., O.P., A.B., S.T.LR., J.C.D., The Local Religious Superior, X-229 pp., 1943.
176. CLARKE, REV. THOMAS JAMES, J.C.D., Parish Societies, XII-147 pp., 1943.
177. CONNOLLY, REV. JOHN PATRICK, S.T.L., J.C.D., Synodal Examiners and Parish Priest Consultors, X-223 pp., 1943.
178. DRUMM, REV. WILLIAM MARTIN, A.B., J.C.D., Hospital Chaplains, XII-175 pp., 1943.
179. FLANAGAN, REV. BERNARD JOSEPH, A.B., S.T.L., J.C.D., The Canonical Erection of Religious House, X-147 pp., 1943.
180. KELLEHER, REV. STEPHEN JOSEPH, A.B., S.T.B., J.C.D., Discussions with Non-Catholics: Canonical Legsilation, X-93 pp., 1943.
181. LEWIS, REV. GORDIAN, C.P., J.C.D., Chapters in Religious Institutes, XII-169 pp., 1943.
182 MARX, REV. ADOLPH, J.C.D., The Declaration of Nullity of Marriages Contracted Outside the Church, X-151 pp., 1943.
183. MATULENAS, REV. RAYMOND ANTHONY, O..S.B., A.B., J.C.D., Communication, a Source of Privileges, XII-225 pp., 1943.
184. O'LEARY, REV. CHARLES GERARD, C.SS.R., J.C.D., Religious Dismissed After Perpetual Profession, X-213 pp., 1943.
185. POWER, REV. CORNELIUS MICHAEL, J.C.L., The Blessing of Cemeteries, XII-231 pp., 1943.
186. SHUHLER, REV. RALPH VINCENT, O.S.A., J.C.D., Privileges of Religious to Absolve and Dispense, XII-195 pp., 1943.
187. ZIOLKOWSKI, REV. THADDEUS STANISLAUS, A.B., J.C.D., The Consecrtaion and Blessing of Churches, XII-151 pp., 1943.
188. HENEGHAN, REV. JOHN JOSEPH, S.T.D., J.C.D., The Marriages of Unworthy Catholics: Canons 1065 and 1066; XV-213 pp., 1944.
189. CARROLL, REV. COLEMAN FRANCIS, M.A., S.T.L., J.C.L., Charitable Institutions.
190. CIESLUK, REV. JOSEPH EDWARD, PH.B., S.T.L., J.C.L., National Parishes in the United States.
191. COBURN, REV. VINCENT PAUL, A.B., J.C.D., Marriages of Conscience, XII-172 pp., 1944.
192. CONNORS, REV. CHARLES PAUL, C.S.SP., A.B., J.C.D., Extra-Judicial Procurators in the Code of Canon Law, X-94 pp., 1944.
193. COYLE, REV. PAUL RAYMOND, A.B., J.C.L., Judicial Exceptions.
194. FAIR, REV. BARTHOLOMEW FRANCIS, A.B., S.T.L., J.C.L., The Impediment of Abduction.

195. Gallagher, Rev. Thomas Raphael, O.P., A.B., S.T.Lr., J.C.D., The Examination of the Qualities of the Ordinand, X-166 pp., 1944.
196. Gannon, Rev. John Mark, S.T.L., J.C.D., The Interstices Required for the Promotion to Orders, XII-100 pp., 1944.
197. Goldsmith, Rev. J. William, B.C.S., S.T.L., J.C.D., The Competence of Church and State over Marriage — Disputed Points, X-128 pp., 1944.
198. Goodwine, Rev. Joseph Gerard, A.B., S.T.B., J.C.D., The Reception of Converts, XIII-326 pp., 1944.
199. Kowalski, Rev. Romuald Eugene, O.F.M., A.B., J.C.D., Sustenance of Religious Houses of Regulars, X-174 pp., 1944.
200. McCoy, Rev. Alan Edward, O.F.M., J.C.D., Force and Fear in Relation to Delictual Imputability and Penal Responsibility, XII-160 pp., 1944.
201. McDevitt, Rev. Vincent John, Ph.B., S.T.L., J.C.L., Perjury.
202. Martin, Rev. Thomas Owen, Ph.D., S.T.D., J.C.D., Adverse Possession, Prescription and Limitation of Actions: The Canonical "Praescriptio", XX-208 pp., 1944.
203. Miklosvic, Rev. Paul John, A.B., J.C.L., Attempted Marriages and their Consequent Juridic Effects.
204. Mundy, Rev. Thomas Maurice, A.B., S.T.L., J.C.L., The Union of Parishes, X-164 pp., 1944.
205. O'Dea, Rev. John Coyle, A.B., J.C.D., The Matrimonial Impediment of Nonage, VIII-126 pp., 1944.
206. Olalia, Rev. Alexander Ayson, S.T.L., J.C.D., A Comparative Study of the Christian Constitution of States and the Constitution of the Philippine Commonwealth, XII-136 pp., 1944.
207. Poisson, Rev. Pierre-Marie, C.S.C., A.B., Ph.L., Th.L., J.C.L., Droits Patrimoniaux des Maisons et des Eglises Religieuses.
208. Stadalnikas, Rev. Casimir Joseph, M.I.C., J.C.D., Reservation of Censures, X-141 pp., 1944.
209. Sullivan, Rev. Eugene Henry, S.T.L., J.C.D., Proof of the Reception of the Sacraments, X-165 pp., 1944.
210. Vaughan, Rev. William Edward, J.C.D., Constitutions for Diocesan Courts, X-210 pp., 1944.
211. Paro, Rev. Gino, S.T.D., J.C.L., The Right of Papal Legation.
212. Balzer, Rev. Rilph Francis, C.P., J.C.D., The Computation of Time in a Canonical Novitiate, X-227 pp., 1945.
213. Dougherty, Rev. John Whelan, A.B., S.T.L., J.C.D., De Inquisitione Speciali, XII-195 pp., 1945.
214. Dziob, Rev. Michael Walter, J.C.D., The Sacred Congregation for the Oriental Church, XII-181 pp., 1945.
215. Eidenschink, Rev. John Albert, O.S.B., B.A., J.C.D., The Election of Bishops in the Letters of Pope Gregory the Great, VII-200 pp., 1945.

216. GILL, REV. NICHOLAS, C.P., J.C.D., The Spiritual Prefect in Clercial Religious Houses of Study, X-140 pp., 1945.
217. HYNES, REV. HARRY GERARD, S.T.L., J.C.D., The Privileges of Cardinals, XII-183 pp., 1945.
218. McDEVITT, REV. GERALD VINCENT, S.T.L., J.C.D., The Renunciation of an Ecclesiastical Office, XIV-179 pp., 1945.
219. MANNING, REV. JOSEPH LEROY, J.C.D., The Free Conferral of Ecclesiastical Offices, VIII-116 pp., 1945.
220. MEYER, REV. LOUIS G., O.S.B., A.B., S.T.B., J.C.D., Alms-Gathering by Religious, XII-163 pp., 1945.
221. O'DONNELL, REV. CLETUS FRANCIS, M.A., J.C.D., The Marriages of Minors, XII-268pp., 1945.
222. PRUNSKIS, REV. JOSEPH, J.C.D., Comparative Law, Ecclesiastical and Civil, in the Lithuanian Concordat, X-161 pp., 1945.
223. SWEENEY, REV. FRANCIS PATRICK, C.SS.R., J.C.D., The Reduction of Clerics to the Lay State, X-199 pp., 1945.
224. VOGELPOHI, REV. HENRY JOHN, J.C.D., The Simple Impediments to Holy Orders, XVI-190 pp., 1945.
225. BROCKHAUS, REV. THOMAS AQUINAS, O.S.B., J.C.D., Religious who are known as *Conversi*, X-127 pp., 1945.

www.ingramcontent.com/pod-product-compliance
Lightning Source LLC
LaVergne TN
LVHW050245080826
844660LV00012B/599

* 9 7 8 0 8 1 3 2 2 3 9 5 7 *